1%

This item was
purchased with monies
provided from the
optional 1% sales tax.

Painfully Shy

Painfully Shy

How to Overcome

Social Anxiety and

Reclaim Your Life

Barbara G. Markway, Ph.D., and Gregory P. Markway, Ph.D.

THOMAS DUNNE BOOKS

ST. MARTINS PRESS ❧ NEW YORK

THOMAS DUNNE BOOKS.
An imprint of St. Martin's Press.

www. stmartin's.com

Book design by Richard Oriolo

LIBRARY OF CONGRESS CATALOGING-IN-PUBLICATION DATA
Markway, Barbara G.
   Painfully shy : how to overcome social anxiety and reclaim your life / Barbara G. Markway and Gregory P. Markway.—1st ed.
       p. cm.
"Thomas Dunne Books"—T.p. verso.
Includes bibliographical references (p.) and index.
ISBN 0-312-26628-6
   1. Social phobia. 2. Self-help techniques. I. Markway, Gregory P. II. Title.
RC552.S62 M367 2001
616.85'223—dc21

                                        00-064479

First Edition: April 2001

10 9 8 7 6 5 4 3 2 1

This book is intended to serve as an informational resource only and should not be taken as psychological or medical advice.

To our clients—
whose courage and
perseverance inspire us

Contents

▼▼▼▼▼▼▼▼▼▼▼▼▼▼

Part One. Spotlight on Social Anxiety

Part Two. Methods for Mastering Social Anxiety: A Comprehensive Approach

Appendixes

Acknowledgments

This book is a result of the inspiration, guidance, and support we've received from many people. Our warmest thanks go to:

- Julie McGovern, our insightful freelance editor and friend, for challenging us to make the manuscript better while offering kind words of encouragement along the way. We couldn't have done it without her.
- Alec Pollard, Ph.D., and Teresa Flynn, Ph.D., of the St. Louis Behavioral Medicine Institute, for being good friends and able mentors.
- Barry Neville, our editor at Thomas Dunne Books, for his vision, and also his wife, Jessica, for putting us in touch with each other. We're also grateful to our editorial assistant, Carin Siegfried, and our copyeditor, Sara Schwager, as well as those other creative people behind the scenes, for working so hard to make this book a success.
- Eric Joffe, for his dedication and perseverance in forming the Alliance for People with Social Phobia.
- Tracie Smith, Cord Harper, and Joe Bellmer, for spreading the message of hope about the treatment of social anxiety disorder to physicians and mental health professionals.
- Melody Boling, Marcia Burton, and their families, for helping with childcare and offering warm support along the way.

- Our delightful son, Jesse, for his patience while we wrote "the book." As always, his combination of wit and wisdom gently reminds us of what's important and brings much joy to our lives.
- Our parents and other family members, for their unconditional love and acceptance.

Introduction:
Courage and Hope for the Journey

Life shrinks or expands in proportion to one's courage.

—Anaïs Nin

Everything that is done in the world is done by hope.

—Martin Luther

This is a book about people who are painfully shy. But more importantly, it's a book about courage. Within these pages you'll read about extraordinary men and women who gathered the courage to do things that made them shudder with fright because they realized the only other option was crawling in a hole, hiding from life, failing to realize their potential.

It's also a book about hope, for hope is what creates courage. Sometimes it starts with only a small seed of hope, but that's all it really takes. With the proper tools and the right attitude, that small seed soon grows into a vision of what life can be—a life free from crippling fear.

You, too, can loosen the shackles of social anxiety and reclaim your life. And remember, you don't have to do it alone. We'll take you through it, step-by-step, supporting you all the way. Read on. Let this book fill you with hope, and may the courageous journey begin.

▼▼▼

Social anxiety disorder, also called social phobia, is extremely common, affecting at least seventeen million people in the United States. It's the most common anxiety disorder and the third most common psychiatric disorder overall. Although there's been a tendency to minimize social anxiety as a minor problem, it isn't. Quality of life can be severely compromised for those with social anxiety disorder. These individuals also run a greater risk for other problems such as depression, substance abuse, and even suicide.

Despite its prevalence and the huge toll it exacts, social anxiety disorder has received little attention until recently. One group of experts has even dubbed it "the neglected anxiety disorder." Indeed, in 1992 when I and my colleagues, Cheryl Carmin, Alec Pollard, and Teresa Flynn, wrote *Dying of Embarrassment*, there was no other self-help book on social anxiety. In contrast, several books could be found on most other anxiety problems, such as agoraphobia or obsessive-compulsive disorder. Individuals with social anxiety suffered in silence, thinking they were the only ones with this debilitating problem.

It has been gratifying to realize the huge need that *Dying of Embarrassment* filled. Yet, more work remains. It's still difficult to find a health care professional who knows much, if anything, about social anxiety. And finding an experienced therapist can be next to impossible in many parts of the country.

Fortunately, our understanding of social anxiety disorder is reaching a new frontier. Soon it will no longer be a "neglected" problem. New research findings are proliferating. Special conferences are being held. Professional journals are devoting whole issues to the subject. Newspaper and magazine articles are reporting the news. The word is getting out that social anxiety disorder is highly underrecognized and that effective treatments are available. Our goal in writing *Painfully Shy* is to continue educating people about the nature of social anxiety, while offering readers the latest information about how to triumph over their social fears.

Who Will Benefit from This Book

We'll go over specific definitions and diagnostic criteria in the first chapter. But for now, know that this book is written for anyone who experiences excessive, problematic anxiety in social situations. Maybe you've always thought of yourself as shy but figured this was a part of your personality that was unlikely to change. Or perhaps you've had trouble advancing at work because you offer little input in meetings and refuse to do any public speaking. You may even have been to a psychologist or psychiatrist and received a diagnosis of "social anxiety disorder" or "social phobia." The situations vary, but the fears—the fear of criticism, the fear of scrutiny, and the fear of disapproval—are the same. This book is written to help you diminish these fears, gain confidence, and feel more at ease in social settings.

Adults aren't the only ones who experience anxiety in social situations. Children may also battle problem shyness or be diagnosed with an anxiety disorder. Third-grader Melissa provides a good illustration. Although she is a bright student, she cannot raise her hand to answer a question, nor can she participate in class discussions. She is embarrassed anytime she has to get up from her desk. This means she won't sharpen her pencils, put something in the trash can, or use the rest room. *Painfully Shy* will help parents, teachers, and school counselors know how to help these children break out of their shells and reach their full potential.

In addition, this book will be useful to family members who often offer the primary social contact for someone with social anxiety disorder. *Painfully Shy* will show family members how truly to support their loved one. Finally, health care workers, mental health professionals, ministers, and others who have relationships with those who are extremely shy will benefit from understanding more about this common problem.

How to Use This Book

Everyone has a different learning style, so approach this book in whatever way best meets your needs. We'll lay out the general framework of the book, and offer some suggestions you can follow if they make sense for you and your situation.

Part One spotlights social anxiety in all its varied forms and provides answers to basic questions which will help you better understand this disorder. You'll get answers to the questions:

- How is shyness different from social anxiety?

- How is it similar?

- How do professionals define social anxiety disorder?

- How common is social anxiety?

- Whom does it affect?

- Why haven't people heard more about social anxiety disorder?

And you'll learn some of the theories about the causes of excessive social anxiety. In short, these first two chapters provide the foundation for the rest of the book.

Part Two contains the latest methods you can use to master social anxiety in almost any situation. Although they're presented in a step-wise order that we've found useful, someone with a question about medication, for example, could go directly to Chapter 9, "Use Medication Wisely," for an answer.

Many of the chapters in this part contain exercises that reinforce the ideas presented in the chapter and start helping you feel more comfortable in social situations. You may benefit from simply reading the chapters, but we think you'll gain more if you actually complete the exercises and practice them regularly. Still, you may not need to do all of the exercises to make progress in overcoming your social anxiety. Some of them may simply not apply to your situation. Again, go at your own pace and do what makes sense.

The last section of the book has appendixes on coexisting problems such as depression and substance abuse and social anxiety related to medical conditions. One appendix is chock-full of practical tips for parents and teachers, and there's a resource section listing useful books, organizations, and web sites.

The Basis of This Book

The information and treatment methods described in *Painfully Shy* are based on both scientific research and clinical experience. As mentioned above, research in the area of social anxiety disorder has grown rapidly over the past few years, and results of this research are reported in professional journals and at conferences. However, much of this information is not accessible to the general public, and most mental health professionals can't attend every conference or read every journal. Thus, one of our goals in writing *Painfully Shy* is to bring the latest breakthroughs to you in a form that is practical and easy to understand. We also hope that psychologists and other professionals will use this book as a resource in their work.

Painfully Shy is also based on our clinical work. Both Greg and I have had extensive training and experience working with people who have anxiety disorders. We are continually awed by the courage and perseverance of the people who come to see us. To face one's fears head-on—to act in spite of anxiety—is a great accomplishment. Although many people have said we could use their names and their stories in this book, we have nonetheless concealed people's identities in the interest of their privacy. In addition, some of the stories are composites of a number of people. This allows us better to illustrate key points while further protecting our clients' privacy.

Finally, as you'll read below, part of this book springs from personal experience.

Barb's Experience with Social Anxiety

When I coauthored *Dying of Embarrassment* in 1992, I never dreamed of telling anyone about my own lifelong struggles with shyness and social anxiety. After all, I was an expert. How could I have difficulty with public speaking, participating in meetings, or going to parties? I thought it was okay to help other people face their fears, but it wasn't okay to admit I'd struggled with these same situations myself.

After the book's publication, I promoted *Dying of Embarrassment* and received much satisfaction from knowing I was helping people learn more about this neglected and misunderstood problem. I continued to feel, however, as if I was doing others with social anxiety a disservice by not sharing my own experiences.

Over the past several years, I've learned of two psychologists, both anxiety disorder specialists, who've acknowledged their own problems with anxiety. Therapist Edmund Bourne, author of the hugely successful *The Anxiety & Phobia Workbook*, wrote in his next book, *Healing Fear*, of his own recovery from a chronic anxiety disorder. And psychologist Thomas Richards, who heads an anxiety disorder clinic in Phoenix, Arizona, used his popular web site, *The Anxiety Network*, to write about his own difficulties.

Reading about these therapists' experiences was a revelation to me. I felt such relief—relief that I wasn't the only psychologist/anxiety disorder expert with my own anxiety problems. I also felt courage—maybe I didn't need to keep my experiences to myself any longer.

Some cynics may claim that Bourne and Richards were just trying to make a buck by talking about their own problems. In this age of Jerry Springer and Jenny Jones, letting it all hang out is what people want, right? Maybe these authors thought their personal stories would add a dramatic angle and sell more books and tapes. I've never spoken to them, so I really have no idea as to their motivation. My guess is, though, that it took guts to reveal themselves in the way that they did, and that they did so in the service of others.

Personally, reading about Bourne's ups and downs with his own recovery normalized my seemingly meandering path toward serenity and freedom from anxiety. We learn from others' stories. We learn from telling our own stories. We learn we are not alone. We learn we are not so different from many other people. Most importantly, we learn there is hope.

It is in this spirit of offering motivation that I include some of my personal experiences with shyness and social anxiety throughout the book—both the triumphs (appearing on *Good Morning America* without completely falling apart ahead of time) and the challenges (experiencing anxiety at the mere thought of certain social situations, and then feeling frustrated with myself that I can still get so anxious).

My husband, Greg, has given me tremendous support in my journey toward healing and is an incredibly good part of "my story." As an example, several years ago when we wrote a book for couples called, *Illuminating the Heart: Steps Toward a More Spiritual Marriage,* the publisher wanted to send us on a national book tour. Greg was thrilled, as he had come to enjoy public speaking and being in the spotlight. I, on the other hand, was filled with dread. We had just been through a lot of stress. Greg's father had recently died after a long battle with cancer, and our son continued to have some health problems. The strain of it all exacerbated my social anxiety. I had lost much of my confidence. I didn't feel as if I could do all of those public appearances. I certainly didn't feel like a "put-together" author/expert. In addition to all of my anxiety, I was lethargic and depressed. I felt no motivation to publicize the book we had worked so hard to write.

I wish I could report that I conquered my anxiety and managed to go on to complete the book tour, but it didn't happen that way. Greg encouraged me in all the right ways, but I just couldn't go through with it. Thankfully, the publisher was extremely understanding, and so was Greg. I knew he was disappointed, though, and I felt horrible about myself as if I were a complete failure. Greg wouldn't let me wallow in guilt for long, though. He reassured me that it was okay and he still loved me. He believed in me and my abilities and had faith that I would—we would—move beyond this low point. "We're a team," he said.

I couldn't agree more. We are a great team. We worked well

together on *Illuminating the Heart,* with me doing most of the writing and he doing lots of advising and editing. Now I'm excited about working on *Painfully Shy* with him. An extremely gifted therapist, Greg has worked for more than a decade with people who have anxiety disorders. He has such a knack for making people feel accepted as they are while still pushing them, bit by bit, beyond their comfort zone. Many of the people he has worked with have overcome long-standing fears and anxieties, going on to live full and productive lives.

Although we're creating this book as a team, we know it can be confusing to switch back and forth between us, alerting the reader to who is saying what. Thus, this book is written primarily in my "voice." "We" refers to both Greg and me, while "I" refers to me (Barb).

Hopefully my experiences with anxiety will help you to feel less alone. Still, I don't want to leave you with a negative impression about the possibilities for recovery from your social anxiety. We all have setbacks and tough times. That's normal and nothing to be ashamed of. Since the book tour "fiasco," I've been able to move beyond feeling that I was a failure and instead see that it was a learning and growing experience. (Why don't we ever grow from the fun times?)

Now, more than ever, there is considerable hope for people like you and me. You *can* overcome the often excruciating pain of living a life that revolves around social anxiety, of always worrying about what other people are thinking of you. It's not easy, and it won't happen as quickly as you'd like. With courage and hope, however, it can be done.

Part One

Spotlight on
Social Anxiety

Chapter 1

When the World's a Stage...
and You Have Stage Fright

All the world's a stage,

And all the men and women merely players:

They have their exits and their entrances;

And one man in his time plays many parts. . . .

—Shakespeare, *As You Like It*

When I first met Gina and asked what brought her to see me, she looked toward the floor and started crying. "I feel like there's something terribly wrong with me. The way I am is not normal." I asked Gina to tell me more.

"I feel like I'm always under the spotlight, as if people are evaluating every word I say, every move I make. Sometimes I feel paralyzed by it. I just know I'm going to do or say something to make others disapprove of me. I don't want to go on like this," she continued.

Gina told me she was single, had never dated, and worked in a pharmacy as a technician. She liked her job but worried about the social aspects of it. For example, when coworkers invited her to eat lunch with them she made excuses for why she couldn't. Recently, someone commented about how she stayed to herself—"Gina thinks she's too good for us." This sent Gina to the bathroom in tears.

Then, twice last week when customers acted grumpy and complained to her about waiting in line, Gina became so upset she thought she might be having a heart attack. Her chest hurt and she could hardly breathe. I told her she was probably having a panic attack, but I suggested she see her physician for a checkup to be on the safe side.

Later in the session I asked Gina what her childhood was like. She told me that while growing up she'd always heard her mother say to others, "She's just a little shy."

Gina thought it was normal that she didn't have many friends. She assumed the popular girls in her class wouldn't want to have anything to do with her, so she mostly kept to herself. Although Gina was bright, she hated school. She dreaded being called on by the teacher to answer a question. She knew she'd freeze up and wouldn't be able to speak. Lunchtime was the worst. She never had anyone to sit by, and she felt too nervous to eat much. She was so miserable, she frequently had stomachaches and begged to stay home. Somehow, though, she struggled through school and began working at the local pharmacy.

Until now, Gina had accepted her mother's explanation that she was "just shy." But lately she worried she was going crazy. "I'm always falling apart at work. I don't know what's wrong with me," she said.

Jim's story is similar to Gina's; he felt as if life was one frightening performance after another. Also like Gina, he had been told more than once that he was "just shy."

Jim explained his main problem to me. "When I talk to people, particularly people in an authority position, or those I think are better than me, I blush," he said. "It starts with a hot, tingling sensation on my neck and chest, and works up to my face. I'm sure everyone notices how red and splotchy my skin gets."

Jim became so bothered by this problem that he mustered up his courage and talked to his physician about it. He thought maybe something physical was wrong. Unfortunately, Jim's doctor was like many other doctors. He knew little about social anxiety and hadn't a clue about what questions to ask in order correctly to diagnose the problem. He dismissed the severity of Jim's situation, and told him, "You're just shy. Don't worry about it."

Jim persisted, though. He no longer believed his problem was simply shyness. He did some research on the Internet, and, to his amazement, he found entire web sites devoted to explaining this condition.

"It helped so much learning that I'm not crazy, and that I'm not the only one with this problem," he told me.

Gina and Jim aren't "just shy." *They're painfully shy.* Although most people have had butterflies in their stomach before giving a speech or have felt a little nervous on a first date, these natural reactions don't come close to the extreme fear and anxiety experienced by people like Gina and Jim. The technical term for the condition is *social anxiety disorder*, or *social phobia* as it's sometimes called. In the rest of the chapter, you'll learn what social anxiety is, at what point it becomes a disorder, and the common symptoms that someone with this problem is likely to experience. You'll also have the opportunity to take a self-assessment test and see where your particular social anxiety problems lie. Perhaps the most important information you'll take from this chapter is the realization that you're not alone—and that help is near.

What Is Social Anxiety?

Social anxiety is a universal experience—one that's necessary for survival. Perhaps it was easier to see its survival value in previous times, when people had to band together to hunt food, build shelter, and ward off enemies. Social anxiety served the function of keeping people close to the "pack." To veer off from the group was to risk death.

Even now, we've evolved in such a way that we're motivated to remain a part of the group. We want to be accepted. We want to fit in. Thus, some social anxiety is normal and beneficial. After all, people who *never* care about others' opinions are often not very pleasant to be around and have a completely different set of problems.

But what exactly is social anxiety? It's the experience of apprehension or worry that arises from the possibility, either real or imagined, that one will be evaluated or judged in some manner by others. We know, this definition is a mouthful. Perhaps it's easier to explain what social anxiety is by listing some ordinary, everyday examples:

- embarrassment after spilling a drink

- "stage fright" before a big performance

- awkwardness while talking to someone you don't know well

- nervousness during a job interview

- feeling jittery before giving a speech

These are common experiences almost everyone has had at one time or another.

Since social anxiety is so universal, how do you know where your reactions fall? Are they within the range of normal? Or like Gina and Jim, does your social anxiety pose more of a problem? In other words, how can you tell when social anxiety becomes social anxiety disorder—a clinical diagnosis?

Recognizing Social Anxiety Disorder

Mental health professionals frequently use *The Diagnostic and Statistical Manual of Mental Disorders—Fourth Edition (DSM-IV)* to make diagnostic decisions. While it's not a perfect system, diagnoses are important for a number of reasons. Without a name for the problem, research vital to understanding a problem and developing effective treatments for it simply doesn't take place. On a practical level, if you try to receive mental health services for a problem that has no diagnosis, you're not likely to get your health insurance to pay.

Let's look at the specific criteria that must be met for a clinical diagnosis of social anxiety disorder. The *DSM-IV* says an individual with social anxiety disorder will:

- Show significant and persistent fear of social situations in which embarrassment or rejection may occur;

- Experience immediate anxiety-driven, physical reactions to feared social situations;

- Realize that his or her fears are greatly exaggerated, but feel powerless to do anything about them; and

- Often avoid the dreaded social situation—at any cost.

Someone may fear just one or a few social situations—public speaking being a common example—in which case the problem is referred to as a *specific*, or *discrete* social phobia. In contrast, *generalized* social anxiety disorder exists when a person is afraid and avoids many, or most social situations.

Once these basic criteria are met for a diagnosis of social anxiety disorder, the individual symptoms can vary, but they generally fall into three categories: the cognitive or mental symptoms (what you think); the physical reactions (how your body feels); and the behavioral avoidance (what you do). Let's look at these areas in more detail.

The mental anguish

People with social anxiety disorder are plagued with negative thoughts and doubts about themselves such as:

- Do I look okay?

- Am I dressed appropriately?

- Will I know what to talk about?

- Will I sound stupid, or boring?

- What if other people don't like me?

- What if people notice I'm nervous?

- What if people think I'm too quiet?

The fear of possible rejection or disapproval is foremost in socially anxious people's minds, and they scan for any signs that confirm their negative expectations.

Let's look at an example. Imagine that George has gathered his nerve to talk to a woman he frequently sees in the break room at work. He has a topic of conversation planned out ahead of time, something fairly neutral such as the nice weather they've been enjoying lately. When George starts talking to her she seems friendly enough, but she yawns several times. George manages to get through the brief conversation, but when he's back at his desk, he berates himself for his performance. He attacks himself: *How could I be so stupid as to talk about the weather? Anyone would find that boring. No wonder she was yawning. She must think I'm a complete idiot.* George didn't consider any other explanation for her yawning; the whole situation was distorted based on his fears and expectations. Alternative explanations, such as maybe the woman had been up late, hadn't even made it into his consciousness.

The pain that such pervasive, negative-thinking patterns causes cannot be underestimated. Without appropriate intervention, these kinds of self-deprecating thoughts can lead to many other complications, including low self-esteem and deep feelings of inferiority.

The physical distress

Many people don't realize that actual physical discomfort can accompany social anxiety. For example, someone may experience a panic attack in a social situation, in which they feel an acute and severe rush of fear and anxiety, accompanied by some or all of the following symptoms: shortness of breath, tightness or pain in the chest, racing heart, tingling or sensations of numbness, nausea, diarrhea, dizziness, shaking, and sweating. Panic attacks usually come on quite quickly, build to a peak in approximately five to twenty minutes, and then subside. It's not uncommon to hear people say that their panic attacks last a lot longer; however, it's probably the aftereffects of the attack that they're feeling, such as residual anxiety and increased alertness to bodily sensations, rather than the panic attack itself.

It's important to note that many people are misdiagnosed with panic disorder when, in fact, they have social anxiety disorder. The key to knowing which of the two is the real problem lies in understanding the root fear. In panic disorder, the person fears the panic attack itself and often feels as if he or she is dying during such an episode. In the case of social anxiety disorder, the fear is centered around the possibility that people might witness the panic attack and the resulting humiliation that would occur. Keep in mind, though, that some people have both panic disorder and social anxiety disorder. The appendix, "Recognizing and Coping with Coexisting Problems" covers this in more detail.

Not everyone with social anxiety experiences full-blown panic attacks, though. Instead, some people are extremely bothered by and focused on a particular physical aspect of their condition. The most common examples include blushing, sweating, and shaking. For example, Patty couldn't lift a fork or a glass of soda without worrying that her hand would shake uncontrollably and that others would notice. In fact, she did have a slight tremor that was exacerbated when she was anxious. She avoided eating or drinking in public whenever possible. Constantly making up new excuses as to why she couldn't go out to lunch with coworkers, she ate alone in her cubicle at work. *If people see me shaking, they'll know how nervous and scared I am.*

Patty thought everyone at work must think she was odd and strange, and this belief made her all the more uncomfortable around them. She thought if she could only control the shaking, she could deal with the rest of her social anxiety problem. Similarly, people with a tendency to blush often believe this is their major problem and will go to great lengths—some people even undergo surgery—to correct this physical "defect."

Regardless of which particular physical symptoms someone experiences, anxiety is never pleasant. Having one's body in a state of constant alert takes its toll and can lead to chronic fatigue, muscle tension, and sleep disturbances.

The toll of avoidance

It's human nature to avoid pain and suffering. From an evolutionary perspective, we're "hard-wired" either to fight or flee from a dangerous situation. It's no surprise then that people with social anxiety disorder tend to avoid or painfully bear situations that they believe will cause them harm. This might mean never attending a party or going to a restaurant. It might mean having few, if any, friends. It might mean never having an intimate relationship. It might mean dropping out of school or working at a job beneath one's potential. *I always think I'll go through with whatever it is, but I usually end up making up some excuse and canceling. I feel like a liar.*

The consequences of avoidance will naturally vary depending upon the person and the severity of their anxiety. In all cases, though, people with social anxiety disorder limit their choices out of fear. Decisions in life are based upon what they're comfortable with rather than what they might truly want to do.

In addition to the outright avoidance of situations, people with social anxiety disorder may engage in other, more subtle methods of avoidance. Examples of partial avoidance include using alcohol to cope with anxiety (drinking before a party in order to be able to go at all) and setting certain parameters on a social situation (only staying at the party a short period of time). In the self-assessment test at the end of the chapter, you'll be asked about your use of partial avoidance. You'll learn as you progress through this book that engaging in any type of avoidance, even partial avoidance, is detrimental to your recovery. In avoiding threatening situations, you never realize that you actually *can* manage your anxiety and cope with your fears. In short, avoidance prevents learning.

Obviously, this is a bit of an oversimplification. In fact, some clients have told us that they have exposed themselves to feared situations repeatedly, and it didn't help. If this has happened to you, don't despair. We'll go over the intricacies of conquering avoidance behaviors in Chapter 8.

You're Not Alone: Social Anxiety Affects Millions of People

A college student, Rachel, believed she had some freakish affliction because she got extremely nervous in any type of group situation. She'd heard about lots of "weird" problems on *Oprah*, but never anything like what she experienced. *I must be the only one with this horrible problem. Why am I like this? Why me?*

While the other girls in her dormitory loved the first day of classes because they usually got out early, Rachel dreaded it. She worried herself sick that the teacher might make them introduce themselves to the class. In fact, she often skipped the first day. She also hated social activities sponsored by the dormitory. On one occasion everyone was asked to wear fifties-style clothes during the day and then attend a sock-hop in the evening. Just the thought of calling attention to herself in this way was enough to send Rachel's anxiety soaring. She told her roommate she was sick and stayed in bed all day.

Like Rachel, you may have thought that no one else shared your problem. But you are not alone. The most up-to-date information suggests that one in eight Americans will, at some point in his or her life, suffer from social anxiety disorder. As we mentioned in the introduction, this makes social anxiety disorder the third most common psychiatric disorder, after depression and alcoholism. Millions of people—from ten to nineteen million depending on the particular survey cited—are affected by social anxiety.

Who are these millions of people?

The millions of people with social anxiety disorder are ordinary people, just like Gina, Jim, Rachel, you, and me. Included in these millions are not only men and women of all ages, but children and adolescents, as well.

In fact, social anxiety typically shows up before the age of twenty, often during the teenage years. However, many people remember being shy and anxious even earlier—as far back as they can remember. Carla's words reflect this: *"Ever since I was a child, I remember feeling different from the other kids. I didn't know how to join in on the playground. I just watched. I was very lonely."*

Current research suggests that several problems seen in the elementary grades, such as school phobia (refusing to go to school) and selective mutism (not speaking at school) are actually manifestations of social anxiety disorder. Because of the early age at which social anxiety can surface, it's important to work toward increasing awareness and intervening as early as possible. We'll cover these topics and explore other ways to help the socially anxious child in Chapter 11.

In addition to the age factor, many people want to know more about whom social anxiety disorder affects. In large studies of the general population, women outnumber men by a ratio of three to two. When looking at groups of people seeking treatment, however, the gender distribution is nearly equal. Social anxiety disorder appears to cut across racial and ethnic lines, although there may be some variations depending on cultural norms. We've personally been contacted by people in countries all over the world—from Canada to India—wanting to learn more about social anxiety.

Some studies show that people with social anxiety disorder are less likely to be married and also are more likely to have occupational difficulties than others. These findings make sense when you think about the "normal" anxiety many people feel when they're dating someone new or going on a job interview. Throw social anxiety disorder into the mix, and you can probably imagine how trying these events can be. Despite these findings, we've worked with many individuals who function very well, people who you'd never suspect had social anxiety. Still, what matters most is how someone feels on the inside. When someone is tormented by anxiety, even if it's not readily apparent to others, it's a problem worth addressing.

You're Not Crazy: Social Anxiety Is Underrecognized, but It's Real and Treatable

Another crucial thing to know about having social anxiety disorder is you're not "crazy." You may, however, frequently feel like you're crazy. A large part of this feeling comes from the general lack of awareness and understanding people have about social anxiety.

We've already mentioned the lack of media coverage about social anxiety disorder, and how this contributes to the general public's ignorance of this common problem. Why, you might wonder, when social anxiety disorder is the third largest mental health problem in the United States, is there not more attention paid it? Psychologist Thomas Richards, whom we mentioned in the introduction, makes some interesting comments about this issue. He muses, "Can you see a movie-of-the-week about a very shy person who rarely leaves the house except to go to work, who has no friends, and is afraid of answering the door at times? This would be highly interesting drama, wouldn't it?" The very nature of social anxiety disorder makes it less likely to receive media attention than other problems.

After *Dying of Embarrassment* was published, I was asked to do numerous radio shows, many of which were call-in formats. I tried to tell the interviewers that I doubted people with social anxiety were going to call and talk on a radio show, much less to an "expert." These radio personalities never seemed to "get it" and were shocked when we had to fill an entire hour of time with absolutely no calls.

Another time a popular, national television talk show called me and said, "We want you on our show if you can bring several articulate, outgoing social phobics with you." This was enough to make *me* feel crazy—what kind of therapist was I that I hadn't cured all these people, turning them into outgoing, social butterflies who wanted to go on national television and talk about their problems?

Unfortunately, this lack of awareness and understanding extends to professional circles. It's still unusual for health care professionals—physicians, psychiatrists, or psychologists—to make a primary diagnosis of social anxiety disorder. It's frequently misdiagnosed as panic disorder or agoraphobia, or it's not diagnosed at all. We have had very few people referred to us who have already been correctly diagnosed, much less been given the appropriate treatment.

In my own case, I was never diagnosed with social anxiety. The mental health professionals I saw focused on my depression and general tendency to worry too much. In fact, I had never heard mention of social anxiety or social phobia until I began my fellowship year at St. Louis University Medical Center's Behavioral Medicine Department. There, while working in the Anxiety Disorders Center, I first learned about social anxiety and began to see patients who seemed to fight, perhaps to a more severe degree, the same fears I had. The people who came to the Center expressed so much relief when learning their problem had a name. It was real, and it was treatable.

Fortunately, we're seeing signs that the situation is changing—more people in the general community, as well as professionals, are hearing about social anxiety disorder. To some extent this is because Paxil, an antidepressant manufactured by SmithKline Beecham, was recently approved by the Food and Drug Administration (FDA) to treat social anxiety disorder. While other medications have been used effectively, this is the first drug to be marketed specifically for social anxiety.

SmithKline Beecham worked closely with the FDA to obtain special permission to launch a publicity campaign geared toward the general public. It's likely you've already seen commercials on television and read advertisements in popular magazines listing the signs of social anxiety disorder and encouraging people to talk to their doctors. SmithKline is also presenting educational programs to doctors, telling them not only about Paxil, but also about other treatments that can be effective.

Medications are often powerful treatments for social anxiety disorder, but they're certainly not the only avenue available to you. Much research has taken place in the past decade, documenting the effectiveness of a particular type of psychological treatment called cognitive-behavioral therapy. This book will show you, step-by-step, how to use these proven methods to prevent social anxiety from limiting your life.

So above all, know this: You're not crazy. The problem you're experiencing with social anxiety is real, and it can be serious. But social anxiety disorder is also very treatable. In the next section, you'll complete a questionnaire to help you assess the extent of your anxiety. Understanding the full range of your difficulties will help you chart your course toward recovery.

Self-Assessment Test:
Do You Have Social Anxiety Disorder?

Let's get started. By going through the checklists below, you'll get a good idea of how your body and mind react to the fear of disapproval, and about the range of social and performance situations that you try to avoid. If you decide to seek help from a physician or a therapist, bring this completed form with you. It will provide the professional with much useful information about you and your situation and may speed up the assessment process.

These are situations in which I'm likely to experience social anxiety:
(Check off any that apply. Put a star by the situations you're also most likely to avoid.)

❏ Talking on the telephone

❏ Being introduced to others

❏ Answering the door

❏ Interacting with clerks at the bank, grocery store, dry cleaners, etc.

❏ Dealing with doctors' offices

❏ Attending church

❏ Buying or returning items at department stores

❏ Driving (for fear of what other drivers are thinking of you)

❏ Going to the gas station

❏ Using public rest rooms (not due to fear of germs)

❏ Eating in front of other people

❏ Writing or signing name in front of others

❏ Attending social events

❏ Hosting social events

❏ Dating

❏ Talking in a small group

❏ Acting assertively

❏ Expressing your opinion

❏ Talking about yourself to others (being the center of attention)

❏ Speaking to a large group

❏ Performance situations, such as playing a musical instrument or taking a test

❏ Other: _____

❏ Other: _____

❏ Other: _____

These are ways I engage in "partial avoidance behavior":
(Partial avoidance means that you may not entirely avoid a situation, but you find some way to limit or control your experience of the situation.)

❏ I use alcohol or drugs before entering a feared social situation.

❏ If I attend a social situation, I stay only a certain length of time.

❏ I'm likely to set other conditions on attendance, such as staying close to certain, "safe" people or staying in a certain place.

❏ I frequently try to distract myself by daydreaming or thinking about other things.

❏ I'm likely to avoid eye contact.

❏ Other: _____

❏ Other: _____

❑ Other: _____

These are the physical symptoms I'm likely to experience when I'm anxious:

❑ Blushing

❑ Shaking/tremors (e.g., commonly occurs with the hands, but it might be the head that shakes, or facial twitching, etc.)

❑ Sweating

❑ Hot flashes/cold flashes

❑ Gastrointenstinal discomfort

❑ Diarrhea

❑ Muscle tension

❑ Heart palpitations or racing heart

❑ Shortness of breath

❑ Tightness in chest

❑ Feelings of weakness (e.g., legs feel like Jell-O)

❑ Light-headedness/dizziness

❑ Choking sensations, lump in throat, dry mouth

❑ Feelings of unreality (almost seems like you're in a fog)

❑ Other: _____

❑ Other: _____

❑ Other: _____

I experience panic attacks, either in social situations, or in anticipation of them:
(A panic attack is a sudden surge of intense fear and anxiety, usually accompanied by

several or many of the above physical symptoms. It will usually reach a peak in five to twenty minutes before subsiding.)   YES ❑   NO ❑

I'm especially likely to experience panic attacks in these situations:

_____

I experience panic attacks approximately _____ times per week.

These are the things I'm likely to be telling myself either before, during, or after a social situation:

❑ I'm such a loser.

❑ I don't fit in.

❑ Everyone can tell how nervous I am.

❑ I don't have anything interesting to say.

❑ I'm so ugly.

❑ I'm boring.

❑ I have to get out of here before I embarrass myself any more.

❑ My voice is quivering.

❑ I sound stupid.

❑ I'm a social misfit.

❑ People must think I'm "crazy."

❑ Everyone thinks I'm too quiet.

❑ If I blow it, it's the end of the world.

❑ Other: _____

❑ Other: _____

❑ Other: _____

Other key questions to ask about my reactions to feared social situations:

Does avoidance of these situations interfere with my normal routine?   YES ❑   NO ❑

Does the fear and avoidance interfere with my academic (school) functioning?   YES ❑   NO ❑

Does the fear and avoidance interfere with my occupational (work) functioning?   YES ❑   NO ❑

Does the fear and avoidance interfere with my social activities and/or relationships?   YES ❑   NO ❑

Does having social anxiety cause me significant pain and distress?   YES ❑   NO ❑

Now you'll want to review your answers. Before doing this, refer back to page 14 where we listed the four specific criteria that must be met for a clinical diagnosis of social anxiety disorder. As you look over your answers, keep these criteria in mind. You'll likely be able to tell whether your anxiety problems fall into this diagnostic category. If you think you have more problems than are covered in this questionairre, refer to Appendix A for information on problems that often coexist with social anxiety disorder.

If you feel overwhelmed at this point, that's natural. We've covered a lot of ground. Rest assured, in the chapters ahead we'll cover each of the areas in the questionnaire. Chapter 5 will show you how to handle the physical symptoms of anxiety; Chapters 6 and 7 will provide you with powerful methods to deal with the negative thinking that accompanies social anxiety; and, Chapter 8 will take you through the process of facing your fears and eliminating avoidance behavior.

Painfully Shy No More: A Look Ahead

We want you to know, we think it's fine to be shy. There's definitely an important place in the world for quiet, sensitive, and reserved people. But no one should have to be painfully shy. Some of you may not even consider yourselves shy. You may feel outgoing in some situations, but anxiety holds you back at others times. In either case, no one should have to bear the physical distress and the mental anguish that come with social anxiety disorder. No one should have to limit one's life because of fear.

There's good news. Now, more than ever, there are ways to minimize the harmful effects of unchecked social anxiety. You've taken an important first step by reading this chapter and by completing the self-assessment questionnaire. In the next chapter, we'll explore factors that may have contributed to the development of your social anxiety, and we'll also describe reasons why it just won't go away.

But before moving on, take some time and allow yourself to imagine a life free from the fear and anxiety you've grown so accustomed to. Imagine a life where you can do what you truly want to do, not only what you're "comfortable" doing. Know that you're on the right track—you *can* reclaim your life.

Chapter 2

What Causes Social Anxiety...
and Why Won't It Just Go Away

Imagine the bow of the violin as life experience and the strings of the
violin as our biological makeup. The bow of life's experience draws
across the violin strings of biology to produce life's music . . . What
kind of music we make depends upon how we deal with what happens
to us in life and also upon what we are made of physically.

—Edward M. Hallowell, M.D.

If the burning question on your mind right now is, "What caused
this?" you're not alone. This is the number one question people
ask after learning they have social anxiety disorder. It's a natural reaction.
Knowing the reason for a problem provides a sense of control and pre-
dictability. Equally important, understanding what causes something
points the way toward change.

Unfortunately, our knowledge is not yet at a point where researchers can definitely say, "This is *the* cause." Most likely, many factors, not
just one, play a role in the onset of social anxiety. Many experts don't
even discuss causes, preferring instead to talk about "predisposing factors." In other words, they look at what aspects of a person's life—be it
faulty genes or negative experiences—make it more or less likely that
social anxiety will develop.

Still, knowing what causes social anxiety is just the beginning. Once social anxiety takes hold, different factors perpetuate the problem. Things like worrying too much and avoiding situations explain why painfully shy people tend to stay painfully shy. Sadly, it's often the very things people do to cope with anxiety—having a drink or two *before* going to a party—that maintain the fear over the long run. Later in the chapter, we'll show how these and other misguided attempts at calming your nerves make matters worse. But first, let's look at why social anxiety strikes in the first place.

What Causes Social Anxiety?

Here we'll look at two major factors—biology and environment—that increase the chances someone will develop social anxiety disorder. Because we're organizing a large amount of material, we'll discuss these factors one by one. Keep in mind, however, that your biological makeup and life experiences combine and interact in such a way that it's difficult, if not impossible, to separate the two forces.

Brain strain: The role of biology in social anxiety

Let me tell you about Garrett. He stands out in my mind because his success in therapy hinged on understanding his biological makeup. He called for an initial appointment after reading an article about my first book, *Dying of Embarrassment*. His case was unusual in that he had already been correctly diagnosed with social anxiety disorder and had tried cognitive-behavioral treatment. At that time, most people seeking help were learning about social anxiety for the first time.

During our initial meeting, Garrett elaborated on what he'd told me on the telephone. "I feel like a total failure," he said. "I did everything my therapist wanted me to do. I attended group meetings and practiced reading in front of others. I did relaxation exercises at home and completed other homework assignments to combat my negative thinking. But I'm still a worthless bundle of nerves when I'm around other people. Why didn't the therapy work?"

I needed a lot more information before I could answer Garrett's question. I had a hunch, though, that Garrett's biological makeup was the major stumbling block.

Over the next hour, I learned a lot about Garrett. He told me that his mother is a nervous person. She worried about everything and suffered from "dizzy spells," as she called them. She often bolted for the door while gasping, claiming she needed more air. The more Garrett described his mother, the more it sounded as if she might have panic disorder, another common anxiety condition. He also told me that his uncle, his mother's brother, was extremely shy and had never married. I wondered to myself if this uncle might have been socially phobic. Garrett described his father as a kind and gentle man but noted that he worked long hours and didn't talk much at home.

I asked other questions: What had Garrett been like as a baby? At what age did he walk and talk? What were his first school experiences like? Garrett didn't know the answers, but he said he'd find them out.

By our next session, Garrett had talked to his mother to find out more about his childhood. His mother said he was a "fussy" baby. He had apparently cried a lot and didn't soothe easily. She also said he resisted any regular eating or sleeping schedule. Many things bothered him: loud noises, unfamiliar people, and new situations.

Garrett didn't attend preschool, and he was rarely left with a babysitter. As a result, the beginning of kindergarten was the first time he'd been away from his parents. Garrett's mother told him several stories about the terrible time she'd had trying to get him to school. He ripped several of her blouses because he clutched her so tightly when she tried to leave the classroom. Apparently, their morning routine went like that for months. Garrett, himself, remembered that the start of first and second grades didn't get much easier. Each new year led to months of distress.

Garrett also answered questions about his previous therapy. From what he could tell me, and from reviewing his records, it sounded like an excellent, state-of-the-art treatment program. Furthermore, I could find no fault with Garrett's efforts. Just as he'd told me, the records showed he regularly attended his appointments, and he completed all of his outside assignments.

Yet Garrett was still a "bundle of nerves." True, he acknowledged that he'd made some progress—he could carry out a few basic social tasks if he really forced himself. But time after time his body reacted as if he were about to fall off a cliff. The intense, physical reaction didn't change much, even with the best, most appropriate psychological treatment.

"So what caused all of this anxiety to start with?" Garrett asked. "With all of these questions you're asking about my parents, do you think it's their fault? And why am I such a loser that I couldn't even get better with therapy?"

First, I made it clear that I was not blaming his parents. I know all too well that parents can get a bad rap for things that are out of their control. Next, I offered my general impressions of his situation. His inborn, biological makeup leads him to see danger quickly and easily, often when there's really nothing to fear.

"For you, anxiety is almost as natural as breathing," I explained. "It's like a needle stuck on a scratch in a record—your brain gets stuck in a fearful, anxious groove and can't get out. Even with all of your good efforts in psychotherapy, your brain didn't unlock and allow your body to grow comfortable with social situations. Instead, you remained on edge, prepared for attack."

I also told Garrett that anxiety runs in families—perhaps he'd inherited his fearful tendencies. His wary nature as an infant and his separation problems as a young child further confirmed a biological component to his anxiety. I stressed that it wasn't his fault. It wasn't his parents' fault. It wasn't anyone's fault. I suggested a referral to a physician for a medication consultation and reassured Garrett there was an excellent chance medicine would help.

Garrett was a bit skeptical at first. He wasn't sure he wanted to take medication for something he'd always considered a "moral weakness." He'd always told himself if he only tried harder, he could overcome his fears. Garrett needed some facts. He needed to know the scientific basis for what I was telling him.

To explain the benefits of medication, I shared with Garrett some of the latest findings about the role biology plays in the origins of social anxiety. The next several pages provide an overview of this research. Most scientific studies have looked at three major areas: genetics, neurobiology, and temperament. As you read about these physical factors, think about how Garrett's story illustrates them. Also, consider your own situation and how your social anxiety might have developed. Later, you'll have an opportunity to answer some questions to further clarify your thoughts about these issues.

Genetics. One of the strongest ways to test for the genetic basis of a disorder is through the study of twins. Monozygotic, or identical twins share the exact same genetic makeup. In contrast, dizygotic, or fraternal twins are no more genetically similar than are any other siblings. In these studies, if a certain condition occurs more commonly in identical twins as compared to fraternal twins, this higher rate of occurrence indicates a genetic component. Unfortunately, such twin studies are difficult to arrange and few have looked specifically at social anxiety disorder.

A large twin study conducted in 1992, however, examined the genetic basis for all anxiety disorders. Psychiatrist Kenneth Kendler, a specialist in genetics at the Medical College of Virginia, along with his colleagues, found that social phobia did, in fact, occur more commonly in identical twins. Among identical twins, in cases where one twin had social phobia, the other twin also suffered from the disorder 24.4 percent of the time. In contrast, among fraternal twins, if one twin had social phobia, 15 percent of their twins also had it. These results indicate genetics is a factor in at least some cases of social anxiety disorder. Most likely, though, there is not a gene specific to social anxiety. Rather, what's inherited is probably a vulnerability to develop anxiety; other factors must be present before social anxiety emerges.

In addition to twin studies, "family studies" are another, more indirect way to test for the genetic basis of a disorder. This type of research examines how disorders cluster among family members. Sometimes, clients are simply asked whether they know of other family members with psychological problems. Other times, researchers interview family members directly to determine the presence of a particular disorder. Some research includes only adult relatives; other studies also include children.

An interesting study conducted in 1996 by Professor Cathy Mancini and her associates at McMaster University in Canada examined the presence of anxiety disorders in the children of socially anxious parents. They found that 49 percent of the children had at least one anxiety disorder; 30 percent had overanxious disorder; 23 percent had social phobia; and 19 percent had separation anxiety disorder. Although there were some problems with this research, results from most of these studies support the idea that "anxiety runs in families." Genetics likely plays some role in this.

Neurobiology. Have you ever asked yourself, "I feel so awful, I wonder if I have a chemical imbalance?" Although the term "chemical imbalance" is a bit unscientific and imprecise, many people relate to it. It's understandable: when anxiety strikes, your body feels completely unbalanced, and it seems that there must be something physically wrong.

Actually, evidence accumulates daily from research centers around the world supporting the idea that social anxiety is, in part, a complex manifestation of neurobiology. What does this mean?

Scientists have proposed that deep within our brain lies a complex, inborn "anxiety circuit." This anxiety circuit is nature's way of ensuring our survival. From an evolutionary perspective, we're programmed to register fear—and to act on it. In fact, the fear circuits in our bodies are some of the most highly developed. Nature's biggest concern is safety and survival, not whether we're enjoying ourselves in the process.

The anxiety circuit gives the brain's messengers—the neurotransmitters—several pathways to travel. For the socially anxious, who studies show may have dysfunctions in their neurotransmitter systems, this means a ready-made path for producing anxiety-ridden reactions. Some studies have even found some anatomical differences in the brains of individuals with social anxiety disorder. This research is still quite new, but with regular advances in technology, it shouldn't be long before more definitive statements can be made.

Temperament

Another area of research closely tied to the causes of social anxiety is temperament. Temperament is defined as one's innate, inborn tendency to experience and respond to the environment in a characteristic manner. Think of it as a style of interacting with the world. For example, a toddler with an active temperament would be expected to have a great deal of energy, always be "on the go," perhaps need less sleep, and so on.

The aspect of temperament we're concerned with is called "behavioral inhibition." This refers to the tendency to be cautious and watchful, especially in unfamiliar circumstances. It's like a checking system. When you're confronted with a situation, you stop and check to see if everything seems the way you expect it to be. If something appears awry, you're likely to move away from the situation. For example, a child with a strong behavioral inhibition system becomes uncomfortable when discovering a substitute teacher in the classroom. The child may stand frozen, appearing unsure of what to do.

Jerome Kagan, a psychologist at Harvard University, has contributed much to our understanding of behavioral inhibition in children. In his research, he monitored the development of twenty-two children with this trait as well as nineteen children who seem uninhibited and found many differences between these two groups of children. When confronted with stressful situations, children with behavioral inhibition will:

- show increased heart rates;

- demonstrate greater muscular tension;

- experience tension in their vocal cords;

- contain higher levels of epinephrine, a substance that puts the brain on alert; and

- display higher levels of cortisol, a hormone present when one is under a constant state of apprehension.

Some of the children Kagan followed are now adolescents. He's found that those who were behaviorally inhibited as young children were more likely to develop social anxiety disorder in early adolescence. Although it seems likely that temperament can predispose someone to social anxiety, as with the other factors we've discussed, it's not enough alone to cause the problems.

There is another interesting physical marker of behavioral inhibition—blue eyes. Among Caucasian children, a "shy" temperament is more common in children with blue eyes. Although the exact mechanisms are not clear, iris pigmentation is associated with the concentration of certain neurotransmitters, and this may account for the connection between the two.

Keep in mind that behavioral inhibition is not all bad. We need some people in the world who don't impulsively jump into every situation that's presented. In fact, psychologist Elaine Aronson finds the term behavioral inhibition too negative. She prefers the phrase "highly sensitive" to describe people who are thoughtful, cautious, and reserved. We'll talk more about Aronson's work with highly sensitive people in the next chapter.

Back to Garrett. As I told Garrett about this research, I noticed him relax his grip on the arms of the chair. His breathing visibly slowed, and his forehead wasn't quite as furrowed. He listened intently and asked pertinent questions. Something seemed to click. Learning there was a physical basis for his anxiety freed him from thinking he was a failure. It wasn't that he hadn't tried hard enough to overcome his anxiety. And it certainly wasn't that he was weak.

An avid sports fan, Garrett came up with the perfect analogy. "What you're saying is that my brain is something like a muscle that's been strained. If I strained a muscle in my leg playing tennis, I wouldn't tell myself it was my fault. I'd realize I should let the strain heal before I tried to put too much weight on it. Maybe my social anxiety is such that I truly do need medication."

I told Garrett his interpretation was quite accurate. Although some people respond to cognitive-behavioral therapy alone, many people have such a strong biological component to their anxiety, they need the extra boost medication provides. It's usually not a substitute for therapy, but it's often a very necessary and helpful addition.

I'm happy to report that Garrett responded well to the medication his doctor prescribed. The medicine, along with a few "booster sessions" of therapy, left him well on his way toward living a life free from crippling fear. You'll learn about the medications commonly used to treat social anxiety in Chapter 9.

Life experience: the role of learning in social anxiety

You may have heard it said, "Biology isn't destiny." This means that even though our biological makeup exerts a strong hand in our development, it's not the whole story. Our environment also shapes us into the people we become. In this section, we'll look at three important ways life experience impacts the development of social anxiety: humiliating experiences, parenting styles, and indirect learning.

Humiliating experiences. Many people with social anxiety disorder recall a specific traumatic event associated with the beginning of their problems. A study conducted in 1985 by Professor Lars-Goran Ost at Stockholm University found that 58 percent of people with social phobia attributed the onset of their disorder to a traumatic experience. Other studies have replicated these findings. Dominic fits this pattern well.

When Dominic described the history of his social phobia, he traced his fears to an event that happened in fifth grade. Once when he wasn't paying attention in class, the teacher called on him to read aloud. He didn't know where they were in the story, so he guessed. When the whole class erupted in laughter, he knew he'd made a mistake. The girl at the desk behind him whispered where to begin reading, but by that time, he was completely embarrassed—there was no way he could gain his composure. He tried to read, but he choked and mispronounced some words.

The next day, he paid closer attention. When he was called on to read, his throat tightened and his mouth felt like it was full of cotton. He asked to be excused to get a drink of water. While in the hallway, he heard laughing. He assumed the kids were making fun of him. From that point on, Dominic was afraid to read out loud. He worried so much about losing his place, he often had trouble concentrating. He continued to experience the sensation of choking. He tried clearing his throat, but it didn't help. Before long, his fear of reading generalized into a fear of speaking to the class at other times. Several weeks later, before giving an oral report, Dominic felt so sick he went into the bathroom and vomited.

Another type of traumatic experience we've learned about from our socially anxious clients is bullying. Leslie remembers being shy but not at all unhappy during elementary school. She had several friends and did well academically. In middle school, however, things began to change. A number of "tough kids" who had gone to different grade schools began teasing her and bullying her. They said things like, "Why are you so shy?" and "Don't you know how to talk, little baby?"

Leslie didn't know how to defend herself. Despite feeling angry inside, she couldn't speak. She'd heard rumors that these were the kind of kids who would beat you up in the bathroom if you simply looked at them the wrong way. Leslie tried to become invisible, so that others wouldn't notice her or pick on her. Unfortunately, the more she tried to avoid these bullies, the more they sought her out. Leslie later artic- ulated that they must have perceived her as vulnerable—an easy target. She believes her shyness might not have developed into an anxiety dis- order if it hadn't been for those negative experiences that year.

For Dominic and Leslie, a specific few events or a discrete period of time stand out in their minds as being significant. For other people, though, a series of smaller experiences can "prime the pump" for social anxiety to develop at a later point.

Remember, too, that interactions occur between your life experi- ences and your biological constitution. Research shows that traumatic experiences can actually alter the brain. For example, the humiliating experiences Dominic and Leslie endured may have contributed to the disruption of their neurotransmitter systems. This may be especially true if they were predisposed to social anxiety in other ways, such as being temperamentally shy and inhibited.

Parenting style. The way you were raised might also have played a role in the development of your social fears. This discussion is not meant to place blame. Most parents are well-meaning, and any child-rearing "mistakes" are not intentional. Still, it's an area that deserves attention.

Elena credits a large part of her social anxiety to her parents limiting her opportunities to develop relationships outside of the family. Her parents, of Mexican descent, worked hard to make a modest living for Elena and her three brothers. Elena provided more details: Her mother worked as a maid in a local motel; her father worked in a factory. They lived in a quiet neighborhood with small, but neatly kept homes. Just down the street were larger, more stately homes. The public school that Elena and her brothers attended was right around the corner.

Elena remembers the exact point when she gave up on having friends. It was a beautiful, crisp fall day with the smell of burning leaves in the air. Elena sat on her front steps, the breeze blowing her long, dark bangs off her forehead. She was waiting for her mother to come home from work. She had something exciting to tell her: Jennifer, a girl that lived down the street, had invited her to a slumber party that weekend. Jennifer had been nice to her since Elena and her family moved into the neighborhood, but this was the first time she'd been asked to do something with her outside of school.

When the bus let her mom off at the corner, Elena dashed down to the street to meet her. Before she could even finish telling her mom the news, her mom let loose a litany of negative comments: "That Jennifer's family is not our kind. They think they're too good for us, the way they drive that brand-new minivan and dress in those designer clothes. I don't see why she invited you to her stupid party anyway. You don't fit in with her crowd. Of course, you're not thinking of going, are you? . . ."

Elena's story illustrates some salient points about how parenting can influence the development of social anxiety. Elena's mother was prone to shyness and anxiety herself, but it was often veiled in irritability and negativity. Allowing Elena to attend the slumber party would mean she'd have to face some of her own fears and insecurities.

Research shows that parents who are socially anxious themselves tend to restrict their child's opportunities for interaction with others. While it's probably not a conscious decision—most parents want the best for their children—it's easy to understand. Especially when children are young, it's often the mother who arranges these "play-dates." At the very least, this means initiating a phone call. It might also mean making "small talk" with the other mom, even spending some time with her. In short, facilitating and allowing your child to socialize usually means you have to socialize, as well.

Although it's tempting to avoid the distress altogether, the implications are great. Social skills, like any other skill, are learned through practice. If children and adolescents don't enjoy numerous and varied opportunities to engage in social activities, their confidence naturally falters. Even many adults need to season their social skills to remain comfortable and at ease around other people.

Other types of learning. There are several other ways learning may have played a role in the development of your social anxiety. In *vicarious learning*, also called *observational learning*, one acquires fear not through direct experience but indirectly, through watching others. Many animal studies have examined this process. For example, monkeys who watch other monkeys behave fearfully around snakes develop this same fear very quickly. Research conducted by Lars-Goran Ost, who was also mentioned above, found that 13 percent of people with social phobia identified observational learning as being an important factor in the onset of their disorder.

Remember, we've already shown that "anxiety runs in families." Although part of this may be genetic, it's also easy to imagine how learning is involved. If you're already predisposed to anxiety and then witness a relative behaving anxiously and avoiding social situations, you'd naturally start to wonder if there was really something to fear. Perhaps you'd also begin to model the family member's behavior.

Observational learning doesn't have to occur within families. We've heard stories from clients in which witnessing someone else endure an embarrassing situation led them to worry about something similar happening to them. Allison's experience fits into this category.

When Allison was in third grade, another girl in the class vomited all over herself, her desk, and much of the floor around her. Of course, many of the students in the class were yelling things such as "gross" and "disgusting." Although the teacher handled the situation well, this event greatly affected Allison. She thought she would never recover if something so humiliating as vomiting in public happened to her.

From that point on, Allison became extremely sensitized to any sensations of nausea. This was particularly a problem after lunch, so she began eating less and less at school. She was hungry in the afternoon and had trouble concentrating on her work, but she didn't want to risk eating something that would make her sick to her stomach. As is often the case, Allison's fears multiplied. She went from being afraid of vomiting at school to being afraid of any situation in which she would be the center of attention.

Taking Stock: What Factors Played a Role in the Development of Your Social Anxiety?

Below are some questions for you to answer. The first group deals with possible biological contributions to your social anxiety. The second group covers environmental factors. Going through this exercise may simply confirm what you already know, or it may reveal some new insights. The questions are in a yes/no format, but feel free to make comments alongside your answers.

I have one or more family members who are shy.

YES ❑   NO ❑

I have one or more family members who are the "nervous type."   YES ❑   NO ❑

My parents and teachers described me as being a shy and quiet child.   YES ❑   NO ❑

As a child, I was typically cautious and reserved when entering new situations.   YES ❑   NO ❑

My nervous system has always seemed very sensitive and re-
active. For example, I startle easily.   YES ❑   NO ❑

I have blue eyes.   YES ❑   NO ❑

**The more of the above items that you checked "yes," the more likely
there is a biological basis to your social anxiety.**

I remember one or more times when I was extremely embarrassed or humiliated as a child.   YES ❑   NO ❑

I remember witnessing someone else being embarrassed or
humiliated, and this event greatly affected me.
                                               YES ❑   NO ❑

I had few opportunities for social interaction while growing
up.   YES ❑   NO ❑

My parents tended to be overprotective of me.
                                               YES ❑   NO ❑

My parents seemed to wish I was more outgoing.
                                               YES ❑   NO ❑

My parents seemed quite concerned about "appearances"—
about what the neighbors thought.   YES ❑   NO ❑

**The more of these items that you checked "yes," the more likely that
there is an environmental basis to your social anxiety.**

Now, take a few minutes to review your answers. Do you notice
a pattern? Are your "yes" responses clustered primarily in the biology
group? Or, did you mark more items related to your environment? Most

likely, you could see pieces of your background in both sections. Remember, it's unlikely that one factor alone caused your social anxiety. Still, some people can determine the relative importance of contributing factors. For example, if Garrett answered these questions, he'd have every item in the biology section checked "yes," except for the one about having blue eyes.

Perhaps you need more information before you can answer some of these questions. You may want to talk to your parents about what you were like as a young child. Be careful not to put them on the defensive, though. They may worry and think they've done something wrong. Share this book with them if you think it's appropriate. Reassure them you're just trying to understand yourself better.

The bottom line is: You don't have to know *exactly* what caused your social anxiety problem to solve it. Sure, it's helpful to have some general ideas about how it developed, and by now, you probably do. But it's not absolutely necessary.

Why Now? The Stress Factor

Here we'll touch on the question of timing. Why does social anxiety develop when it does? Why does it ebb and flow in its severity? Stress, it seems, is a huge factor.

In some cases, individuals are predisposed to anxiety problems but don't develop a full-blown disorder until stress overwhelms them. Adam's situation was like this. A quiet child who had done well in school, Adam had several close friends. He got along well with his parents and participated in a youth group at his church. His world was disrupted, however, when his father's company relocated and the family moved across the country. During January of his junior year of high school, Adam had to start all over making friends.

His parents thought he was handling the adjustment fairly well, but they'd been so caught up in the move, they hadn't noticed his withdrawal. He'd become moody and irritable. He worried constantly about what the other kids were thinking about him. His new school was so big, no one made an effort to include him, and he had trouble initiating anything on his own.

Many kids in Adam's situation would adjust in time. But because Adam already had a number of predisposing factors in his background—a positive family history for anxiety and a quiet, shy temperament—he didn't adjust. Rather, his anxiety spiraled out of control. It wasn't until he failed his first semester in college that his parents realized the extent of his problems.

Stress can also explain why someone who has recovered from social anxiety disorder may experience a setback. Becky had been on medication to treat her social anxiety for about a year and had participated in group psychotherapy. Becky also made huge strides in overcoming her fears. She'd gone into business for herself and started dating. Things changed dramatically, however, when her mother died after a brief battle with cancer. Obviously, when a close relative dies, it's important to grieve, and grieving can take a long, long time. But Becky didn't just grieve over her mother's death. She reverted back to her old pattern of avoiding practically all social contact. She isolated herself at a time when she most needed others' support.

Stress is inevitable, and it's not always negative. Even positive events like being promoted or getting married can be stressful. If stress isn't coped with in a healthy way, though, it can take a toll on any progress you've made.

Think back over your own life. How has stress played a role in the course of your social anxiety?

What Maintains Social Anxiety Once It Starts?

So far we've looked at possible causes, or predisposing factors, of social anxiety, and we've shown how stress can set it off. Now let's explore what maintains social anxiety. Why doesn't it simply go away on its own? After all, a certain percentage of people with depression improve without treatment. In contrast, such spontaneous remission rarely happens in cases of social anxiety disorder. Why does the fear of disapproval tend to be so chronic and unrelenting?

Avoiding isn't the answer.

With any type of phobia, avoidance is a defining feature. People who are afraid of heights avoid top floors of buildings. People who are afraid of flying don't travel by plane. People who are afraid of driving on highways take the back roads. Avoidance is the automatic reaction to fear. And the immediate reduction in anxiety is a huge payoff. But it's certainly not the best long-term answer to the problem.

Avoidance maintains anxiety, even makes it worse, for several reasons. We've already mentioned some of this material in Chapter 1, but it's so important, it's worth repeating.

First, avoidance prevents a process called *habituation* from taking place. With habituation, your body becomes accustomed to a certain situation—it learns not to react so strongly. Habituation only takes place with repeated exposure, or contact, with the feared situation. So if you practice avoidance, your body doesn't have a chance to calm down, to learn on a physical level that it's not in danger. Second, avoidance prevents your thinking patterns from changing. When you avoid something you fear, you don't learn that you'd survive, and maybe even thrive. Finally, avoidance lowers your self-esteem. Over time, as you continually avoid situations, you begin to lose your confidence and feel like a failure.

We'll lead you through the step-by-step process you can take to overcome avoidance in Chapter 8.

Thinking can cause more trouble.

Faulty thinking patterns also keep many people stuck in the anxiety spiral. People with social anxiety disorder make two fundamental errors in the way they think about social or performance situations. These errors are called *probability* and *severity distortions*.

Probability distortions involve overestimating the likelihood that something will go wrong and people will judge you negatively. Some examples include:

- I'm sure everyone will notice my face is red when I have to introduce myself at the employee orientation meeting. They'll think I'm strange.

- People will see how nervous I am when I give the report in class and they'll think I don't know what I'm talking about, that I didn't prepare.

Thoughts such as these come automatically when you're anxious, and they seem perfectly logical at the time. Although it's possible some people will judge you harshly, it's not as likely as you think. Other people have a lot on their minds, and may not even notice you're blushing or nervous. Who knows? They may be worrying about their own performance. Still, nagging questions remain. What if they notice? What if they think I'm "strange"?

The big "what if" questions lead to severity distortions, which see receiving criticism or disapproval as a catastrophe. Consider these examples:

- When people see me blush, they'll think I'm weak and incompetent. No one will want to have anything to do with me. I'll be all alone.

- When my classmates notice how nervous I am, they'll laugh at me. I can't stand to have people make fun of me. I'll fall apart.

It's natural to want people to like us. But even if people disapprove of us sometimes, the consequences usually aren't as horrible as you imagine. We'll go over in depth how to change these destructive thought patterns in Chapter 6.

Worrying makes it worse.

Worry is a major issue for people with social anxiety disorder and one of the more challenging aspects to conquer. It's another important part of what maintains social anxiety.

Worry involves projecting fear into the future. It's that barrage of "what if" questions we've mentioned before and the associated antici-pation and dread of something dire happening. People with social anxiety disorder worry about social events for weeks, even months, before they take place. While this heightened anxiety could be a plus if it led to useful preparation (for example, practicing for an upcoming piano con-cert), it's usually unproductive. More typical is that all of this worry leads to procrastination—and even more worry.

Worry also keeps your body in a constant state of physical tension. Your neck may feel tense. You may have more headaches than usual. Perhaps you can't sleep well. The increased tension from worrying makes it more likely you'll suffer from the acute physical symptoms of anxiety when the actual event occurs. Because you're already like a stretched rubber band, it doesn't take nearly as much to make you pop. In addition, the constant state of tension leads your thoughts in negative directions, and you're more likely to make the probability and severity errors we discussed earlier.

Why is worry so difficult to overcome? In part, it's because of the superstitious quality of worrying. Somehow you think if you worry enough, you can prevent something horrible from happening. And if nothing terrible occurs, the idea that worrying did help is re-inforced. Or you think to yourself, "It was just luck. Next time I will probably screw up."

Paying attention (to the wrong things) can backfire.

Another important element in the social anxiety spiral is one's focus of attention. This is a relatively newer area that's described by psychol-ogist Ronald Rapee in his recent book, *Social Phobia: Clinical Applications of Evidence-Based Psychotherapy.*

According to Rapee, when socially anxious people enter a situation they perceive as potentially threatening, their attention goes in two di-rections. First, they focus on a picture in their mind, a mental image, of how they believe they must appear to others. This picture is usually inaccurate and distorted. At the same time, socially anxious people scan the "audience," the people around them, for any indication of disap-proval. Because they're looking for negative feedback, they'll probably find it. Or, they'll see disapproval when it's not really there. This negative feedback then reinforces their distorted internal snapshot and further exaggerates it. Let's look at this process in action.

Devon was in graduate school working on his doctorate degree in history. As is common in large universities, introductory freshman courses are taught by graduate students. Devon agreed to teach American history. He needed the extra income, and he thought teaching would be a good experience. He hadn't imagined, however, how frightening teaching a group of a hundred freshmen would be for him.

The first day of class, Devon was so nervous he felt sick to his stomach. He thought his voice sounded weird as he spoke into the microphone. He couldn't remember a thing, so he had to read from his notes. When he tried to turn the pages, his hands shook as if they had a life of their own. As the first few weeks went on like this, he began forming a picture in his mind of how he must appear. He imagined his hands as huge and clumsy, even grotesque, while the rest of his body looked stiff and lifeless. As he focused on this image, he was sure the students couldn't help but notice him shake as he turned the pages of his lecture notes.

Devon was shocked at how the students behaved. People in the back row were sleeping. He noticed many students yawning. A few even left during the middle of his lectures. "They must be completely bored," he thought. "How could they not be bored with me having to read my notes like this." Devon was convinced someone would complain about him to the department chairperson.

Devon's anxiety prevented him from focusing on the task at hand. He wasn't able to teach a subject that he actually knew and loved. He was too focused on his hands and what the students were thinking of him.

You'll learn strategies for dealing with these sorts of attentional problems in Chapter 7.

Low mood exacerbates the situation.

Mood is a final factor to consider in the social anxiety cycle. You may find when you're in a cheery mood you're able to do more things socially, and with more comfort than usual. Your good mood might simply be because of a sunny day or the approaching weekend. Whatever the reason, you find you're generally more outgoing on days when things are going well.

You may also find the reverse is true. When you're feeling down in the dumps, you may be more likely to hide out in your house, not wanting to talk to anyone.

We frequently have clients tell us they have "good days" and "bad days." While to some extent this is true for everyone, the consequences for people trying to overcome anxiety are greater. When people believe they can only perform socially when all conditions are good, they continue to limit their opportunities.

Many of the techniques in this book can help you with your moods as well as your anxiety. Keep in mind, though, if you find yourself in a gloomy mood more days than not for several weeks, you might be suffering from clinical depression. If this is true for you, talk to your doctor right away. Appendix A will also offer some suggestions on coping with both depression and social anxiety disorder.

Putting It All Together

Let's briefly review. Refer to the diagram "A Model of Social Anxiety." You can see at the top of the diagram the factors that increase one's vulnerability to social anxiety—the biological and the environmental contributions. The arrows going back and forth between these factors indicate that they interact with each other. For example, we mentioned that traumatic experiences can lead to biochemical changes in the brain.

In the middle of the diagram, you see "The Stress Factor." If you're predisposed to social anxiety, stressful life events can propel you into the social anxiety spiral. We described Adam, who developed social anxiety after a stressful time when he had to change schools. Stress can also make symptoms of anxiety fluctuate over time. Remember Becky who had a major setback with her social anxiety following her mother's death.

A Model of Social Anxiety

Factors that can make you vulnerable to social anxiety:

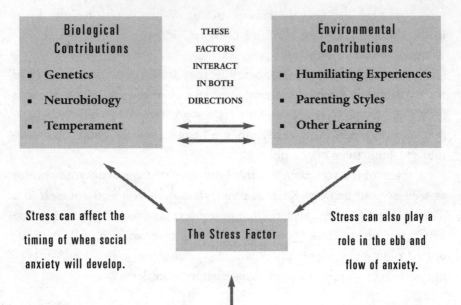

Biological Contributions

- **Genetics**
- **Neurobiology**
- **Temperament**

THESE FACTORS INTERACT IN BOTH DIRECTIONS

Environmental Contributions

- **Humiliating Experiences**
- **Parenting Styles**
- **Other Learning**

Stress can affect the timing of when social anxiety will develop.

The Stress Factor

Stress can also play a role in the ebb and flow of anxiety.

Factors that play a role in maintaining social anxiety, once it begins:

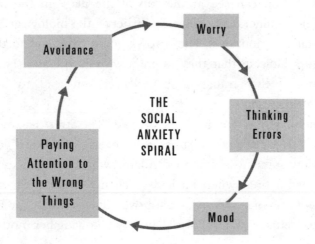

Avoidance

Worry

Paying Attention to the Wrong Things

THE SOCIAL ANXIETY SPIRAL

Thinking Errors

Mood

At the bottom of the diagram in a circular shape you'll see the maintaining factors we discussed: thinking errors, avoidance, worry, attention problems, and mood. These factors overlap some, and they tend to play off of each other. For example, when your mood is low you're more likely to worry and avoid. And then, the more you worry and avoid, the lower your mood drops.

Because of this downward spiraling effect, it can seem it takes a monumental effort to overcome social anxiety. To some extent, it's true. Overcoming fear does require a lot of effort. But learning the latest breakthrough methods can help tremendously, and that's the subject of our next section. In the following chapters, we'll show you step-by-step how to regain control of your life and free yourself from fear. You'll learn you don't have to stay painfully shy. In short, you'll learn to live the life you were truly meant to live.

▼▼▼

Part Two

Methods for Mastering

Social Anxiety: A Comprehensive

Approach

Chapter 3

Practice Acceptance

Acceptance is the only way out of hell.

—Marsha Linehan

Christy appeared visibly anxious during our first meeting. Her arms shook, and she sat mostly with her head down, eyes staring at the floor. In her mid-thirties, married with no children, Christy came to see me because she had "lost her voice."

Several months before our first appointment, Christy had been sick with a cold and sore throat, and subsequently developed laryngitis. She recovered from her illness but continued to have difficulty speaking above a whisper. Doctors ran all sorts of tests but could find nothing apparent that was wrong. Her next stop was a speech therapist, who was quite helpful in many ways; however, he felt Christy's problem was related to anxiety, and he referred her to me.

I asked Christy some general questions to get an overall picture of her background. She said she'd always been agonizingly shy and withdrawn. She never spoke at school and had difficulty making friends. She grew up a devout Catholic, and despite her shyness, she met a man at church whom she later married. At the time I saw Christy, she was working in a small diner doing mostly food preparation; her husband, Will, worked for a sign company. They lived in a small town, several hours away from our office.

I asked Christy to describe herself. "A nobody . . . worthless," she whispered. "A complete failure." As she continued, her head shook slightly. "I know my husband is disappointed in me because I haven't gotten my voice back. I'm such a problem."

"What about before you lost your voice. Did you feel so bad about yourself then?" I asked.

"Yes, but I hate myself even more now," Christy answered. "I never did have a very strong voice, and it was embarrassing. When I said something, people always asked me to speak up. It would be great to be more outgoing and talkative, but I never have anything interesting to say. Will has lots of friends from work, and he knows a lot of people from playing sports. Sometimes I feel jealous that he has friends and I don't."

Christy teared up as she added, "I've always been nervous and jittery around other people, even before I lost my voice. Like right now. I know you've noticed how shaky I am. My head won't stay still sometimes. I hate for people to see me like this."

Although Christy could find absolutely nothing positive to say about herself, I liked her right away. I could tell she was a warm and caring person who had a lot of potential.

We agreed to work together, although the distance between us would make it difficult to meet regularly. Christy set the goal of getting her voice back. She didn't think she could stand it if she had to continue whispering the rest of her life. She also wanted to work on becoming less shy.

As for my goals, I needed first to verify Christy's physical condition with her physicians. I wanted to make sure they'd ruled out all possible medical causes for her lack of speech. After that, my next step focused on helping Christy learn to accept herself—to treat herself as kindly as she did others. I knew she'd have a difficult time making progress on her goals until she eased up, at least a little bit, on the vicious self-criticism. I believed that Christy needed to accept herself and her situation before she could make changes in her life, especially a change so great as speaking again. We'll return to Christy's story later in the chapter.

If you're like many people with social anxiety, you can relate to Christy's disdain for herself, even if you've never experienced her inability to speak. You probably see no value to your quiet, reserved approach to life and would trade social anxiety disorder for practically any other problem. Of course, we've written this book to help you change— to become more comfortable in social situations and to improve the way you manage your anxiety. But we must proceed carefully. Techniques designed to help people change must be carefully blended and balanced with an ongoing posture of "acceptance."

What Is Acceptance?

Acceptance is difficult to explain, but once people experience its power firsthand, they understand why it's a necessary and important first step in overcoming any problem.

Acceptance is an attitude.

Acceptance is way of looking at ourselves and the world around us. It implies a willingness and an openness to see things as they truly are, without judgment. For example, if you're feeling anxious, you're feeling anxious. That's all. It doesn't mean it's horrible or catastrophic.

It doesn't mean the anxiety will last forever. It doesn't mean you won't be able to handle it. It doesn't mean anything except that you're feeling anxious at a particular moment.

We're so busy putting things into categories—"this is good" or "this is bad"—that we miss the actual experience of the moment. Certainly, it doesn't come naturally to suspend judgment, tolerate uncertainty, and turn off the ongoing internal commentary that plays in our minds. But all any of us can truly know is what's happening right here, right now.

Acceptance doesn't equal approval.

Many people think acceptance means approval, and this confusion causes them to balk at the whole idea. In the way we're discussing it, however, these two aren't equivalent. Acceptance does not equal approval. For example, accepting the fact that there is poverty in the world doesn't mean you approve of poverty.

Acceptance also doesn't mean you're giving up. Accepting your doctor's diagnosis of cancer doesn't mean you'll refuse treatment and just roll over and die. In addition, acceptance doesn't preclude taking appropriate action. Recognizing that you're anxious and experiencing shortness of breath doesn't mean you won't use the coping skills you have for calming down. Acceptance is simply paying attention to the way things are and taking appropriate action.

Acceptance alleviates suffering.

Perhaps the greatest benefit of learning the art of acceptance is that it alleviates unnecessary suffering. We're not saying you won't feel any more pain, because you will. But the kind of acceptance we're talking about can lead you to peace amidst the pain, calm in the center of chaos, serenity in spite of suffering. Does this sound too good to be true? In a way, it is, because acceptance doesn't simply happen overnight.

We'll share a personal example of how acceptance helped us transcend suffering. Although the story isn't in itself about social anxiety, it poignantly illustrates how acceptance works in the "real world."

For the first three years of our son Jesse's life, he had a multitude of health problems. One of our major concerns was his chronic vomiting. When he was an infant, our pediatrician reassured us that his "spitting up" was normal. Since this was our first child, we had no way to compare how much (buckets) or how often (after every meal) was normal. We had an inkling that his vomiting was somewhat unusual when we saw others' horrified reactions as they witnessed the event. When we began introducing solid foods, we hoped the vomiting would stop. Unfortunately, the situation grew worse. Jesse stopped gaining weight at nine months, and started losing weight about the time of his first birthday.

Overwrought with worry after a particularly difficult weekend, we decided the time had come (perhaps we'd waited too long) to change pediatricians. Our new pediatrician took the matter seriously, completed extensive testing, and made the diagnosis of *gastroesophageal reflux*. We hoped an end was near when Jesse began taking a medicine frequently prescribed to treat reflux. To our dismay, however, the first medicine didn't work. We tried many other medicines. None of them worked. He still vomited daily—often several times a day.

This wasn't the way we'd envisioned our life with our firstborn child. In addition to our worry about his physical health, this problem greatly diminished our quality of life. It was a major challenge getting ready in the morning. Many times we'd be walking out the door when Jesse would vomit on himself and on at least one of us, sending us back to the bathtub. More than once he threw up on the dog. We didn't go out much—it's hard to find a baby-sitter mature enough to deal with this situation. We stayed awake all night listening for sounds of vomiting (he often did it when he was in bed). We spent hours and hours theorizing about what was wrong with him. We went to medical libraries and read anything that might apply.

During one office visit, the doctor spent a lot of time with us and gave us a good heart-to-heart talk. He told us that we had to accept Jesse's vomiting—we should stop fighting it. It wasn't life-threatening at this point, he said; Jesse's weight had stabilized. The only thing to do was wait until he outgrew the problem. This wasn't what we wanted to hear. We wanted the problem fixed, solved, ended. How could we go on dealing with a child who vomited on a daily basis? Somehow, though, the doctor's message of acceptance sank in. We realized we weren't being fair to ourselves, or Jesse. We had restricted our life too much. The doctor was right. We had to start living, in spite of the vomiting.

What did acceptance involve for us? First, it meant grieving. We cried. We allowed ourselves to feel sad. As much as we'd tried to gain control of the problem, it was out of our control. Next, we "let go" of trying to prevent the vomiting. If we was going to vomit, so be it. We started getting out of the house more, carrying a bucket and a change of clothes wherever we went. We praised each other when we handled a tough situation. For example, we vividly remember the rainy Halloween night when he started to vomit while trick-or-treating at the shopping mall—how we quickly dumped the candy he had already collected onto the floor so the pumpkin-shaped bucket would be "available." We laughed about our situation a bit more. We impressed ourselves with our ability to clean up vomit one minute and eat dinner the next. We supported each other, and sought support from friends and family whenever possible.

As we accepted the situation, little by little, our suffering diminished. We handled things better, we enjoyed Jesse more, we were more relaxed. This attitude of acceptance carried with it other benefits: Our thinking gained clarity, and we trusted ourselves more. We knew it could not be healthy for anyone, much less someone so young, to vomit so much. Another year and a half had passed and he'd still not outgrown the problem. When we asked our pediatrician for a consultation, he continued to assert that it probably wasn't a big deal, and he even suggested that we might have "conditioned" Jesse to vomit. The doctor nonetheless referred us to a pediatric gastroenterologist for another opinion. After another round of more invasive tests, the GI specialist found nothing conclusive. Next, we saw a psychologist who specialized in working with children and their parents. Was it possible the doctor was right, that we'd subtly reinforced our son's vomiting? The psychologist didn't think so, and she encouraged us to continue seeking medical answers.

Two weeks after his third birthday, Jesse was awake all night coughing and vomiting. When we took him to the doctor's office the next morning, we saw an associate of our regular pediatrician. She noticed that Jesse was having difficulty breathing and hospitalized him. The next morning, the same doctor visited us in his room. She said, "I reviewed Jesse's chart from front to back, and I believe I know what's wrong with him. He has asthma and probably severe allergies." Looking back on it now, we're amazed that no one had mentioned this as a possibility to us before. In fact, one of the theories we'd developed ourselves had to do with allergies, but Jesse's first pediatrician saw no validity in it. Jesse received intensive treatment for his asthma while in the hospital, and he continued to take breathing treatments daily for the next several years. He's doing much better now, vomiting only rarely when his asthma or allergies flare up.

As you can see, acceptance doesn't come quickly or easily. It's a process, much in the same way in which grieving someone's death is a process. Only after you go through the shock, the denial, the anger, and the despair can you move forward with a spirit of patience and trust. Practicing the art of acceptance taught us to seek answers while at the same time tolerating uncertainty. We couldn't control what was happening in Jesse's body. We couldn't force the medical professionals to take us seriously. We couldn't change or control any of the events. All we could do was to take charge, as best we could, of our reactions to those events. Each new twist and turn, each new sign and symptom, presented us with an opportunity to embrace the paradox of suffering—and acceptance. As twentieth-century philosopher, D. T. Suzuki, said, "Unless we agree to suffer, we cannot be free from suffering."

Why Do We Fight Acceptance?

Acceptance doesn't come easily to most of us. We're certainly not raised to think this way. Quite the opposite, Western culture teaches us that if we put our foot down and refuse to accept something, it will magically change. Let's explore why it's so difficult to adopt an accepting attitude, especially when it comes to accepting ourselves.

We're bucking cultural norms.

One reason we resist accepting our quiet side is that it doesn't match the cultural ideal. How many times have you seen a television show or a movie where the main character was reserved, cautious, and thoughtful, and where this was seen as positive? We can't think of a single example. Most often, the media portray popular characters as outgoing. Shy or quiet characters, when they are seen, often assume the role of a victim. Is it any wonder we have trouble accepting ourselves as okay?

In Elaine Aronson's book, *The Highly Sensitive Person*, she describes some extremely important research dealing with this issue of culture. The study, conducted by Xinyin Chen and Kenneth Rubin of the University of Waterloo in Ontario, Canada, and Yuerong Sun of Shanghai Teachers University, compared children in both cities to determine what traits made children popular. Among the group of 480 students in Shanghai, "shy" and "sensitive" children were the most sought-after as friends. In contrast, among the 296 Canadian children, shy and sensitive children were the least desirable. You can see, then, that whether you're accepted by others can have little to do with your personally and much to do with the prevailing cultural norms.

Not measuring up to the ideal personality type can have an enormous impact on how you view yourself. For example, I still remember one horrible day in high school when a math teacher called attention to my quietness. He told the whole class that I was the quietest student he'd ever had in his twenty-two years of teaching. Of course, everyone turned around to look at me, as if I was some kind of freak. I was humiliated and felt deep shame. I truly believed there was something wrong with me. It didn't even cross my mind that there was something wrong with a teacher who would make such a statement. Unfortunately, an accumulation of such experiences led me to hate myself for being so quiet.

Being in a minority can make accepting yourself difficult. But sometimes simply having an understanding of these cultural factors can make the task of acceptance a bit easier. When I'm having a bad day and wish I was more outgoing, it helps to remind myself of the study comparing children in China and Canada. I tell myself that it's okay to be sensitive and quiet. If I lived in China, I'd be very popular!

We're questioning the accuracy of family messages.

Accepting ourselves may mean questioning the messages we've learned not only from the culture at large but also from our families. Perhaps you picked up on subtle, or not so subtle, signs from your family that they'd prefer you to be more sociable, not so sensitive. In addition, they may have mislabeled your sensitivity, thinking you were behaving like a prima donna rather than a painfully shy child.

I remember an example of when this happened in my family. I was seventeen years old when my grandfather died. I was not only sad about my grandfather's death, I was extremely anxious about attending the funeral as I had never been to one before. I locked myself in the bathroom, yelling through the door that I wasn't going. My father, himself grief-stricken and clueless about why his daughter was acting this way, yelled back, "I can't believe you could be so selfish. How can you say that you won't go to my father's funeral?" Of course, I felt horrible about myself.

What my father didn't realize, and what I couldn't articulate even to myself, was that I was threatened by the mere thought of this unfamiliar situation. I didn't know what to expect at the funeral. I didn't know what would be expected of me. How was I supposed to act? I hated the idea of having to make conversation with my distant relatives. What was I supposed to say?

I survived the funeral, and my father forgave me for the scene I'd made when I initially refused to attend. But I know he didn't understand. How could he? Parents aren't taught how to recognize and deal with a socially anxious child. Unfortunately, the label "selfish" stuck with me, and it took me a long time to question the validity of what my dad had said.

Sometimes memories get seared into the brain without the appropriate context surrounding them. In my own journey toward self-acceptance, I've had to revisit that incident and examine the circumstances surrounding my father calling me "selfish." I had to decide that he wasn't right—he had completely confused my anxiety with selfishness.

Consider your own family. Were there times when your anxiety was misread? Did you receive messages about yourself that simply weren't true? It can be difficult to dissect these experiences and develop your own interpretations. But learning to see ourselves clearly and to accept what we see is important work to do.

We think if we punish ourselves enough, we'll change.

Accepting ourselves unconditionally is also difficult because we must give up the fantasy that if we punish ourselves enough with negative thoughts, we'll change. It's as if we think we can whip ourselves into shape by saying things like:

- I'm weak for feeling any anxiety.

- I'm abnormal because I'm quiet.

- There's something wrong with me if I don't have lots of friends and an "active" social life.

- I'm a loser.

- I'm defective.

- I'm weird.

- I'm boring.

We cling to the belief that by berating ourselves, we'll transform into "social butterflies." But as you've probably learned from experience, this strategy doesn't work well. In fact, the more we yell at ourselves to "buck up," "snap out of it," or "get tough," the more anxious we become. The frightened little child inside of us doesn't respond favorably to such a mean dictator. Instead, we need to find ways to accept the anxious part of our selves, to hold that part by the hand and gently say, "You're okay."

We don't believe we deserve self-acceptance.

The messages we receive from our culture, our family, and ourselves become deeply ingrained, in part due to sheer repetition. It's not that we hear "you're too quiet" once or twice; we hear it over and over again from many different sources. Because these negative messages bombard us, and because we never stop to question whether they're true, we internalize the feeling that we are, indeed, defective. We don't believe we're deserving of acceptance, at least not now. Similar to a woman who puts her life on hold until she loses thirty pounds, we put conditions on self-acceptance. We say to ourselves:

- Maybe I'll feel okay about myself *if* I can go through with that presentation next month.

- Maybe I'll feel okay about myself *if* I get up my nerve to ask that woman in my Tai Chi class out for a date.

- Maybe I'll feel okay about myself *if* I get a decent job.

What types of conditions do you place on yourself? Do you accept yourself as you are today? Or do you feel you must change *before* you can accept yourself?

Remember, acceptance doesn't mean you're giving up and not trying anymore. In contrast, it means you're looking at yourself and your situation realistically. Most people with social anxiety disorder take too negative a view of themselves. Of course, there are aspects of your life you want to work on. But as we've said before, it's much easier to work toward change if you're not wasting energy criticizing yourself for perceived flaws.

We believe we're giving up control.

The final barrier to self-acceptance, and perhaps the most difficult to overcome, is the belief that we're exerting some sort of meaningful control when we fight against something. Again, this is a Western way of thinking: We must fight to conquer. In contrast, Eastern philosophy emphasizes "going with the flow," moving with, not against, the resistance. This shift in thinking can be frightening because it seems we're giving up control, and it can feel like a terrible loss. In reality, however, we're not losing; we're gaining tremendous strength. Instead of giving away our power by letting other people determine our worth, we're saying to ourselves, "I accept myself today, exactly the way I am." By relinquishing control, we gain it.

Learning and Practicing the Gentle Art of Acceptance

We realize this idea of acceptance sounds good in theory, but you're probably wondering, "What do I do? How can I accept myself and my circumstances when I'm so totally miserable?" These are legitimate questions, and we'll answer them below.

To illustrate, let's return to Christy. Remember how she was so relentless in her negative comments about herself? After I'd explained the concept of acceptance, I told her it was time to get practical. There were concrete steps she could take to begin changing the way she felt about herself and her problems. Her face brightened, and she seemed eager to learn more.

Step 1: Recognize the nonaffirming thought.

The first step, I explained to Christy, is to become aware of the constant stream of "self-talk" that runs through your mind. "Everyone talks to themselves. It's perfectly normal," I reassured her. "While some of this self-talk may be positive or neutral, you'll probably be shocked at the sheer volume of negative, self-critical thoughts you also have. If you make the effort to monitor this negative self-talk, you'll get a better idea about why you often feel overwhelmed and hopeless."

We went over a few examples. I had plenty of notes from my initial session with her, and I read back some of the things she'd said about herself: "I'm worthless" and "I'm a nobody." Christy looked a little startled when she heard someone else say the words. I asked Christy to carry a small notebook in her purse for a few days and to jot down any negative thoughts she had about herself. I encouraged her to write her thoughts immediately after she noticed them. "If you wait, you're likely to forget," I said.

But we don't really forget, do we? On a deeper level these messages stay with us, wearing us down and eroding our feelings of self-esteem.

Step 2: Apologize to yourself.

Next, I instructed Christy to apologize to herself immediately after she noticed she'd made a negative comment about herself. I acknowledged that this might seem a bit awkward at first, but I stressed how important it is to do.

"Do you ever speak as cruelly to other people as you do to yourself?" I asked her.

"No. Just the opposite," Christy answered. "I'm always trying to make sure I don't hurt other people's feelings. If I accidentally say something hurtful, I'm quick to apologize. I probably say 'I'm sorry' too much."

"So why not tell yourself, 'I'm sorry'? Explain to yourself that you're just learning about the damaging effects of this critical self-talk, and that you're going to work at being kinder and more understanding. It won't happen overnight, but it's important to start somewhere."

Step 3: Question the validity of the thought.

The next step, I told Christy, is to examine the negative statement you've made about yourself and ask these questions:

- What is the evidence that this statement is true?

- Who says it's true?

- What gives him or her the right to decide it's true?

- So what if it's true? Does it matter?

I explained to Christy that she doesn't have to firmly believe the answers she comes up with at this time. Just going through the process of answering them will yield important insights and help loosen the grip of the thought. If possible, she could write out the answers to these questions at the same time she made note of the thought. Otherwise, she could wait until later in the day to go through this questioning process. I asked her to initially write the answers on paper. Later, these steps would come more naturally and she wouldn't have to write everything down.

Step 4: Replace the thought with an affirmation.

Finally, Christy and I discussed the next step in dealing with critical self-talk: replacing the negative thought with a more positive, self-accepting one. Some people call these affirmations. Some examples you might consider using include:

- I accept myself as I am today.

- I am okay just as I am.

- We need quiet, thoughtful people in the world.

- I have many gifts to offer the world.

- My anxiety causes me much pain, but part of this pain comes from not accepting who I am.

- I choose today to stop berating myself for my social anxiety. I will remember that everyone has problems. That's part of what makes us human.

- If I accept myself, it won't matter so much what other people think.

Many people have a favorite affirmation or two that they write on an index card and refer to routinely. Others like to post a few of these in places they see often, such as on the bathroom mirror or the refrigerator door.

Christy really liked the idea of having something she could do outside of the session. Eager to begin, we set up another appointment.

When we met again, Christy looked prepared and ready to get to work. She'd brought her journal in—a small, spiral notebook she could carry discreetly in her apron at work. We talked generally at first about how the experience had been for her. She said she felt a little uncomfortable sharing what she'd written, that it was probably "silly." I told her she didn't have to share it, and that I understood. I reassured her that it was great that she'd taken the time to write her thoughts down;

many people don't follow through like she did. Before I could say anything else, she handed me the notebook. She didn't think she could read it out loud without feeling self-conscious, but she said that I could.

Christy had included a lot of helpful detail in her journal, noting the time and the setting. Let's look at her first entry.

Christy's Journal
Mean Things I Say to Myself

> *Monday morning, 8:05 A.M.: I'm at work. Standing at a counter cutting vegetables for the salad bar. Everyone is talking about their weekends. My head starts to shake. My hand shakes too. I can hardly keep the knife from cutting myself. I think everyone must think I'm so strange. I'm just a strange person who whispers and shakes.*

> *Questions:*
> *What is the evidence? I do shake, and I do whisper. That part is true. I guess I shouldn't say I'm strange though.*

> *Who says it's true? I do, I guess. No one's really said anything to me. I guess I don't know that they think I'm strange. Maybe they think I have some kind of disease or something.*

> *What gives them the right to decide? Who's to say what "strange" is? Maybe I'm different than the people who usually work here. Maybe I'm not what they're used to. Does that mean I'm strange?*

> *So what if it's true? What if I am strange? My husband still loves me. After all, being strange is better than being an ax murderer or something.*

> *Affirmation/Accepting Thought: I'm a worthwhile person even if I have this anxiety problem. Everyone has something they have to deal with.*

Christy did a great job, especially since this was her first time keeping any type of journal. We laughed at the part about not being an ax murderer. I was starting to see a spark in Christy; she had a sense of humor.

As we went through several other entries, Christy became more adept at questioning her negative self-statements and developing helpful affirmations. Toward the end of the session, she wrote out this affirmation on an index card and vowed to repeat it to herself often: *"I accept my shaking and my whisperlike voice as a part of my life today. This doesn't mean I like it, but I can tolerate it, learn from it, grow from it."* On the back of the card, I wrote down the Serenity Prayer: *"God, grant me the serenity to accept the things I cannot change, the courage to change the things I can, and the wisdom to know the difference."*

Christy found the most difficult part of this whole exercise was apologizing to herself. "I still believe the negative things I'm saying to myself, so it seems fake to apologize. I'm just going through the motions," she explained.

This was to be expected; the process of self-acceptance is just that, a process. "It's not something you simply figure out once, and then 'just do it' like the Nike commercials tell us to," I told her. "You've been beating yourself over the head with your critical words for a long, long time. I know it's hard, but try to be patient."

Christy kept her journal for several months, and little by little she began accepting herself more. She even noticed a big improvement in her shaking. She still felt stuck, though, in that her voice remained a whisper. "No matter how hard I try, I can't speak at a normal volume," she lamented.

I agreed it must be frustrating and perhaps even frightening for her to not have her voice back. She might be disappointed that our sessions hadn't "cured" her. I would probably feel that way, too, if I were she. I suggested we try a visualization exercise to see if we couldn't find another way of looking at her situation.

I first learned about this visualization exercise from psychologists Jane Hirshmann and Carol Hunter, authors of *When Women Stop Hating Their Bodies*. In working with women who were obsessed with losing weight, they asked them to imagine what would happen if they knew there was absolutely no way they could ever lose weight. It was a physical impossibility. The purpose of this exercise was to foster self-acceptance and to help these women realize the futility of putting their lives on hold until they achieved a specific culturally sanctioned weight. We've used a variation of their idea to address acceptance of other situations.

I asked Christy to form an image in her mind of what she wants to change, what she's having difficulty accepting. She wanted to stop whispering and start speaking in a "normal" volume and tone of voice. Next, I asked her to imagine that some freak accident of nature has released a harmless but potent gas into the atmosphere. This gas makes it impossible for the very thing you want—getting your voice back—to occur. You realize the gas has been released and there's no way to reverse its effects. This means you will whisper for the rest of your life.

I gave Christy some time to immerse herself in this imagery. Next, I asked her to consider these questions:

- Now that you know you will always whisper, how will you choose to live your life? Would you do anything differently?

- Will you continue to berate yourself for the way you talk? Remember, it's not your fault that this gas was released, preventing any change from taking place.

- Will you find a way to handle the situation? To tolerate it?

- How can you cope more effectively? How can you take better care of yourself?

- If you weren't worrying so much about your voice, how else would you expend your energy?

This was a powerful exercise for Christy, but the answers didn't come to her all at once. She thought about these questions many times after our session.

When we next met, Christy appeared perkier than I'd ever seen her, almost bubbly. She told me that she had wanted to volunteer at the Humane Society for a long time. She'd gotten up her courage once before, prior to losing her voice. Something came up, though, and she wasn't able to follow through. Then, after she'd lost her voice, she decided there was no way she could attempt volunteer work. Would they even want someone who couldn't speak normally?

After our last session, Christy realized she couldn't put her life on hold waiting for her voice to return. She went to the Humane Society and asked about the possibility of volunteer work. The director was apparently quite receptive and invited Christy to attend an upcoming board meeting. She said they desperately needed a secretary for the meetings. Could Christy take notes? she asked. Christy was thrilled, and agreed.

Christy and I worked together for several years. This was quite a commitment on her part, especially given the distance she traveled to my office. During our sessions, we worked on many of the methods for mastering anxiety that you will learn in the coming chapters. Christy learned to better manage the physical symptoms of her anxiety. She didn't shake quite as often, and when she did, it didn't bother her so much. She gradually exposed herself to new social situations. For example, she started attending the adult Sunday school class at her church, something she'd previously been too afraid to do. She continued to serve as secretary for the Humane Society board, and she helped care for the animals. She especially loved working with the animals, she told me, because they didn't care if she whispered.

As Christy became more comfortable with herself and more content with her life, we needed to see each other less and less. Also during this time period, Greg and I made the decision to move from St. Louis to Jefferson City to be closer to family. This increased the distance between us and made the drive completely out of the question for Christy, so we ended our formal treatment. It was sad to say good-bye to Christy; I had grown quite fond of her. She promised to keep in touch, though, and true to her word, I did receive several letters from her.

One day, a few years after I'd moved, I received a phone call. A pleasant but unfamiliar voice on the other end of the phone said, "Barb, do you know who this is?" I had no idea as to the caller's identity; it was a complete mystery. Then she said, "This is Christy. I got my voice back." Now I was the one who was speechless!

When I regained my composure, we talked for a while. Of course, the scientist part of me wanted to know what had happened. How did she regain the ability to speak above a whisper? Being a deeply religious person, Christy thought it was a miracle, and she was probably right. Miracles happen, but I also believe that this was a miracle bathed in acceptance. Although Christy's therapy contained many components, and certainly her faith played a huge role in her ultimate recovery, I believe developing an attitude of acceptance was key and something that couldn't be bypassed.

Equally miraculous, though, Christy told me that by the time her voice returned, it didn't matter as much. More important than being able to speak, she said, was finally realizing she had something important to say.

Chapter 4

Commit to Change
(A Little at a Time)

Be not afraid of going slowly, be afraid only of standing still.

—Chinese Proverb

The first time I saw Nolan, a twenty-one-year-old college student, I could tell he wasn't thrilled to be in my office. He sat with his arms crossed, kept his head down, and responded to my initial questions with few words. Although this can be typical for shy people, I sensed there was more involved. I followed my instincts and dispensed with my usual questions. Instead I said, "Nolan, I'm wondering if it was your idea to see me, or if someone else encouraged you to come." I thought I saw him begin to grin as he looked up at me for the first time.

"How did you know?" he asked.

"A lucky guess," I replied. "Actually, I see my fair share of people who'd rather be at the dentist having their teeth drilled than talking to a psychologist."

"Yeah. That's pretty much how I feel. My parents made me come," he acknowledged.

Nolan opened up a bit after that. He said he had always lived at home and was a student at a nearby college. It was taking him a while to get through school because he found it difficult to take a full course load. He said it was because he "didn't handle stress well." He didn't work except to do some lawn care for a few neighbors. He had no friends. When he wasn't in class or studying, he stayed in his room listening to music or playing computer games. Nolan didn't know why his parents were "on his case"—he just wished they'd leave him alone.

Because Nolan wasn't sure why his parents wanted him to see me, I suggested they accompany him to his next appointment. Reluctantly, he agreed.

I learned a great deal more at the next session. Nolan sat quietly while his parents did most of the talking. Mrs. Baxter began.

"I'm very worried about Nolan," she said. "He rarely leaves the house except to go to school. I know he's shy; he always has been, but I believe he's getting worse. He doesn't have any friends left, and the few friends he did have went out of town for college. He won't even go out to buy his own clothes or shoes. I have to go to the store, buy things I think will fit, and bring them home for him to try on. He won't get his hair cut, either. He wears it long in a ponytail."

Nolan jumped in, "I like my hair this way."

Mr. Baxter added his perceptions. "I think we coddle Nolan. We should *make* him do more things. For example, he never helps out with errands. My wife and I both work full-time. It would be nice if Nolan went to the grocery store sometimes."

By the end of the session, I was reasonably sure that Nolan suffered from social anxiety. I also wondered whether some family dynamics might be complicating the situation, but I'd have to wait and see. During the remaining time, I provided Nolan and his parents with some basic information about the nature and treatment of social anxiety disorder. Mr. and Mrs. Baxter needed no convincing. "How often can Nolan see you?" they asked. "We want him to get started right away." In contrast to his parents' enthusiasm, Nolan appeared hesitant, perhaps even angry.

Although Mr. and Mrs. Baxter were motivated by concern, I had to slow them down a bit. We didn't know if Nolan was ready to accept my diagnosis, much less dive right into treatment. Ultimately, it was Nolan's decision whether he wanted to make changes in his life. There would be things they could do to help, but he would have to do the work—they couldn't do it for him. I asked Mr. and Mrs. Baxter to step into the waiting room; I wanted to talk with Nolan by himself.

It was a tricky situation. His parents were concerned and wanted him to begin treatment, but I strongly suspected Nolan wasn't ready for major change. I needed to build a relationship with him first, to show him I had something to offer—something that would benefit him, not just his parents.

I presented Nolan with an option. Perhaps we could meet for a limited number of additional sessions, maybe two or three. This would ease his parents' worries and hopefully give him a bit of breathing room at home. During our sessions, we could discuss whatever he wanted. I promised him I wouldn't push him into anything.

Nolan agreed. He didn't see that he had much to lose by coming back for a few times.

We're not finished with Nolan's story, but before we continue, we need to examine the process of change. As you probably know from personal experience, change doesn't happen in one fell swoop; rather, it takes place in stages. Below, we'll describe these stages and illustrate their importance. You'll learn what stage Nolan was in, and how this affected his treatment.

The Stages of Change

Three psychologists, James Prochaska, John Norcross, and Carlo DiClemente, have devoted their careers to studying the process of change. Combined they have more than fifty years of clinical and research experience in this area. Their research has included thousands of people who have tried with varying degrees of success to make all kinds of changes in their lives—everything from losing weight to quitting smoking to overcoming psychological distress.

In the course of their research, Prochaska, Norcross, and Di-Clemente found six stages people encounter in the process of changing:

- precontemplation

- contemplation

- preparation

- action

- maintenance

- termination

Just like any other process, people spend varying amounts of time in each stage. But every person who undergoes a significant change in his or her life will pass through them.

This team also has written an excellent book, *Changing for Good*, for people who want to make changes in their lives. In addition, the six stages of change identified by them have been applied in programs sponsored by organizations such as the National Cancer Institute and the Institute of Drug Abuse.

So what does each of these stages include? What do they mean? Why are they so important? We'll answer these questions below. Then, later in the chapter, we'll offer tips on moving from one stage to another.

Stage 1: Precontemplation

The first stage in the change cycle is called precontemplation. As the name implies, people in this stage haven't begun to think about change. They may not realize they have a problem, they may not know change is possible, or they may have given up hope. As a result, they aren't ready to overcome their distress. It's common for someone in precontemplation to say:

- "This is just how I am."

- "I don't have a problem."

- "What's the point?"

Many people with social anxiety disorder have struggled for so long they can't imagine their life any other way. They've come to think of their fear and avoidance as almost normal. The possibility of enjoying a full and satisfying life, free from fear and anxiety, doesn't even enter their minds.

People in precontemplation can seem like they're in denial. "Why doesn't he simply admit he has a problem?" family members complain. It's true, denial can play a role in the precontemplation stage; however, it's often related to lack of information. Many people may not know they have an anxiety disorder—one that's serious but also treatable.

When people in the precontemplation stage seek help, it's often because of pressure from others, as was the case for Nolan. Although he sometimes wished he had more of a social life, he didn't recognize his loneliness as a solvable problem. Also, because his parents had accommodated him so much, he was never forced to consider changing. Remember how his mother bought all his clothes for him? She also filled his car with gas, bought his textbooks at the bookstore, and made sure there was food in the house. In addition, his parents didn't require him to pay rent, which allowed him not to work. Ironically, his environment made it possible for him to ignore many of the harmful effects of his anxiety.

Another hallmark of the precontemplation stage is a feeling of demoralization. Nolan felt this way. His older sister had graduated from college, found a good job, and was engaged to be married. What was wrong with him, he often asked himself, that his life was such a wreck? He felt thoroughly hopeless. He couldn't even imagine moving away from home.

Precontemplators must take several steps before they can move to the next stage. First, people in this stage need to develop greater awareness of themselves. Too often what's on the surface masks the real issue. For example, all Nolan's father saw was a son who was "lazy" and didn't help around the house. Nolan, in turn, accepted his father's interpretation and also thought of himself as lazy and unhelpful. In fact, these labels were inaccurate. Nolan wasn't lazy and unhelpful, but he was anxious and depressed. Nolan also minimized his situation and made excuses for his behavior. "I have too much studying to have friends," he told his mother when she expressed her concern.

Let's return to my work with Nolan. I kept my word about letting him take the lead during our sessions. At first, he mostly talked about the music he liked and the classes he was taking. It didn't take long, however, before he raised other topics. The issue of being compared to his sister, and his related feelings of hurt and anger, was a big concern. He believed there was no way he could ever live up to his sister's achievements, so why should he try? He felt his parents favored her and that they thought of him as their "problem child."

As Nolan and I talked about this and other issues, I was able to point out how many of his anxious responses and subsequent avoidance behaviors fit the description of social anxiety disorder. Soon, he agreed to read a brochure and watch a video on the topic. He started to see that much of his life had been governed by his extreme shyness, and he felt sad about all the experiences he had missed. We also discussed what it would mean for him to make changes in his life—to become less anxious, more responsible, and no longer be the "problem child." What impact would these changes have on him? On his family?

In addition to gaining awareness of his problem, Nolan, like all precontemplators, needed to cultivate hope. After all, without hope there's little reason to contemplate change. Why would anyone bother to take the risks and exert the required effort unless there was the promise of better times ahead?

For Nolan, simply learning that precontemplation is a predictable part of the change cycle lessened his despair. He began to ask questions about what treatment for his social anxiety would involve. He started to talk about his goals for the future, and his mood improved. He'd taken that all-important step—that leap of faith—of simply entertaining the idea that his life could be better. This glimmer of hope marked a new beginning for Nolan's and my work together, and signaled his transition into the contemplation stage.

Stage 2: Contemplation

In contrast to the previous stage, people in the contemplation stage readily acknowledge they have a problem. However, they're still struggling to integrate their new self-awareness and are unsure how to proceed. Statements you're likely to hear from someone in the contemplation stage include:

- "I want to change, but I don't know how."

- "I don't know if I'm ready yet."

- "I feel stuck."

I remember one woman who was clearly in the contemplation stage. She called in response to seeing me interviewed about social anxiety on the local news and asked if I had time to talk with her on the phone. When I told her I had a few minutes, she launched into a list of questions. Did most of my clients improve? Did I think cognitive-behavioral therapy would work in her case? What did I think about medication? Should she see a psychiatrist first? I answered her questions as best I could and said we would discuss these issues more in our first meeting. She said she needed to check her schedule and would call back.

She did call back, but not to set up an appointment. She had more questions she wanted answered first. She told me she'd been to another anxiety disorder specialist. What did I think of his approach? Was I sure I could help her? She didn't want to take any chances, she said.

The calls continued for another few days until, finally, she set up an appointment for the following week. Can you guess what happened next?

She left a message canceling her appointment. She apologized profusely for taking up so much of my time but said she wasn't ready. "I need to think about it more," she said. Although I could easily have been annoyed, I understood she was ambivalent about change. She'd also fallen into the trap of expecting some kind of guarantee.

We're all cautious about change, aren't we? After all, it can be frightening. Change leads us into unknown territory, causing us to rethink who we are and what we believe. It would be easier if we knew ahead of time how everything would turn out. Unfortunately, life doesn't offer us such assurances.

Still, the contemplation stage is necessary. People need time to think things over before they can begin preparing for change. The trouble lies with analyzing too much, never making the move from thought to deed. I hoped this wouldn't be the case for the woman caller I mentioned above.

Stage 3: Preparation

In the preparation stage, people have made a decision to change, but they haven't worked out all the details yet. They're more optimistic than in the previous two stages and might think or say things like:

- "I'm not going to let anxiety control me any longer."

- "I know I can overcome my fears."

- "I'm going to do something about my problems."

The main task of this stage is, as its name implies, to begin preparing for the action stage. We'll use Janna's story to illustrate.

Janna returned home from her first semester of college determined to make some changes. The fall term had been rough. She hadn't gotten along well with her roommate, Sheri, who was quite outgoing and frequently invited other people to their dorm room. Sheri didn't exclude her, but Janna still felt uncomfortable, unable to think of anything to say. Janna sensed everyone thought she was a "nerd" because she didn't join in the laughing and joking around. Sometimes she just wanted the room to herself so she could study rather than needing to go to the library for some peace and quiet. She didn't think that Sheri would understand, so she never said anything.

Janna missed her family terribly, and she went home each weekend. Still, she knew she missed out on some of the campus activities by coming home so often. By the time the semester break rolled around, Janna hadn't made any friends.

Adjusting to college can be difficult for many people, but these problems weren't new to Janna. She'd been slow to make friends all through grade school and high school. In addition, she knew her extreme shyness kept her from participating in activities she'd probably enjoy. For example, she loved music and had always wanted to join the marching band in high school, but she could never bring herself to try out. She didn't think she could perform in front of others, especially with the pressure of being judged. She vowed to herself that she'd make a fresh start in college, but here she was again, retreating further into her shell.

Fortunately, Janna enjoyed a warm, open relationship with her mother, and they talked a lot about Janna's situation during the holidays. Janna's mother had encouraged her daughter to seek professional help before, but Janna had always said she could handle things herself. However, her mother now sensed an attitude of readiness, and together they developed a plan.

Janna agreed to make an appointment at the student counseling center the first week she was back at college. She'd heard a few other girls talk about going for various reasons, and they'd apparently had positive experiences. Janna also knew she wouldn't make any friends if she wasn't there, so she agreed to stay on campus a few weekends a month. She and her mother practiced how to talk to Sheri. Janna needed some time when she could count on their room not being a party zone. She was still unsure of her ability to be assertive, but she promised her mom she'd try. By the time the semester break ended, Janna felt more hopeful than she had in months. She'd successfully accomplished the tasks of the preparation stage; now she was ready to put her plan into action.

The Later Stages of Change

So far in this chapter we've emphasized the first three stages in the change process. They're the ones most often overlooked and the ones you most need to know about right now. Still, it's helpful to have an overall picture of the process, so we'll briefly describe stages 4, 5, and 6 below.

STAGE 4: *Action.* Most people equate change with doing something, and that's what the action stage is all about. It involves the nuts and bolts work of overcoming a problem. The remaining chapters in "Part Two" cover methods for mastering social anxiety and constitute the "action" part. Reading and following the exercises in these chapters will go a long way toward helping you overcome your social anxiety.

STAGE 5: *Maintenance.* In maintenance, changes made in the action stage are consolidated. The task of this stage is to make sure change lasts.

STAGE 6: *Termination.* In the termination stage, there is essentially no longer a problem. Changes made are completely integrated into your life. Many people never reach this stage, and that's okay since some problems don't easily allow for a full "termination." For example, many therapists in the field of substance abuse believe that one never fully recovers from alcoholism. In the case of social anxiety disorder, it seems that people's experiences differ. Some people feel fully "recovered" while others periodically recycle through these stages.

What Stage of Change Are You In?

Now that we've described the stages of change, let's find out where you are in the process. In their book *Changing for Good*, Prochaska, Norcross, and DiClemente list three simple questions to ask yourself. We've changed them to fit the case of social anxiety disorder. Read each question and then circle yes or no.

1. Are you seriously considering trying to overcome your social anxiety within the next six months? Yes or No

2. Are you planning to try to overcome your social anxiety in the next thirty days (and perhaps taking small steps to do so)? Yes or No

3. Are you now actively involved in trying to overcome your social anxiety? Yes or No

Now look at the grid below to determine your current stage of change.

Q1	No	Yes	Yes	Yes
Q2	No	No	Yes	Yes
Q3	No	No	No	Yes
Stage of Change	**Precontemplation**	**Contemplation**	**Preparation**	**Action**

Remember that every stage has its purpose, and the action stage isn't the only place where progress occurs. Before the chapter's over we'll offer you specific suggestions for things you can do at each stage. But first we need to discuss the important issue of timing.

Timing Is Everything

Prochaska and his colleagues not only delineated the six stages of change, they also demonstrated the importance of matching one's efforts to these stages. For example, imagine that while conducting a yearly physical, the doctor tells his patient that he'd better quit smoking. He lists all the reasons why and writes a prescription for a new medication to help decrease the urge to smoke. He also tells him to attend a smoking cessation group at a nearby hospital. The patient leaves, never fills the prescription, and never attends the group. The physician offered a perfectly legitimate and often helpful change strategy, but the patient wasn't ready. He wasn't in the right stage of change for this approach to work.

People seeking help for anxiety disorders face this same situation. If they're not ready for change, even the best intentions won't work. Let's look at two examples of such "mismatches."

Margie had done considerable reading about social anxiety disorder. In fact, she probably knew more than many professionals. Motivated in part by her young daughter, she had already made a commitment to herself to change. She wanted to be able to do all the things that parents do with their children, such as take them to play groups or to birthday parties. The way she functioned now, she avoided anything that involved other people. But she didn't want her daughter to be so isolated—like her.

From her reading, Margie knew some of the basic approaches she could try. She could learn relaxation skills, change her thinking patterns, gradually expose herself to anxiety-arousing situations. But she also knew herself well enough to know she couldn't do it alone. It would be too easy to say, "I'll do that tomorrow when I'm in a better mood." She decided it would help keep her on track if she worked with a therapist.

Unfortunately, and all too common, Margie's HMO assigned a therapist for her. She ended up seeing a psychologist who was very warm and caring, but who wanted to talk a lot about her childhood, trying to get to the roots of her anxiety.

Margie was beyond all that. Sure, there were things in her past that she knew contributed to the way she felt. But she also knew that talking about it at this point wouldn't help her change. She already had insight; what she needed was action.

Now let's look at an example where the mismatch went in the other direction. In this case, I was working with a woman, Joan, in her middle forties who had suffered with social anxiety for most of her life. When she first came to see me, I missed the fact that her husband had been the one who wanted her to get help. He had recently been promoted to a new position that required him to entertain business clients. He wanted Joan to accompany him to work-related social functions, something she didn't think she could do because of her shyness. But I didn't know this. All I saw was a bright and seemingly motivated woman who wanted to overcome her social anxiety.

Because I didn't recognize she was actually in the precontemplation stage, I didn't plan her treatment accordingly. I spent several weeks teaching her relaxation and coping skills. Then I helped her construct a list of situations she feared, ranking them from least frightening to most frightening. I taught her how to carry out these exposures and assigned her "homework" to do between sessions. I began wondering what was going on when she canceled several sessions in a row.

Fortunately, she came in again and we discussed what had happened. This is when I learned of her husband's job promotion, and that it was he who wanted her to change, not she. Of course, I now realized that none of my interventions had been appropriate—my timing was way off. In contrast to Margie in the previous example who needed less talk and more action, Joan needed to talk. There were plenty of issues she needed to address before she could deal with her social anxiety.

These examples drive home the point: It's important to match your efforts to your stage of change. But how do you know what strategies to try at each stage? That's the subject of our next section.

Tips for Each Stage

Think about when you determined your stage of change by answering three simple questions. If you didn't already complete this exercise, take a few minutes and do so now. The list below offers tips and suggestions to try at each stage. Find your particular stage, then read through the list. Notice that some are simply points to think about while others require more action. Select at least one or two of the ideas to implement.

Things You Can Do When You're in the Precontemplation Stage:
- Recognize that you may feel "safe" in this stage. You may not be happy about your social anxiety, but at least it's familiar, and you know what to expect. In addition, there may not be as many demands placed on you because of your anxiety. Allow yourself to recognize these aspects of your situation—it's an important step.

- Even if you've tried to overcome your social anxiety in the past and feel like you've failed, don't give up on yourself. Most people who are successful "changers" have tried many times before they succeed. It's all part of the process.

- Try to increase your awareness about how your social anxiety is preventing you from living the life you want to live. What things do you wish you could do that you currently avoid?

- Be open to events in your environment spurring you on in the change cycle. For example, a woman whose son was graduating from high school in a few months really wanted to overcome her fears enough so that she could attend the ceremony.

- Reading educational and self-help materials can be a big help at this point, but give yourself permission to simply read. Do not complete any exercises yet.

- Make use of the Internet and read about other people who share similar fears (see the "Resources" section for specific web sites).

- Realize that you are more than your social anxiety. You are a whole person who has many strengths and a few challenges.

- Accept yourself as a person who has a particular problem—a problem that you can overcome when you are ready.

Things You Can Do When You're in the Contemplation Stage:
- Review the questionnaire you completed in Chapter 1 and take a good look at the extent of your social anxiety. How many aspects of your life are affected? What are the consequences of anxiety on your personal relationships? Your job? Your health? Your feelings about yourself?

- Visualize the consequences of not overcoming your social anxiety. What will your life be like twenty years from now if you're still struggling the way you are now?

- Continue learning about social anxiety. If possible, talk to other people with this problem. Consider attending an anxiety disorder support group; if you speak to the leader, you probably could simply listen. Go with the intention to gain insight and awareness, not to make changes.

- Watch a videotape about social anxiety disorder. SmithKline Beecham Pharmaceutical Company has produced an excellent video in which people talk openly about their experiences with social anxiety. Although it's put out by a drug company, the video doesn't push medication. See the "Resources" section for information about how to obtain the video.

Things You Can Do When You're in the Preparation Stage:

• Write out a list of the benefits of overcoming your social anxiety. Carry this list with you and read it often.

• Realize that once you move into action, you'll need to devote extra time and energy to carrying out your plan. Make any necessary adjustments to your schedule.

• Set a date for when you will institute your plan of action. To capitalize on the high level of energy that typically occurs at this point in the change process, make the date sooner rather than later—within thirty days if possible.

• Make your decision to overcome your social anxiety public. Tell your spouse, another family member, or a friend about what you've learned and what you plan to do. Tell them you'll be devoting some time to following the methods in this book. Ask for whatever support you'll need.

• Write out your plan. If it's in writing, you're more likely to follow it. It doesn't have to be long or complicated; it might simply consist of: "I will spend thirty minutes each day completing the exercises in *Painfully Shy*."

Acceptance Revisited

This is a good place to remind you to practice acceptance. Understandably, you may be impatient with yourself to "hurry up and change." It doesn't help to rush yourself, though. If you do, the frightened, ambivalent part of yourself will likely rebel and sabotage your efforts. Remember, there's no right or wrong timetable—no perfect way to change. Wherever you are in the process is exactly where you need to be.

Most likely, you've been socially anxious for much of your life. You can't expect to overcome your fears in a short period of time. We wish there was a way to speed up the process so you wouldn't have to suffer any longer. Unfortunately, there's no quick fix. Allow yourself time to go at your own pace through each of the stages of change.

It's also important to give yourself credit for the steps you take, regardless of how small they might seem to you. Reread the quote we included at the beginning of the chapter. This Chinese Proverb advises, "Be not afraid of going slowly, be afraid only of standing still." Too many socially anxious people minimize their efforts. They think to themselves, "Big deal. Anyone can do what I did." But that's not the point. What matters is that you challenged yourself, and you took a step. Each and every step—even "baby steps"—brings you closer to your goal of becoming less painfully shy.

In addition, don't think you have to change in a perfectly linear fashion. Most people don't move in a straight line. More typically, they cycle through the stages of change several times. For example, you may make significant progress while in the action stage but have stress set you back, leaving you in the contemplation stage once again. Remember, this is normal.

So what's the bottom line? Don't rush through the stages; don't skip any stages; and don't worry if you recycle through the stages. Thankfully, slow and steady progress—even with a few setbacks sprinkled in—works just fine.

Chapter 5

Treat Your Body Well

A relaxed and healthy body is less prone to fearful thoughts and
feelings.

It's that simple: If you take good care of your physical body,
you are likely to experience less anxiety.

—Edmund Bourne, Ph.D.

Claire walked into my office carrying a can of diet soda in one
hand and a day planner in the other. Attached to her purse was
a pager. She sat on the edge of the chair, her foot softly tapping the
carpeted floor. I asked Claire what had brought her to see me.

"I'm completely stressed out," she said. "There are not enough
hours in the day to finish my work. And now my boss wants to add
more responsibilities to my job that I don't think I can handle."

I learned that Claire worked for an insurance salesperson. She had
done clerical and administrative work for him until now, which had kept
her plenty busy. Although she apparently liked her boss, he was young
and trying to establish himself. He put in long hours and demanded a
lot of Claire. He expected her to be in the office whenever he saw clients,
including many evenings and Saturdays. Now he had asked Claire if she
wanted to learn the sales end of the business.

"I don't think I could sell anything," said Claire. "I've always been shy and quiet. I like the organizational parts of the job, but I'm not ready to tackle interacting with clients any more than I already do."

"Whenever I fill out forms with clients, I'm so nervous my hand shakes," she continued. "I don't like anyone to watch me write. I'm afraid they'll think I'm incompetent, you know, with my trembling and taking so long."

I asked Claire to tell me more about being "stressed out." She said she'd been to her primary care physician before seeing me because she felt "rotten" most of the time. "I thought I was just run-down," Claire said, "but the doctor told me my blood pressure and cholesterol were both bordering on being too high. She thought I needed to learn some stress-management techniques and take better care of myself."

Claire did need to attend to her health, and she needed to make it a priority. She admitted she didn't exercise, ate too much fast food, drank a lot of caffeine (four or more cups of coffee plus diet soda throughout the day), and often went to bed late. She rarely did anything just for fun; everything revolved around her job.

Claire's case is not unique. Patients frequently tell me they're jittery and nervous, and I later learn they're drinking more than a pot of coffee a day. Or, people complain they feel "blah" and "down in the dumps," and I discover they work sixty to seventy hours a week. It's easy to forget that how we feel is not just a psychological issue; our emotional well-being is every bit as much related to our physical condition.

Indeed, research from many areas points to a strong mind-body connection: How we treat our body affects how we feel, and how we feel affects how our body functions. An exciting and truly revolutionary example of this is Dean Ornish's research with heart-disease patients. Ornish is a well-known cardiologist and author of *Dr. Dean Ornish's Program for Reversing Heart Disease*. Using very sophisticated methods such as PET scans and angiography, he demonstrated that the process of atherosclerosis (the narrowing of the arteries of the heart) can be reversed without drugs when patients radically change their lifestyles.

In his study, one group of patients followed a low-fat diet (10 percent or less fat), walked three times a week, regularly practiced yoga and meditation, and attended a support group with other heart-disease patients. The control group received excellent medical care and also followed a low-fat diet (30 percent or less fat), but did not make the other lifestyle changes. The results showed that while the patients' arteries in the control group were more clogged a year later, the group following Ornish's program had significantly increased blood flow to their hearts.

Of course, making lifestyle changes is not easy. It takes commitment, discipline, and a vision that life will be richer for having made the changes. In this chapter, we'll see what changes Claire made in her lifestyle, and how these changes led to her experiencing greater confidence and self-esteem—and much less social anxiety. In reading about Claire, you'll learn what lifestyle factors you may need to target in your own efforts to minimize social anxiety.

Make Caring for Yourself a Priority

A major step in treating your body well is to think of yourself first. Maybe this sounds selfish, but too often we don't take time to exercise or enjoy something fun or relaxing because we we're busy putting other people's needs ahead of our own. Socially anxious people can be particularly susceptible to this because we tend to be sensitive to other's feelings and want to be helpful. Plus, sometimes we're not as assertive as we should be. Of course, sensitivity and caring can make us wonderful friends, but we need to learn to treat ourselves as well as we treat others.

Claire had been raised to think that taking care of yourself was somehow "selfish." It was better to think of others first and worry about yourself later. I showed Claire a quote from the popular book, *Simple Abundance*, by Sarah Ban Breathnach. The book quotes Eda LeShan on the topic of self-nurturing: "When we truly care for ourselves, it becomes possible to care more profoundly about other people. The more alert and sensitive we are to our own needs, the more loving and generous we can be to others."

What help will Claire be to her boss if she runs herself ragged and becomes physically ill? What effect will her less-than-optimal health have on her other relationships? Will her harried lifestyle play a role in her problems with anxiety worsening? Claire needed to consider the answers to these questions.

It didn't happen immediately, but Claire started to realize that becoming alert and sensitive to her own needs was the foundation for everything else. There was no way she could reach her full potential if she didn't tend to her health. After all, one's physical body is the vessel of the inner self; it can't be ignored without paying the consequences.

Exercise: An Effective Antidote for Anxiety

Each New Year's Day, fitness centers everywhere become crowded with people who've resolved to start exercising more—to get in shape. But for people prone to anxiety, exercise is much more than getting in shape. It's an integral part of reducing tension and worry, managing negative moods, and alleviating nervous suffering.

Many studies have documented the benefits of aerobic exercise such as running, biking, swimming, or brisk walking. From a purely physical standpoint, the goal of aerobic exercise is to strengthen the cardiovascular system and increase stamina. From a psychological perspective, however, exercise can do much more. Research has demonstrated that twenty to forty minutes of aerobic exercise leads to reduced anxiety and positive increases in mood, effects which last for several hours after the workout. Energy and concentration also receive a substantial boost from exercise. Perhaps most significant, a regular exercise program can enhance your general sense of well-being and quality of life.

Despite the promise of these benefits, anyone who has tried to start an exercise program knows how difficult it can be to stick with it for more than a few weeks. Like Claire, some people may feel selfish for taking time out for themselves. People also complain they're too busy to exercise, they don't have energy left over after work to exercise, or it's boring and they lose their motivation. But for people with social anxiety, there's another obstacle—embarrassment.

Embarrassment related to exercise is something I know too well. I remember in my grade-school physical education classes how teams were selected. The teacher picked two of the best athletes to be the captains, and they each took turns picking whom they wanted on their team. Invariably, I was the last to be picked. Then, no matter what the sport, I tried to be as far away from the action as possible; I didn't want to risk further humiliation by dropping the ball, or whatever the case might have been.

Given my past, the thought of writing anything about exercise seems ludicrous to me, but here we go. Hopefully, you'll realize I understand where you're coming from, and you can rest assured I won't ask you to do anything too threatening. I know my experiences helped me empathize with Claire's fears about exercise. Let's return to her story.

Claire knew she needed to exercise; her doctor had told her so. If she couldn't bring her blood pressure under control with diet and exercise, she would have to take medication for it. We discussed possible options, such as exercising at home. Claire had bought a *Sweatin' to the Oldies* videotape a few months ago, but so far it was just gathering dust on a shelf. Claire didn't think she could discipline herself to exercise at home, but the thought of going to any type of fitness center was overwhelming.

Anyone can feel a little nervous about exercising in public if they haven't done it in a while. But for people with social anxiety, the insecurity runs much deeper. Do you relate to any of these things Claire told me?

- "I don't know what kind of clothes to wear. I don't want to stand out."

- "I don't like the way I look. I don't want people to see me."

- "I'm so awkward. I'm afraid I'll trip or something and people will laugh at me."

- "I don't know how to deal with the whole locker-room scene."

- "What if it's crowded and I have to stand around waiting to use the equipment? I'll feel so uncomfortable."

- "I wouldn't want to have to talk to anybody."

For Claire and others with social anxiety, it's not only going to a gym that's a problem. Even walking in a familiar neighborhood can spark anxiety. Claire had already tried walking in her subdivision, but she felt extremely uncomfortable. She crossed the street frequently to avoid passing by neighbors or other walkers. "Everyone must wonder why I zigzag back and forth so much," she said.

Claire had another problem when it came to exercise: She had a bad knee. It bothered her when she went down stairs and at other times, too. She needed to know what exercises were safe to do and which ones she should probably avoid. Although she balked at first, I convinced Claire to call the YMCA. I had heard of a new program for people like her—not necessarily people who were socially anxious, but people who, for a variety of reasons, didn't feel comfortable exercising in the usual workout area and needed extra assistance designing a program to meet their needs.

The next day, Claire called the Y and spoke to someone who sounded so understanding that she set up an appointment for an introductory meeting. This particular YMCA did indeed have a special exercise room where only a limited number of people were allowed at one time. These were all people who weren't regular exercisers, at least not yet. And the hard-core, muscle-bound jocks who can be rather intimidating to us unathletically inclined people, were on a completely different level of the facility.

In addition to the benefit of privacy, the staff was trained to work with people who had special needs of some sort. They knew not to push too hard—to start slowly. Claire developed a warm relationship with one of the staff members, and this helped motivate Claire to work out three or four times a week. The program included not only aerobic exercise but also stretching and weight training. She learned what aggravated her knee and was able to avoid those things.

Over time, Claire's energy increased and in general, she felt more relaxed. Also, as her body grew stronger, she began to feel stronger emotionally. She entertained new possibilities for her life. For example, she started thinking about whether she might want to consider learning insurance sales as her boss had suggested. Maybe she would, maybe she wouldn't. At least now she was giving herself the choice. In addition, she began asserting herself a little more with her boss. She told him she couldn't work every evening because she wanted to go to the Y.

Claire had taken some important steps. She was caring for her body, helping to control her high blood pressure, among other things. No, exercise hadn't changed her personality; we wouldn't want that to happen. Exercise did, however, give her some much-needed confidence and self-esteem. In essence, she'd begun to take her needs seriously and to treat herself with the respect she deserved.

We know it might be hard to believe, but what happened for Claire can happen for you. Here are some general tips:

- Be sure to check with your physician if you have any health concerns.

- Call your local YMCA. They might have a program similar to the one Claire found.

- Whether it's at home, a gym, or a park, try to exercise three to four times a week, thirty minutes at a time doing some type of aerobic activity you enjoy. Keep your exertion level moderate. And of course, work up to this slowly.

- Avoid exercising two to three hours before your usual bedtime, especially if you have trouble sleeping.

- If concerns about embarrassment are getting in your way of exercising, the skills you'll learn in the chapter, "Think It Through," will help. Learning the diaphragmatic breathing method we describe later in this chapter should also help.

Food and Mood

A complete discussion of nutrition is beyond the scope of this book. In the "Resources" section you'll find a listing of books you can refer to for more in-depth coverage of the topic. For our purposes here, we want to make a few main points.

First of all, be aware that certain foods and other substances can actually make people anxious. Most people are aware of the effects of coffee, but there are other offenders, as well. In addition to coffee, watch your intake of these things:

- colas

- chocolate

- caffeinated tea

- nicotine

- alcohol

- some over-the-counter cold medicines, particularly pseudoephedrine

- some herbal nutritional products containing ephedrine

Keep in mind that people's bodies react differently. For example, one person may feel quite jittery taking a decongestant while another person feels no increased nervousness. Similarly, you can build up a tolerance to caffeine, nicotine, and alcohol. Any efforts to cut back on these substances must be done carefully to reduce withdrawal symptoms.

It's also probably no surprise that many people use food as a major form of stress reduction. And people with anxiety problems may find that eating calms them down. Certainly, this calming effect may be due to the property of the food itself. However, another reason why you turn to food may surprise you. Dr. Barry Jacobs of Princeton University has found that certain repetitive movements, such as licking or chewing, increase serotonin levels in the brain. Perhaps chewing gum when you're anxious would work as well as that bowl of ice cream!

It all gets back to taking care of yourself. If you're feeling anxious and you think food is the answer, ask yourself: Am I really hungry right now? If you are hungry, try to eat something that will truly satisfy. If you're not really hungry, ask yourself: How could I best meet my needs right now? Consider taking a warm bubble bath or writing in a journal.

Maybe you need a nap. Most of us aren't adept at soothing ourselves, but it's definitely a skill worth cultivating.

There's one final piece of advice regarding what to eat and what not to eat: Use common sense. Test out what kinds and how much food make you feel good. Many people with anxiety find they need to eat smaller meals more frequently to counteract any tendencies toward hypoglycemia. When blood sugar drops, you're likely to feel dizzy, light-headed, and shaky. You may interpret these sensations as anxiety, but it may also be that you need a snack.

Rest and Relaxation: The Keys to Balance

Despite the importance of getting enough rest, many of us are sleep-deprived. In fact, one study showed that up to a hundred million Americans don't get as much sleep as they need. Another study documented that sleep time has decreased by 20 percent since the invention of the electric light. We're no longer constrained by the setting of the sun. We can stay up late to finish that report, do another load of laundry, or zone out in front of the television.

For people prone to social anxiety, adequate sleep is crucial. It can mean the difference between thinking about an issue realistically and becoming needlessly upset over something that's not really important. In other words, when you're overly tired, you're more likely to misread social situations and interpret them negatively.

For example, Claire was much more likely to think clients in the office thought she was "slow" and "incompetent" when she had stayed up too late the night before. As a part of her plan to take better care of herself, Claire decided to avoid watching the ten o'clock evening news. There was usually some story on that upset her. She had already read the newspaper anyway, so it wasn't that she was uninformed. Plus, after the news she usually kept the television on to see what guests were on the late shows. Of course, something usually caught her attention— or she was too tired to turn off the TV—and she wouldn't wind up in bed until midnight.

How much sleep is enough? Although many people require approximately eight hours each night, individual needs vary. The general rule of thumb is if you're sleepy during the day, you probably need more sleep.

Many sleep experts also recommend a twenty- to thirty-minute nap during the afternoon, citing improved concentration and functioning. Unfortunately, corporate America doesn't generally allow for this. But if you work at home and can take a quick catnap, it's definitely worth trying.

It's also important to pace yourself throughout the day. Give yourself periods of downtime after you've worked hard on something. Sure, maybe it can't be a long break, but even stretching your legs after a long period of sitting can refresh you.

Look at the activities in your week. Maybe you're one who thrives on busyness, but many people who tend to be socially anxious find adopting a slower pace is beneficial. We tend to become "overstimulated" easily, especially around a lot of people. It helps to have time to process all we've taken in. Of course, these are generalizations, and there are always exceptions. The point is, look at what's filling your time and determine if it's something you truly value.

Lastly, take time to relax and simply have fun. You can't work effectively if you don't sometimes play. And if you can "play" outdoors, all the better. Sunlight nourishes, energizes, and regulates our bodies. Unfortunately, most of us are light-deprived as well as sleep-deprived. The book, *Beyond Prozac*, listed in the "Resources" section, contains several chapters on the benefits of light.

The Hidden Power of Breathing

Intellectually, we know that breathing is fundamental to life, but we usually take this amazing process for granted. We don't pay attention to how we breathe, and for many of us prone to anxiety, our breathing patterns become problematic.

Imagine you're entering a room full of people you don't know.

You're worried about what they will think of you. What happens to your breathing? Most likely, it will become rapid and shallow. You may even feel short of breath, as if you're gasping for air.

Recall from Chapter 2 how human beings are biologically pro-grammed to respond with "fight or flight" when confronted with a dangerous situation. This rapid and shallow breathing actually leads to complex physiological reactions that prepare your body to respond quickly to an emergency. This system worked exceedingly well in previous eras when threats to survival were often physical, such as fighting off an enemy while hunting for food. But when you're afraid to enter a roomful of people because you fear scrutiny or disapproval, there's no need for these physical changes. You are breathing in excess of your metabolic needs. This is called overbreathing, or in its extreme form, hyperventilation.

Overbreathing and hyperventilation can produce a number of physical symptoms, such as light-headedness, dizziness, shortness of breath, heart palpitations, tingling sensations, chest pain, tremors, sweating, dry mouth, difficulty swallowing, and weakness. Does this list sound familiar?

When you experience many of these physical symptoms at once, you're probably in an acute state of hyperventilation. In fact, 60 percent of all panic attacks are accompanied by acute hyperventilation. But you don't have to be huffing and puffing or gasping for air to be hyperventilating. Even slight alterations in breathing patterns can produce physiological changes in your body's chemistry, thus leading to some of the symptoms listed above.

Here are some signs indicating you may be chronically over-breathing:

- You sigh or yawn a lot.

- You breathe through your mouth.

- You breathe from your upper chest. In other words, you notice your chest moving in and out when you breathe.

- You breathe rapidly, perhaps eighteen to twenty-two breaths per minute.

So how does hyperventilation relate to social anxiety? Let's look at a few, brief examples. Dave thought he sounded "breathless" when he spoke to others, and this breathlessness became more pronounced as speaking occasions grew more formal. But even if he was just talking with coworkers at the office water fountain, he was self-conscious about the way he sounded. According to Dave, being breathless all the time was not very masculine, and he worried people would think something was "wrong" with him. Of course, the more he focused on his breathlessness, the more he exacerbated the problem. His anxiety led to rapid and shallow breathing which, in fact, did make him appear breathless.

Many people can become sensitized to bodily sensations, and these sensations then trigger anxiety. Dave was so sensitized to his breathing that he couldn't walk up a flight of stairs without feeling a surge in anxiety. The natural change in his breathing to accommodate the increased exertion led to catastrophic thoughts: "What if I have to talk to someone at the top of the stairs and I sound breathless? or "I have to sound like I'm in control, not all out of breath and anxious." These anxious thoughts then lead to more shallow breathing, and the spiral continues.

Fortunately, with training and practice, you can learn to exert conscious control over your breathing patterns, and this in turn can help you manage your anxiety. The breathing technique we'll describe is called many names: diaphragmatic breathing, abdominal breathing, controlled breathing, or paced breathing. Regardless of the name, this slow and deep manner of breathing is a powerful natural relaxant—one you can use to alleviate anxiety in all types of social situations.

What is diaphragmatic breathing?

Have you ever noticed how a baby breathes? How his or her belly rises and falls rhythmically with each breath? We're born knowing how to breathe the "correct" way, and we still breathe this way when we sleep. But years of stress and bad habits can prevent us from routinely doing what once came naturally.

The diaphragm is a large, umbrella-shaped muscle that separates the chest cavity from the abdominal cavity. It is intimately involved in the process of inhaling and exhaling air. As you inhale, the diaphragm descends to allow room for the increased air volume. Then as you exhale, the diaphragm rises upward as air is released from the lungs.

Let's look at what happens if your muscles are tense, as they might be when you're anxious. If your stomach muscles are tense when the diaphragm descends to accommodate the air being inhaled, the diaphragm meets with resistance. It cannot move as far down as it ordinarily would. There isn't as much room for air to flow in and your breathing will be shallow. Poor posture can also prevent the diaphragm from moving freely as it needs to.

Before you get started, there are three main points you'll need to remember about diaphragmatic breathing:

1. Inhale and exhale through your nose. Breathing through your mouth increases the possibility of hyperventilating.

2. As you inhale, your abdomen should extend outward. You can think of this as making room for the air you're taking in. As you exhale, your abdomen flattens as you push the air out. This may be exactly the opposite of how you normally breathe, especially when you're anxious.

3. Concentrate on slowing down your breathing to approximately eight to ten breaths per minute. This is just a general guideline. You don't have to count your breaths each time.

Although this may not be the way you're accustomed to breathing and may feel awkward at first, remember this is the way our bodies were designed. It's truly a healthier way to breathe.

Learning diaphragmatic breathing

We'll take you step-by-step through the process of breathing this way; then we'll show you how to apply this skill to your daily life.

The easiest way to learn this form of breathing is to lie on the floor or on a firm bed and place a light tissue box on your abdomen, directly above your navel. Concentrate on taking slow breaths as you watch the tissue box rise and fall. Remember, the box should rise as you inhale—to make room for the air—and fall as you exhale. Also remember to breathe through your nose. Practice this twice a day, five minutes each time.

After you have practiced for a few days, do the same procedure but without the tissue box. Instead, place one hand on your abdomen, with your little finger resting just above your navel. Feel your hand rise and fall as you inhale and exhale. Practice this for a few days until you feel comfortable. Then, do the same thing but with your hands at your sides.

Next, continue this breathing practice, but vary your body position. For example, practice diaphragmatic breathing while lying on your side. Then try it sitting up. Finally, see if you can breathe this way while standing. Remember, it may take a few weeks of regular practice to become proficient breathing diaphragmatically in a variety of positions.

Using diaphragmatic breathing

Your diligent practice is soon going to pay off. You're ready to branch out and apply this way of breathing throughout your daily activities.

Begin by "checking in" with your breathing frequently throughout the day. Perhaps you're at work, the phone rings, and your supervisor asks about a report you haven't yet finished. It's a good time for a breathing check. Are you breathing abdominally? Are you breathing slowly and deeply? If you find you're breathing rapidly and from the chest, take a few minutes to consciously breathe from you diaphragm.

Check your breathing when you're rushing, when you're stressed, and when you're relaxed. Notice how your breathing changes depending upon what's going on around you. To some extent, this is normal. We all tend to overbreathe when we're upset or anxious. But again, we do have some conscious control over how we breathe. By deliberately choosing to breathe in a more calming manner, we give ourselves the opportunity to think more clearly about our reactions to events, rather than simply responding in a knee-jerk fashion.

After you've done these mini-check-ins for a while, begin to apply diaphragmatic breathing when you're in an anxiety-arousing situation. Try to catch your anxiety early on; you'll have a much greater chance for success. In other words, don't wait until you're in a severe panic state and then decide to try breathing techniques to stop the panic. It won't work nearly as well, especially without a lot more practice.

Claire practiced diaphragmatic breathing at home twice a day for two weeks before she tried using the skill at work. She remembered how I'd said not to apply this way of breathing in anxious situations until she had some solid practice behind her.

She gradually began integrating the diaphragmatic breathing into her daily activities. She did brief breathing practice sessions at work to get the hang of doing it with distractions going on around her—the boss talking on the phone, the radio playing, the mail being delivered, and so on. Claire grew more confident in her ability to slow her breathing down in a variety of situations.

Next, she wanted to use her breathing skills in more stressful situations, to see if she could calm herself down even a bit. For Claire, the worst thing was having to write in front of clients. Remember how she worried about taking too long to fill out forms? And about how her hand might shake?

Claire could usually tell when her boss was wrapping up, about to send clients over to her desk to complete the paperwork. So she concentrated on implementing her diaphragmatic breathing throughout the time when her boss was talking with clients. It wasn't that she completely ignored her other work to pay attention to her breathing. She just made a conscious effort to ask herself questions periodically: Am I holding my breath? Am I breathing from my chest? Am I breathing too rapidly? Then, she made adjustments to her breathing pattern accordingly. Much to her surprise, Claire realized that she wasn't quite as nervous by the time the clients came to her desk.

Of course, the diaphragmatic breathing didn't totally take away Claire's anxiety. She still struggled with her anxious thoughts, and sometimes she still felt shaky. But at least Claire had learned the basics of a coping skill she could continue practicing while honing her ability to calm her body down. It was a solid start.

Moving Ahead

In this chapter we've looked at several ways you can take care of yourself physically and how this is an important part of your recovery program. You can't ignore your physical health and expect to feel good emotionally. It simply doesn't work. Many of the things we suggested such as exercising more and breathing diaphragmatically take time to develop into habits. And sometimes it can seem like too much of an effort in the beginning. But keep at it. Try to focus on the benefits you'll receive: less tension and worry, greater peace of mind, and a well-deserved sense of accomplishment. These things will help you as you move ahead to the next chapter, "Think It Through."

Chapter 6

Think It Through

Change your thoughts and you change your world.

—Norman Vincent Peale

My son Jesse, almost eight years old, peered over my shoulder as I began writing this chapter. He read the quote above and asked, seemingly shocked, "That's not true, is it?" I tried to relate the saying to something he could understand—baseball.

I reminded Jesse of an evening several years ago when he was learning to bat. Despite Greg's best coaching, Jesse missed every ball. In frustration, Jesse stormed inside and flung himself on the floor crying, "This is too hard. I'll never get it right." After he calmed down, we encouraged him to change what he was telling himself. Instead of saying that he'd never succeed we suggested the alternative, "Learning something new is hard. It takes time and practice." Who knows if what we said registered, but the next evening he hit several balls in a row.

Jesse listened intently as I reminisced about this experience. I asked him, "Do you see how when you changed your thinking, you were able to change what you were doing? That's what the quote is about."

He assumed his batting stance and took several pretend swings. "But I didn't change the world," he said. "It's still round."

Obviously, changing your thoughts won't alter the actual shape of the world. Still, learning strategies to deal with the cognitive components of your social phobia—your thoughts, expectations, and beliefs—will make a huge difference in your life. In this chapter, we'll teach you how to think things through in a way that challenges your fears and calms your nerves.

Realistic—Not Necessarily Positive—Thinking

First, we need to distinguish between realistic and positive thinking. Although we opened this chapter with a quote from Norman Vincent Peale, best known for his book, *The Power of Positive Thinking*, we're not advocating his specific approach. Why not? Isn't it good to try to think positively? Not always. Let's look at an example to see the differences in these two approaches.

Imagine you have a business lunch tomorrow with some people you don't know. You tell a friend that you're worried about how it will go. You're afraid the others in the group will notice you're anxious, and you worry you won't have anything intelligent to say.

Now imagine possible responses from your friend. The following examples show the difference between "positive thinking" and "realistic thinking."

POSITIVE THINKING	REALISTIC THINKING
What are you worried about? It will go great.	The lunch will probably go well. You always seem to make a nice impression and you're usually quite articulate. But if it doesn't go smoothly, it's not the end of the world.
No one will even notice that you're anxious. You'll be fine.	It's possible someone will notice you're anxious, but if that happens, will it matter that much?

How would you feel if your friend made comments like the ones on the left? Positive thinking assumes a best-case scenario, but as you know, life doesn't always cooperate. As a result, well-meaning comments such as, "Everything will turn out," or "Don't worry, you'll be fine," can sometimes ring hollow. Rather than feeling reassured, you may end up feeling unheard or misunderstood. Positive thinking doesn't address your concerns—exaggerated though they may be—about the possibility that something unpleasant will take place or the consequences that may ensue.

Granted, not everyone is a communications expert. In some situations, even I find myself searching for the best thing to say. Most people's attempts to reassure you with a brief positive comment are genuine. And perhaps a simple word of encouragement *is* all you need.

Sometimes, though, comments such as those in the realistic column may help you more. They address your worries without making them into a catastrophe. You're more likely to feel validated and heard because the responses recognize the possibility that situations don't always go as planned. Social blunders happen. Anxiety happens. STUFF happens. You get the idea. Realistic thinking says, "Something bad might happen; if it does, I can cope."

Most socially anxious people aren't in danger of too much positive thinking, though. Just the opposite—they're likely to think too negatively, which is equally unrealistic. This was certainly true for Corey.

Corey was beginning his student teaching in a third-grade classroom. He had spent a week simply observing the teacher and getting to know the children. The teacher seemed supportive, and the children were friendly, but Corey was petrified nonetheless. He didn't know how he'd ever manage to assume more of the teaching responsibilities when he felt so nervous inside. He was sure his hand would shake uncontrollably when he wrote on the blackboard. He knew the kids would misbehave right when the principal walked by the room. He imagined the teacher telling him he should consider another profession.

Corey's negative, unrealistic thoughts were getting the best of him. He was envisioning one catastrophe after another. Instead of assuming the worst, Corey needed to search for the truth. He needed to ask himself, "What is the evidence for this thought?" and "What evidence do I have that this will happen?"

In the rest of this chapter, we'll walk you through this process. You'll see how focusing on the facts leads you to feel much less overwhelmed. Only when your thinking becomes more balanced—more realistic—will you feel comfortable in social situations and truly at ease with yourself.

Keeping Track of Your Thoughts

We've mentioned before that each of us has a stream of automatic thoughts running through our minds. These thoughts are often undetectable, yet powerful nonetheless. It's much like having background music playing while you work. Most of the time you don't even notice it's on—you simply go about what you're doing. But have you ever felt that different music affects your mood or even your energy level? Perhaps also your ability to concentrate? The automatic self-talk playing in your mind can affect all of these things, and much more.

To work with our thoughts and make them more adaptive and realistic, we first need to know what they are. We can't allow our self-talk to remain background music, affecting us without us knowing it.

One of the most useful things you can do is keep a running record of your thoughts on paper. We saw what an effective tool this was for Christy in Chapter 3 as she journeyed toward self-acceptance. There's simply no better way to learn about your thought processes than to write them down.

Below is a format we've found helpful, but feel free to adapt it to your needs. Use any type of notebook you like and make the same headings at the top. Leave space to jot down a few words about the situation and perhaps the date so you can easily monitor your progress. Most importantly, write down any thoughts you're having either in anticipation of or during a social situation. In other words, what are you telling yourself? What do you fear will happen? How do you feel about it? You can use a number in the third column to represent how you feel or write a few words as a description.

Thought Diary

Situation	Thoughts/What am I telling myself?	How anxious or shy do I feel?*
_____	_____	_____
_____	_____	_____
_____	_____	_____

*Shyness/Social Anxiety Scale

0	1	2	3	4	5	6	7	8	9	10
None		Slight			Moderate			Quite a bit		Extreme

Most people aren't accustomed to keeping a thought diary such as this, and obstacles frequently occur. Below we'll describe these common problems and offer some tips on how to solve them.

"I don't have any thoughts. I'm just anxious!" Sometimes people feel their anxiety comes from "out of the blue," and they have difficulty identifying specific trigger thoughts. Joe, a college student I'm working with, told me about a situation that happened recently where he encountered this problem. He needed to do some research for one of his classes. As he walked though the library doors, he immediately felt an overwhelming sense of dread. His heart raced, he perspired profusely, and he became so dizzy he thought he might faint. But because he wasn't paying attention to his thoughts, he hadn't a clue as to what was going on. "It happened so fast," he said. "I wasn't thinking about anything. I just needed to check out a book for a paper I'm writing."

In studying the situation more closely, Joe remembered he had seen a group of students from the same class walking up the library steps ahead of him. "Come to think of it, it crossed my mind that I should speak to them but I looked down, pretending not to notice them," he said. As we talked about the incident, Joe recalled several thoughts that had flashed through his mind:

- They have friends; I don't.

- If I said "hi" they probably wouldn't know who I was.

- I hope I can avoid them in the library.

- No one ever asks me to study with them.

- I do everything alone. I'm such a freak.

Joe was amazed that he could have all these thoughts running through his mind without him noticing it. Once he did, he could see why he'd felt so anxious. He picked up right away how one negative thought led to another more devastating than the first, and how this made him feel even worse.

When you run up against situations like Joe did—you know you're anxious but you don't know why—you'll need to investigate. Review what you were doing prior to feeling anxious. Did you see anyone in particular? Did you talk to anyone? What was going on around you? Try to remember precisely when your mood changed. Joe recalled he had been in a good mood before entering the library. He was eager to check out the book he needed so he could finish his paper. He enjoyed this particular class, and it wasn't an effort for him to write. He hadn't felt at all anxious until he saw those other students, which then triggered an onslaught of unrealistic, negative thoughts.

Even if you don't know exactly what you're thinking at the time, develop the habit of writing anyway. Write down, "I don't know for sure what I'm thinking but I wonder if it has something to do with _____." Generate several possibilities; don't commit yourself to one. Often times, simply going through the process of writing in your thought diary helps you ferret out important insights. It certainly takes practice and patience, but if you persist, you'll become adept at noticing your thoughts and seeing the connections to your social anxiety.

"I don't have time to write down my thoughts." It's true, it can be a chore in the beginning to keep a detailed thought record. But keep in mind, you don't need to write down all your thoughts. That would be impractical if not impossible. Pick times when you feel at least moderately shy or anxious, perhaps when physical symptoms mount as well. For example, Joe's experience in the library was a good one to journal. His anxiety came on quickly and mysteriously, along with a good dose of physical distress. Try to write down your thoughts while you're still in the situation, but sometimes that's not feasible. Do so as soon as you can, though, while the thoughts are still fresh in your mind.

Also remember, you won't need to write down your thoughts forever—even doing it for a week or two will yield plenty of good information. After you've gotten some practice with monitoring and challenging your thoughts, the process will become more natural and you won't have to physically do it each time. You'll develop mental shortcuts that will prove effective, as well. But don't rush the learning process. Most people need to write out their thoughts—think them through on paper—in order systematically to make changes in their outlook on life.

Yes, keeping a thought journal takes time, but it's certainly not time wasted.

"My thoughts sound stupid when I see them written out in black and white." Some people find that when they write down their thoughts, they're surprised at how foolish they sound. Remember how initially Christy didn't want to show me her thought diary? Even if you don't plan on showing what you've written to another living soul, you may still feel embarrassed.

This reaction isn't all bad. It means you're gaining perspective through the sheer act of putting pen to paper. Thoughts that seemed perfectly logical in your head now look irrational on paper. What's more, writing your thoughts down is one of the most direct routes for bringing unrealistic thoughts into consciousness. Only when you're fully conscious of your thoughts do you gain the power to change them.

Let's assume you've kept a thought diary for a period of time. What do you do with this information? How can you keep these thoughts from controlling you? To answer these questions we'll introduce you to Kim. You'll read some of the entries from her thought diary, and you'll see what she learned from diligently monitoring her thoughts. Later, you'll also learn how she began to confront and change her deeper beliefs, allowing her to feel more confident than she had in a long time.

Handling Unrealistic Thoughts: Kim's Story

Kim had been on maternity leave for two months. She'd hoped by now she'd be back in her regular-sized clothes, but she wasn't. She thought she still looked pregnant, and she was sure everyone at work would stare at her. Kim had always focused a lot on her appearance; this tendency was even worse now. She couldn't stop thinking about how "fat" she was and how everyone would notice.

Kim also worried about her competence at work. She had been promoted to a supervisory position not too long before she had the baby and hadn't yet learned all the details of her new job. She felt sure she'd mess something up and people would say she shouldn't have been promoted, that she didn't deserve it. To make matters worse, she was scheduled to give a major presentation her first week back at work. She couldn't imagine having to stand in front of all those people when she felt so fat, ugly, and stupid.

Kim saw me off and on throughout her pregnancy. She'd taken medication for her social anxiety and depression in the past but when she learned she was pregnant, she and her doctor decided she should try therapy instead.

The mental and physical changes related to her pregnancy, plus adjusting to not taking the medication, were a lot to handle at once. Kim was resilient, though, and it helped that her husband was very supportive. She managed to keep her anxiety and depression under control and mastered many of the techniques in this book. When she began feeling overwhelmed about returning to work, she realized her thoughts were again wreaking havoc. Fortunately, she knew what to do. Kim began tracking what she was telling herself and wrote it all down in her thought diary. In addition, she called me for an appointment.

The first thing Kim did when I saw her was apologize for needing to come back in. "I already know what to do. I should be able to manage on my own," she said.

I reminded Kim about the process of change and about how setbacks are normal. "Even star athletes need coaches to help them out of slumps," I said. I praised her for recognizing her difficulties early on and for taking steps to get back on track.

Kim brought her trusty thought diary to the session. Below are a few of her entries:

Kim's Thought Diary

Situation	Thoughts/What am I telling myself?	How anxious or shy am I now?
Going back to work soon	*Everyone will stare at me. They'll think I should've already lost this weight.*	*Extremely. I wish I could call in and say I needed more time off. But what reason would I give?*
Same	*I waddle when I walk. Everyone will laugh at how I walk.*	*Same*
Same	*I know I've forgotten half of my job. People will think I'm dumb.*	*Same*
Thinking about presentation	*I will be boring. I should have a more entertaining style. I'll sound flat—lifeless. Everyone will know I'm nervous.*	*Wish I could get out of it! What lie could I come up with?*

Kim and I carefully went through each of the thoughts she'd written down. As we did, I taught her some techniques to help her gain some distance from her thoughts. She needed to step back a bit and gain perspective.

Call a spade a spade. The first thing you must do to deal with automatic thoughts is identify and label them appropriately. Recognize your socially anxious thoughts for what they are—misleading and maladaptive. Thoughts running through your mind such as, "Everyone is staring at me" "I'm such a loser," are simply not true—they're manifestations of social anxiety. It can be an enormous help to relabel these thoughts and realize you don't have to pay attention to them.

This technique of "relabeling" your thoughts is used in the treatment of obsessive-compulsive disorder (OCD), an anxiety disorder in which people are plagued with obsessive thoughts (e.g., I will be contaminated by germs) and compulsions (e.g., I must wash my hands over and over). In his book *Brain Lock*, UCLA School of Medicine psychiatrist Jeffrey M. Schwartz describes OCD's intrusive thoughts as the brain misfiring. He instructs people to tell themselves, "It's not me—it's my OCD."

In our experience, the thoughts of social anxiety sufferers are equally intrusive and unpleasant. After all, who would enjoy being barraged with thoughts like the ones in Kim's diary? No one wakes up one morning and says, "I'd like to worry all day long about what other people think of me." And although it's probably not as simple as the brain misfiring, relabeling anxious thoughts as being at least partly biological can be quite helpful. Telling yourself, "It's not me—it's my anxiety," relieves you of some of the guilt and shame you may feel about having the thoughts in the first place.

Kim needed to talk to herself along these lines: "The thoughts I'm having about my weight and people judging me are not about my appearance. They're the work of social anxiety. I'm under a lot of stress right now so it's understandable why these thoughts are coming back. I'm nervous about leaving the baby at the day-care center, and I'm still not getting enough sleep. I don't have to pay attention to these anxious thoughts."

Cultivate mindful awareness. Another very useful method for dealing with negative automatic thoughts is "mindful awareness." Similar to the accepting attitude we described in Chapter 3, mindful awareness is an ancient Buddhist concept involving being conscious of your thoughts, yet not clinging to them. Instead of holding on to your thoughts and obsessively analyzing them, you allow your thoughts to gently and effortlessly flow through you. This can take some practice. For many people, "letting go" doesn't come naturally—especially when anxious thoughts can seem so believable at the time.

I refreshed Kim's memory about using the breathing skills (presented in Chapter 5) to help her develop mindful awareness and let go of her anxious thoughts. Whenever she caught herself worrying about going back to work and what her coworkers would think of her, I encouraged her to take a break from what she was doing, sit in a comfortable chair, and begin her paced breathing. She quickly remembered the routine. As she slowly inhaled she said to herself, "This is just a social anxiety thought. It's not the gospel truth." When she exhaled she said, "I'm letting go of this thought. It's not serving me well." When Kim practiced breathing in this manner for as little as five minutes, she was able to soothe herself effectively.

You can also add imagery to your breathing and mindful awareness exercises. As you're relaxing in your chair, imagine tying each negative thought from your thought diary to a different-colored balloon. In your imagination, let the balloons go, one by one, feeling peace and relaxation descend upon you as you watch them infuse the sky with vibrant hues.

Kim liked the balloon imagery. She found it helped deepen her relaxation and her ability to let go of negative thoughts. But imagery techniques don't work for everyone. Some people are simply able to form pictures in their minds more easily than others. With or without imagery, it doesn't really matter. The main idea is to nurture mindful awareness—gently to release your anxious thoughts—in whatever way works best for you.

Realize your thoughts are not you. We've made this point before, but it's worth repeating. Although the pain of social anxiety cuts deeply, it doesn't tarnish who you are as a person.

Kim and I discussed how everyone has an inner core that isn't touched by unrealistic, negative thinking. It's the part of the self that remains objective, believing without a doubt that there's value in one's humanness, and does not care at all about performance or perfection.

Kim only needed to cradle her baby in her arms to experience this point in a profound way. Her daughter needed her, and it made no difference what she looked like, whether she made a mistake at work, or what other people thought of her. All her baby cared about was having a loving, attentive mother available to meet her needs.

We'll return to this idea of being more than your thoughts later in the chapter when we talk about core beliefs. But first, let's see how you can keep those negative thoughts from even cropping up.

Challenging Your Expectations

Following the suggestions in the previous section will go a long way toward making you feel more in control of your automatic thoughts. Eventually, though, wouldn't it be nice if you didn't have to deal with them in the first place? Is that too much to hope for? We think not. Sure, you might always have a few residual negative thoughts to deal with here and there, but it's certainly possible to cut down on the quantity and pervasiveness of them. To do this, we need to look closely at what you expect will happen in specific social situations.

Recall in Chapter 2 we discussed how your expectations play a sizable role in keeping you locked in the anxiety spiral. A 1996 research study conducted by psychologist Edna Foa, noted for her research on anxiety disorders, illustrates this. Foa and her colleagues compared individuals with and without social phobia about their expectations regarding various social events. They asked the subjects questions about the probability of something happening to them, such as someone not saying hello. They also asked the subjects what they thought the consequences would be, should this event actually occur.

The results indicated that the socially anxious people overestimated both the probability and the severity of negative social events. In other words, they expected negative social events to be more likely to occur and the consequences of these events to be more severe. But these differences were found only when they were asked about social events, not other situations.

In addition, Foa's research demonstrated that one of the best predictors of "treatment outcome"—the extent to which people improve with treatment—is whether they modify their estimates of the consequences of negative social events. Those individuals who learn that unpleasant social situations aren't the end of the world, and that they can cope with such situations if they occur, are the ones who make the most progress.

As you can see, revising your expectations is crucial to overcoming social anxiety successfully. Using Kim's thought diary, let's see how her expectations contributed to her distress.

What Are the Odds? Kim's first entry reads: "Everyone will stare at me. They'll think I should've already lost this weight." Kim needed to ask herself how likely it would be that this would occur. What is the evidence for this thought?

It can help to assign a number value to your estimations. This forces you to be more precise in your thinking. It also gives you another way to chart your progress. I showed Kim the following scale and asked her to rate how likely she thought it was that her coworkers would stare at her and think she should've lost more weight.

What are the odds of _____ occurring?

(what you expect/fear will happen)

0%	10%	20%	30%	40%	50%	60%	70%	80%	90%	100%
definitely		not			fifty-			highly		definitely
won't		too			fifty			likely		will
occur		likely			chance					occur

I reminded Kim that when she's making her assessments to let her fear do the talking. I didn't want her to base her expectations on what she knows intellectually; such knowledge can often have little impact on what one actually believes.

Kim kept a record of these percentages in her thought journal. Initially, she guessed there was a 90 percent chance that her coworkers would stare and notice her weight.

Let's look at the proof Kim had that her fears would come true. To examine the evidence, she asked herself:

- If it was someone else in my position, would I stare? Would I think poorly of that person for being heavy after having a baby?

- Do my coworkers have a history of staring at other people?

- Have I witnessed my coworkers talking negatively about others in the past?

- What would staring mean? How would I know if people were staring at me? How many seconds could people look at me before it would be considered staring?

Kim and I went through these questions together. She acknowledged that if the situation was reversed, she wouldn't give a second thought to how someone looked after having a baby. She would be more interested in seeing pictures of the baby, asking the new mom questions about how they were doing, and things like that.

In response to the second and third questions, Kim did say several women in the office were prone to gossiping. She'd heard them talk about others' appearances before. One day she overheard them talking about someone's outfit that they thought looked "hideous." Kim told me she'd felt quite uncomfortable hearing this conversation take place. "I wonder what they're saying about me?" she said.

Unfortunately, many offices have a few people who are like the women Kim described. There's not much you can do except rise above it and realize it's not your problem. Although these women bothered her, Kim admitted that only two or maybe three were like this. The other fifteen or so people in the office were quite nice, not at all the gossipy type.

After talking through her responses to the questions, Kim revised how likely it was that people would stare and notice her weight. She now guessed it to be about 30 percent. That's a significant difference from her initial 90 percent assessment. By examining the evidence for her thoughts she was able to revise her expectations to be more realistic. Although Kim expressed some relief in knowing her fear wasn't as likely to occur as she'd originally thought, she still worried about the remaining 30 percent chance. "What then? How would I handle it?" she asked.

How Bad Would It Be? Next, Kim needed to examine whether she was exaggerating the severity of what would happen if her prediction came true. Again, I asked her to rate her expectations using the following scale.

How bad would it be if _____ occurred?

(what you expect/fear will happen)

0%	10%	20%	30%	40%	50%	60%	70%	80%	90%	100%
no		not a			moderately			horrible		worst
problem		big			terrible					possible
at all		deal								catastrophe

At first, Kim assumed she wouldn't be able to handle any scrutiny or disapproval. Images played in her mind like a bad movie. She thought if anyone simply looked at her the wrong way, she'd assume they were thinking she was fat, she'd start crying uncontrollably, making a complete fool of herself. She even imagined her boss yelling at her for being so emotional.

Based on these fearful images, Kim placed her severity rating at 80 percent. "The only thing that keeps me from saying 100 percent is I know I wouldn't lose my job because of all the bureaucracy in our department," she noted.

Kim needed to closely examine her expectations to get them more in line with reality. I asked her to consider the following:

- How bad would it be if my coworkers stared at me? Why couldn't I say to myself, "What's their problem? Didn't their parents teach them it's impolite to stare?"

- So what if I did cry at the office? Is that a crime?

- If my coworkers did comment on my weight, would I crumble? Sure, I'd probably be upset and hurt. But again, who has the problem? Instead of getting down on myself, I could silently say, "What's up with these rude people?!"

- Do their opinions reflect at all on my value as a person?

Kim could easily see that if people stared at her, she could tell herself it was their problem—not hers. She was stuck on the part about crying at the office, however. She insisted it wouldn't be "appropriate" and that she would be viewed as highly unprofessional. She continued to think it would be a catastrophe if it happened.

"Have you ever seen anyone else cry while at work?" I asked her.

Kim remembered a time just before her maternity leave when one woman was having a really bad day. Her uncle was quite sick in the hospital and she was naturally worried about him. "She did cry once after getting a phone call about his condition. But she had a good reason to cry—I don't."

Kim didn't change her mind overnight about it being horrible if she cried at work. Her expectation of it being a catastrophe was deeply tied to one of her core beliefs: It's not okay to show signs of emotion because it means you're weak. However, this belief only applied to herself. It was quite acceptable for other people show emotion.

I pointed out this double standard to Kim. "So it's okay for other people to be human, but it's not okay for you." Kim could see what I was trying to get at and said she'd think about it more. She obviously still had some work to do in this area, but that's understandable. The way we think about things can become quite ingrained.

We alluded above to the fact that one's expectations are tied to one's beliefs. We'll address this final, important cognitive component in the next section.

What Matters Most

Deep down inside, everyone has ideas about how they must look or act or feel. These basic beliefs are the underlying principles that give rise to your thoughts or feelings, especially those which come to your mind automatically. Remember Joe? He was so anxious about his encounter in the library that he subconsciously had several negative thoughts. That's because his belief system told him he had to be the most popular person at school to have friends.

As we discussed in this chapter, however, monitoring your thoughts and challenging your expectations cause you to confront these basic beliefs. This is critical to make deep and lasting progress in overcoming social anxiety.

See if you hold any of the following beliefs. Many people with social anxiety do.

- My worth depends upon what others think of me.

- My worth depends upon my accomplishments.

- Anxiety and fear equal weakness.

- I must be perfect for others to accept me.

- I must be perfect for me to accept myself.

- I cannot function when I am anxious.

- I cannot tolerate criticism or rejection.

- Everyone must like me or it's horrible.

We already mentioned one of Kim's beliefs—displaying emotions is inappropriate and equals weakness. Look over the thoughts in Kim's diary one more time. Do you have any ideas about other basic beliefs she holds?

Kim recognized she was putting a lot of pressure on herself to look and act a certain way. She felt she needed to be perfect to be acceptable, not only to others but also to herself. She set unrealistically high standards that anyone would have difficulty measuring up to. Kim also placed a lot of emphasis on her performance at work. Of course, it's important to do one's best, but Kim expected much more than that. And now that she had a new baby to care for, she needed to give herself time to adjust and regain her energy.

I asked Kim to consider what was most important in her life right now. What did she value most about herself? What were her greatest blessings? What gave her the greatest joy? Kim's list was short, but it got straight to the heart of the matter.

- It's important to me to be a loving mother and wife—to take care of and nurture my family.

- It's important to me to live a moral life, to be kind to others, and to help those in need.

- It's important to me to use my strengths and talents as best I can, not only in my work but in everything I do.

Kim and I talked about what she'd written. She was able to see that the opinions of others had very little relevance to the things most important to her. For example, if someone at work didn't think her presentation was perfectly polished, it wouldn't make much of a difference in her life. In fact, Kim realized that none of the things she typically worries about truly affect what matters most to her—the ability to love and be loved.

Our discussion made me recall a quote I'd once read, a fitting close to this topic of "thinking it through."

What other people think of me is none of my business.

—Ellen Degeneres

Chapter 7

Focus on the Task at Hand

Concentrate all your thoughts upon the work at hand.
The sun's rays do not burn until brought to a focus.

—Alexander Graham Bell

It was the 1997 NBA finals with the Chicago Bulls facing the Utah Jazz. Superstar Michael Jordan had been sick with the flu, and Bulls' fans feared the worst: Michael wouldn't play. Yet Jordan did play, winning the game for the Bulls and giving perhaps the best performance of his career.

Think of why the Bulls won the game. Jordan, fighting a fever, got out on the court. He wasn't thinking of his aches and pains but instead was focusing on the task at hand—winning the basketball game. It worked, and the Bulls went on to win their fifth NBA title.

Now let's switch gears. Imagine yourself giving a speech. You know the topic well, but instead of concentrating on what you're supposed to be saying, you're imagining the audience noticing the beads of sweat on your brow. They hate my performance, you think. As a result, you lose your place, stumble over facts you know, and appear less than the expert you are.

Paying attention to the wrong things—in this case, how you think the audience is evaluating you—leads to more anxiety and interferes with your ability to present your speech.

In this chapter, we'll show you how to overcome this problem of focusing on unhelpful things in the situations you deal with on a regular basis. We'll describe strategies for strengthening your powers of concentration and dealing with distractions. You'll discover how learning these skills will help you feel more relaxed and confident, leaving you able to put forth your best effort for the task at hand.

Lessons from Sports Psychology

I'm inundated with sports at my house. My husband, Greg, pitched for his college baseball team. He enjoys almost all other sports, as well. Jesse has definitely followed in his father's footsteps. He enjoys watching sports, playing sports, reading about sports, and perhaps his favorite, talking about sports. Not being athletically inclined, I've never had much of an interest. In the past, I would be doing quite well if I could name the teams playing in the Super Bowl. But living with my two sports enthusiasts, I've had to adapt. One way I've survived is by developing an interest in the psychology of sports.

Something that's fascinated me is how many of the challenges athletes face are similar to those of people struggling with social anxiety. Athletes work under immense pressure and public scrutiny. To perform at their peak they must learn to block out distractions, such as:

- high expectations from themselves and others

- frustration over mistakes

- criticism from coaches and judges

- the presence of loved ones they want to impress

- the scrutiny of the media

Although we probably don't have the media tailing us, many of us face similar distractions when we encounter social or performance situations. We expect a lot of ourselves, we worry if we make a mistake, and we wonder how other people will judge us. We feel pressure to do our best. While some people do better under pressure, perhaps even feel energized by it, this isn't always the case.

Look at New York Yankee second baseman Chuck Knoblauch. During the 1999 season, Knoblauch went through a period where he made several wild throws to first base on routine plays. He couldn't figure out what had happened. The more he thought about it and worried about it, the more difficult it became for him to perform. He continued to have trouble making what should be easy throws for a baseball player. One television replay actually showed Knoblauch watching his own hand as he threw the ball, rather than looking at his target as he should have been. Knoblauch was concentrating intensely, but on the wrong thing.

Knoblauch's example is not unique. Many athletes—even those at the top of their game—go through slumps where they don't perform well. Some, unable to deal with their setbacks, never recover.

One such athlete is Mark Wohlers. During the mid-1990s, Wohlers was one of the top relief pitchers in baseball. He was successful under pressure, pitching in playoff games and the World Series. Then, for some inexplicable reason, he could no longer throw the ball for strikes during the 1998 season. The more pressure he felt, the more he obsessed about his performance, and the more difficult the task became. He was sent back to the minor leagues and is now out of baseball. There was no physical injury that could explain his severe drop-off in performance; it was due to his inability to focus.

Isn't this similar to our own struggles with social situations? The more we concentrate on our perceived shortcomings, the worse we perform. Whether it's introducing ourselves at a meeting or asking someone for a date, if we're not focusing on the "right" things, we're more apt to fail. Don't worry, though. There are things you can do to improve your ability to zero in on what's truly important. But if you lose your focus from time to time—we all do—it's not the end of the world.

Sports psychology offers many techniques to help enhance concentration. Yet these are skills that anyone can learn and benefit from, not just athletes. Before we describe them, however, we need to take a brief "time-out" to cover the basics of what you should and should not focus on when you're feeling anxious. In the next few sections, we'll explain the importance of determining your focus and show you how to get "in the zone," that state of focused attention in which your abilities naturally flow through you.

Determining Your Focus

In some situations, it's easy to determine where your focus should lie. For example, a baseball player should concentrate on the game. A surgeon needs to concentrate on the details of the operation. But in social situations, it's more difficult to decide, "What should I pay attention to?" Plus, when we're in these situations, we're usually not consciously thinking, "Okay. I'll focus on this now." Usually, it's our anxiety—and our faulty thinking—that leads us to focus on one thing or another. That's why many of us can benefit from some basic, explicit instruction on what's helpful and what's not helpful to focus on during social situations.

This was the case for Ross, an extremely shy and quiet young man who was studying to become a doctor. He had done well in medical school, scoring at the top of his class. But when he began his residency training, more social interaction was expected of him, and he floundered. Only a few months after beginning the program, Ross felt like he was on the verge of breaking down. He wasn't sleeping or eating well, and he was tense and nervous most of the time. His major fear was that he wasn't performing up to par in his residency and that he'd be expelled.

As Ross explained his situation to me, he spoke of his extreme nervousness during Rounds—a time when residents go from room to room with their professors. They interview patients in front of the group, make decisions aloud about the proper diagnosis and treatment, and explain their reasoning. There was enormous pressure to come up with the "right" answers quickly, and the residents were quite competitive with each other.

Ross began worrying about Rounds days before, and his anxiety during the actual event was overwhelming. He described it as a surrealistic-like feeling in which he felt unable to focus on what he was supposed to be doing. He was acutely aware of his every move, such as how he was standing, how his arms were positioned, and, especially, how his eyes were directed. He worried about every detail imaginable related to eye contact:

- If I don't have good eye contact, I will look suspicious. People will think I'm up to no good.

- If I look at people too long, they'll think I'm staring, and that would be rude.

- If there are a lot of people in the room, I don't know whom to look at: the patient? the professor? the other students?

- I feel like my eyes are constantly darting around. I know everyone will think I have "shifty-looking" eyes.

Once Ross started focusing on how his eyes looked, he entered into an endless, useless loop of self-defeating thoughts. He became stuck, unable to change his focus.

The first thing I did with Ross was explain how unhelpful it is to focus on your performance *while* you're trying to perform. Ross was second-guessing his every move—actually, his every blink. His attention was so fixed on how his eyes appeared to others that there was no way he could adequately concentrate on the content of what was being said during Rounds.

Just hearing this information was helpful to Ross. He hadn't realized he was contributing to the problem by focusing on the wrong thing. He mistakenly believed that if he tried hard enough, he could control his eyes—in effect, force them to "look normal."

Read through the list below and make note of any areas you tend to focus on. Think about how concentrating on these things is unhelpful, how this misplaced attention only fuels your anxiety and negative thinking, and how it makes it more difficult to do your best.

Unhelpful Things to Focus on During Social/Performance Situations

Your Physical Symptoms
- blushing
- sweating
- shaking

Your Appearance
- how you look, in general
- your hair
- your weight
- your clothes

Body Language
- how you're standing
- where your hands/arms are
- eye contact

Evaluation Concerns
- what type of impression you're making
- how your performance is going
- what other people are thinking

Were you able to recognize the areas you tend to focus on? Many people with social anxiety have global evaluation concerns, but also one or two more specific areas they pay attention to. For example, Ross was bothered by general worries about his performance, but he mostly focused on how his eyes looked to others.

Knowing where your mind naturally tends to fixate is the first step in learning to shift gears. But what next? How do you train your mind not to dwell on these unproductive areas? And how can you improve your ability to concentrate on what you're supposed to be doing? To answer these questions, we'll return to sports psychology.

Getting "in the Zone"

When athletes play well, they often state later that they were "in a zone." They're describing a state of focused attention where their abilities naturally flowed out of them and they performed at their peak. The zone is an almost Zen-like meditative state in which distractions simply have no place in your mind. Instead, you're mentally free to execute skills as you've been trained, and you're focusing only on the task at hand.

University of Chicago psychologist Mihaly Czikszentmihalya calls this state of focused attention "flow." For decades he's studied people who have experienced such periods of peak performance in all sorts of situations, and he's found that these occurrences share common characteristics. When you're in "the zone" or a state of "flow":

- All of your attention is focused either on the skill being performed or input from your senses relevant to the skill.

- You're not evaluating your performance while you're executing the skill.

- You're not concerned with others' expectations during your performance.

- You are not consciously aware of your awareness at the time.

- You are in control of your actions and reactions, despite feeling an almost altered state of consciousness.

- You feel invigorated and exhilarated.

Keep in mind, when we talk about a "skill" or a "performance," this can mean anything: a concert, an interview, a presentation, a test, meeting someone new, and so on. For Ross, participating in Rounds during his medical training was certainly a performance. It seemed to him that he was on display, for everyone to judge his competence as a doctor. As another example, I sometimes feel like I'm in a zone when

I'm immersed in my writing. I'm tuning out distractions, and the words seem to be almost channeled through me. But if I worry too much about the end product and how my work will be perceived by others, the words simply don't come and I'm stuck with a bad case of writer's block.

So how do athletes and other peak performers get in the zone?

First of all, they recognize that slumps, even failure, are part of the game. For example, a good batter in baseball fails to get a hit 70 percent of the time. A relief pitcher may fail one day and be back pitching well in the same situation the next day. This acceptance of "failure" is crucial because it allows the player to put the past behind him and focus only on what he must do to succeed in the present.

Second, they practice. Even the most successful hitters practice their craft on a daily basis. They continually hone their abilities so they feel confident of their skills in the actual game.

The practice isn't only physical, though; athletes also practice mentally. Mark McGwire has said that everyone looks at his huge arms, but that his mind is much more crucial to his ability to hit the ball. If you watch McGwire before he comes up to bat, he's not sitting on the bench talking to the other players; he's off by himself. He usually has his eyes closed as he mentally prepares for what he needs to do when it's his turn at the plate. McGwire has talked openly of how he worked with a psychologist to help him overcome devastating injuries and improve his performance on the field.

Phil Jackson, former coach of the Chicago Bulls, used meditation techniques to help the team improve its performance on the court. He so strongly believed in it that he often had meditation experts spend days at a time training the players on proper form and technique.

According to Jackson, most of the members of the team found practicing meditation to be extremely valuable. But even the few who were less than enthusiastic found some good in it. For example, team member Bill Cartwright often bantered about how he liked the meditation sessions because he was able to take a nap. Although the goal of meditation isn't to fall asleep, most people do feel refreshed and better able to concentrate afterward.

You don't have to be Mark McGwire or a player for the Bulls to

learn ways to increase your concentration and improve your performance. In fact, the diaphragmatic breathing skills you learned in Chapter
5 help relieve anxiety and leave you better able to focus on what you
need to do. There are also numerous relaxation and meditation techniques you can learn to accomplish the same goal.

In this chapter, we'll show you how you can relax your body and
calm your mind—achieving a state of focused attention—using what's
called applied relaxation training. We'll describe each stage of this approach and then show you how to apply it to your everyday life.

Applied Relaxation Training

Applied relaxation training combines several well-known and
proven relaxation techniques in a way that allows you to relax
rapidly even in anxious situations. Imagine being able to enter a stressful
social situation knowing you could relax your body in a brief period of
time. Imagine how much confidence this would provide. Instead of worrying about your body going haywire, you'd be free to focus on the
situation itself. It takes time and practice to reach the point of being able
to relax on command, but it can be done.

Applied relaxation training was developed in the late 1980s by the
Swedish physician, Lars-Goran Ost, who is well-known for his work in
anxiety disorders. Ost wanted to find a way to help his phobic patients
more easily enter their feared situations. To do this, he creatively combined several relaxation techniques in a way that armed his patients with
exactly what they needed—a powerful, fast, and reliable method to relieve their anxiety. By employing these relaxation techniques, even severely phobic patients were able to manage their anxiety while facing
their fears.

Applied relaxation training involves six stages, and each stage builds
on the previous one. This isn't a quick fix, so you'll have to be patient.
Devote about twenty to thirty minutes a day to practice, and give yourself one or two weeks to become comfortable with each stage. Keep in
mind, the earlier stages will take more time to master than the later

ones. As you become more adept at these relaxation techniques, it will take less practice time and become more a matter of refining and applying your skills.

Stage 1: Progressive Muscle Relaxation (PMR)

The goal of this first stage is to recognize the difference between how your muscles feel when they're tense and how they feel when they're relaxed. You might think you'd automatically know this, but many people experience chronic muscle tension without even realizing it. By practicing PMR you'll begin to quickly scan your body for muscle tension and you'll be able to relax any trouble spots on command.

To learn PMR, you may find it helpful to tape-record the instructions below. Another option is to purchase a professionally recorded relaxation audiotape. Refer to the "Resources" section to find out how to order one. After you've gone through the procedure several times, though, you'll become familiar with the procedure and you may not need a tape.

These are the instructions:

1. Find a comfortable, quiet place to sit or lie down.

2. Take a deep breath from your diaphragm.

3. Tense each muscle group following the list below. Notice what the tension feels like. Hold the tension for five to ten seconds.

4. Release the tension. Focus on how relaxed the muscle feels.

5. Take another deep breath.

6. Repeat procedure with each muscle group.

Below are the major muscle groups. Tense and release each one in order. If you experience pain in any of the areas, stop immediately and omit them in the future. In particular, people with back or neck pain should be cautious when tensing the muscles in these areas.

Your head:
- Clench your teeth and pull the corners of your mouth back in a forced smile.

- Close your eyes tightly.

- Open your eyes as wide as you can.

Your neck and shoulders:
- Press your head to your right shoulder, then your left.

- Press your chin toward your chest.

- Tilt your head toward your back. Don't force it too far, though.

- Raise your shoulder up toward your ears in a big shrug.

Your arms and hands:
- Tighten your hands into fists.

- Tighten the muscles in your upper body by making a fist and bending your arms up at the elbows.

- Press your hand firmly into the surface where you're practicing.

Your chest:
- Take a deep breath and puff out your chest.

- Tighten your chest muscles.

Your back:
- Arch your back.

Your abdomen:
- Push your abdomen out as far as you can.

- Pull your abdomen in tight toward your spine.

Your hips, legs, and feet:
- Tighten your buttocks.

- Push the soles of your feet down into the floor. If you're lying down, press your heels.

- Point your toes downward.

- Flex your toes upward.

Practice relaxing your body this way at least once a day. It should take approximately fifteen to twenty minutes to go through the entire process. Remember, the goal at this stage is to really notice the difference between tension and relaxation. This will make it easier to master the next stage.

Stage 2: Release-Only Relaxation

In this stage you omit the first part of PMR, the tensing part, and instead focus only on relaxing each of the muscle groups in turn. This will shorten the time the process takes and allow you to reach a state of deep relaxation more quickly.

Begin in a comfortable position, either sitting or lying down. Focus on your breathing for a few minutes. Concentrate on taking deep breaths from your diaphragm. Now progress through the muscle groups and gently tell yourself to relax each muscle and allow the tension to slip effortlessly away. You can intensify the relaxation by imagining the muscle being heavy and warm. After you've progressed through your entire body, spend a few minutes breathing deeply. Scan your body for any remaining tension. Focus on any muscles that are still tense and spend a moment relaxing those areas.

Try not to rush through this stage. It may seem easier than progressive muscle relaxation, but it's actually more difficult because you're relaxing the muscles entirely through the power of your mind.

Stage 3: Cue-Controlled Relaxation

The next stage in applied relaxation training is called "cue-controlled relaxation." It's a simple idea that involves pairing a word with a relaxed physical state. With enough repetition of this pairing, the body learns to associate the relaxed condition with the word. With enough time spent conditioning your body and mind in this way, you can use the word to direct your body to calm down, even in anxiety-arousing situations.

Keep in mind, you can select any word or short phrase to be your cue. Many people use a single word, such as "relax" or "calm" but you could just as easily use the phrase "relaxed body, calm mind." You also can use a physical gesture as your cue—either alone or in combination with a word or phrase—such as touching your hand to your side or touching your right hand to your left forearm. The details don't matter much; what counts is whether the cue works for you.

Here are the instructions:

1. Take a few deep breaths. As you do, imagine all your worries are floating away.

2. Using release-only relaxation spend a few minutes scanning your body for tension, letting all of it slip away. (If you need more than a few minutes in the beginning, that's fine.)

3. Once you're relaxed, silently say a cue word, such as "calm" or "relax" every time you exhale.

4. Continue inhaling deeply through your nose, holding the breath for a few seconds, and then exhaling while silently saying your cue word or phrase. Spend a few minutes on this step.

With practice, you should be able to relax your body completely in about two to three minutes. Again, this may take several weeks of practice to get to this point. In the beginning, especially, do as many brief, minirelaxation sessions as you can using your cue. This will enhance the conditioning process. In other words, the frequent pairing of a relaxed state with the cue is what will give you the power to use the cue later, when you're anxious and need to redirect your focus.

Stage 4: Differential Relaxation

The purpose of this stage is to become accustomed to relaxing your body in different positions and situations, not just while you're lying down or sitting comfortably in a quiet room. Sure, it's great to be able to relax while you're at home. But the purpose of applied relaxation training is to eventually be able to relax quickly while in a stressful situation.

If you've been practicing the relaxation exercises while lying down, the next step is to do them in a comfortable chair. If you've already been practicing in a favorite chair, try moving on to a harder, straight-backed chair. We're mainly talking about practicing the cue-controlled relaxation, but it may also be helpful to review the other two methods—progressive muscle and release-only relaxation—in different contexts as well.

Try adding distractions when you practice relaxing. Have the radio on or TV on in the background. Practice in a different room than you usually do. Practice standing up. The idea is to gradually add more "real-life" aspects into your sessions.

Another aspect of differential relaxation is to become skilled at using only the muscles you need for a particular task and keeping the rest of your muscles relaxed. For example, sometimes when I'm typing I notice my shoulders are scrunched up toward my ears. They don't need to be; I don't need my shoulder muscles to be active when I'm typing. When I notice this, I take a deep breath and release the tension from my shoulders, letting them drop to their normal resting position.

Pay attention as you move throughout your regular activities. Are you tensing muscles that aren't needed for the task?

Stage 5: Rapid Relaxation

The purpose of this stage, rapid relaxation, is to shorten the time needed to relax down to about thirty seconds and to do so frequently throughout the day.

Recall how in the cue-controlled relaxation instructions you picked a word, such as "relax" or "calm" to say to yourself as you breathed deeply and scanned your body for tension. In this stage you'll pick another kind of cue—a reminder to relax throughout the day. For example, you might select your watch as a reminder. You can even put a piece of colored tape on it or tie a string around the band to remind you in the beginning. Every time you look at your watch during the day it will remind you to:

- take a deep breath;

- say "relax" or whatever word works for you, as you exhale;

- scan your body for any tension; and,

- release the tightness from these muscles.

You don't have to rely on your watch to remind you. You could put a sticker on your phone, and every time you hang up the phone do the above steps. The idea is to have some kind of reminder that you'll frequently notice throughout the day.

Stage 6: Applied Relaxation

You're now ready to begin applying your relaxation skills when you're in anxiety-producing situations. Keep in mind, this technique will probably not take away your anxiety completely. It will, however, be a powerful tool to help you manage your anxiety so you can focus on the task at hand.

One of the keys is to catch your anxiety when it's at a mild level. You'll learn that you can function even in spite of anxiety, especially when the anxiety isn't overwhelming yet. If you wait until you're in a full-blown panic attack it will be much harder, if not impossible, to bring your anxiety under control using relaxation techniques alone. This is one reason why practicing the previous stages is so crucial. By doing so, you've gained plenty of experience in regularly scanning your body for tension recognizing what areas of your body tend to tense up first.

As soon as you notice any sings of tension or anxiety, begin these steps:

1. Take two or three deep breaths, using your diaphragmatic breathing skills.

2. Think your cue word to yourself as you continue to breathe slowly and deeply.

3. Scan your body for tension and focus on relaxing those muscles that feel tense.

Try to be patient with yourself; as we've said, this takes a lot of practice. And remember, bringing your anxiety level down even a notch or two will help you better focus on the task at hand.

A Few More Tips

In addition to regular use of applied relaxation, there are a few other things you can do to maintain your calm in an anxiety-provoking situation. The more tricks you have up your sleeve, the better prepared you'll be to do what you need to do.

Rate your anxiety and watch it ebb and flow.

Anxiety is not an all-or-nothing condition; it exists on a continuum. Recall how to rate your anxiety using a numerical scale of 0 to 10, with 0 being the most relaxed you've ever been and 10 being a state of severe panic. When you're feeling anxious, assess where you are on the scale. For example, say to yourself, "Oh, I'm at a 7 now. I think I'll take a few deep breaths and see what happens to my anxiety level." After taking a few minutes to focus on your breathing, reassess your level. You'll likely find that your anxiety has decreased, even if only by a point or two. Realizing that your anxiety level doesn't remain constant can reassure you that you won't remain in a high-anxiety state forever.

How you approach this activity makes a huge difference in the results you'll see. If you're telling yourself, "This rating-my-anxiety thing better work or I'm really in trouble," you'll only make yourself more anxious. Instead, adopt an attitude of curiosity. Say to yourself, "I wonder what will happen to my anxiety level if I do this . . ."

Notice and describe concrete objects around you.

Another trick you can try if you're having trouble maintaining your focus is silently to describe to yourself simple objects in your environment. For example, talk to yourself about the carpet: "This carpet has a low pile, it's tweedy-looking, with mauve and blue in it. Goes nicely with the cream-colored walls . . ." Sometimes it can help to make physical contact with an object. Touch the table you're sitting at, for example, or the material of the chair cushion beneath you.

What does this accomplish? Remember that anxiety is typically future-oriented, concerned with all the catastrophes that might happen. By describing your surroundings, you ground yourself in the present, preventing your anxiety from escalating any further. Before long, you're not noticing your racing heart or your trembling hands quite as much. Granted, you're still not paying attention to the task before you, but at least you're focusing on something neutral. Once you've settled down a bit, you can then redirect your attention to what you're supposed to be doing.

Focus on other people.

Although it may seem like you're the only one who suffers with social anxiety, in reality, there are many others who share your concerns. Remember the statistics we reviewed in Chapter 1? As many as one in eight people has social anxiety disorder. That means if you're in some type of gathering, perhaps a meeting for example, chances are there will be other people around you who are uncomfortable.

One client I worked with did an experiment of sorts. She hated the monthly department meetings she was required to attend. She felt that she was the quietest one there, and that people must think she was a "scared, little mouse." At one meeting, she decided to keep track of how many times people spoke. She actually kept tally marks on a pad of paper, discreetly of course. To her surprise, she learned that she wasn't the most quiet. In fact, she discovered that there were several people who said absolutely nothing. My client learned that while she wasn't the most outspoken of the group, she certainly wasn't the quietest either. By taking the focus off of herself and instead noticing other people, she was able to shift gears and relax.

Why not try your own experiments? Be creative. Notice who tells the most jokes, who tries to placate the group, and who tries to stir up trouble. Again, this will keep your focus off yourself and your anxiety. An added benefit: You might learn something that will help disprove some of your beliefs.

If you're feeling brave, why not look around to see who might be feeling similar to you, and see if you can help. For example, if there's a quiet person at a party standing alone, he or she may be feeling anxious and not know how to approach someone. If you can redirect your thoughts for even a brief while, you might be able to make someone else feel a bit better.

This approach of looking out for others always helps me. As I mentioned earlier in the book, when I was to appear on *Good Morning America*, I was apprehensive, to say the least. Waiting in the hotel lobby the morning of the show for the "driver" to take me to the set was nerve-wracking. I could feel my heart racing, my mouth felt as dry as chalk, and I knew I was sweating off all my makeup that took me an hour to apply. I was worried I'd freeze up on national television, making a complete fool of myself. And what if the host, Charlie Gibson, asked me something unexpected? On top of all these worries, the driver for the show was late. What should I do?

Then I saw someone who looked more nervous than I did. He was a young man, pacing, looking repeatedly at his watch. The night before, *GMA*'s producer had called to brief me. She told me I would go on the show with another person, someone with social anxiety. The man in the lobby looked about the age of the person she'd described. I wondered, could it be him? I gathered my nerve, walked over to him, and asked, "Are you going on *Good Morning America* this morning?" When I learned I was correct in my hunch, I redirected my attention. Instead of focusing on my own anxiety, I tried to help this brave gentleman feel more relaxed, despite the fact that our driver was really, really late by now!

So if you can, focus on other people and their needs. We all have our struggles, and if we can help lessen someone else's load, we'll help ourselves in the process.

Remember, you are the expert.

This last tip applies to situations in which you're giving a presentation or a speech. It may also apply to other times when you're in a position of authority and sharing information with others.

When my friend and editor, Julie McGovern, reviewed this chapter she pointed out a basic tenet of speech-making that says, "As long as you're prepared, you have nothing to be nervous about. For the moment you are speaking, *you* are the expert on the subject. You know more than your audience does—that's why you've been chosen to speak." I'm a bit embarrassed to admit it, but this idea had rarely crossed my mind, at least not at times when it would have helped me to relax. When I'm nervous before giving a presentation, I forget that I know more than the audience does—that I'm there to share helpful and valuable information with them.

I'm going to remember this principle the next time I'm asked to give a speech. And I'll also try to remember that being the expert doesn't mean I must give a flawless presentation or know every single thing about a topic. After all, surely the audience hasn't come to judge me, but instead they have come to learn. This thought alone will put me at ease.

How Does All This Work in Your Everyday Life?

Remember Ross and how he was self-conscious about his "shifty-looking eyes?" He couldn't help but think about how his peers and professors were constantly judging him during Rounds. He was so anxious he couldn't pay attention to the patients and their needs. Could applied relaxation and the other techniques we've presented really help? Let's take a look.

Recall that Ross benefited from me simply explaining how futile it is to focus on your performance *while* you're trying to perform. Now, whenever he began worrying about his "shifty-looking eyes," he told himself, "I can't control how my eyes look right now. I need to focus on other things."

I also believed Ross would benefit from applied relaxation training.

He focused so much on his eyes because he was anxious; if he could reduce his anxiety level, he'd be better able to consciously choose to focus on more productive things.

Ross was a little reluctant to try this approach. He understood learning the relaxation techniques would take time, and he wanted instant results. He worried that any day he'd be kicked out of his residency program. He didn't think he could afford to wait possibly weeks for the relaxation training to pay off. But short of taking an antianxiety medication, an option Ross didn't want to consider yet, there wasn't a quicker way. He agreed to give it a try.

Once Ross set his mind to do something, he did it in earnest. He set his alarm twenty minutes early each day to practice the relaxation techniques. In the evening he skipped turning on the television and found that he didn't really miss it. The relaxation practice helped him unwind from his busy day at the hospital much better than sitting in front of the TV.

While Ross was working his way through the stages of applied relaxation training, we went over some of the other tips he could use right away. He learned how to rate his anxiety level and watch it ebb and flow. This helped him realize his anxiety wasn't simply stuck at an unbearably high level. He also learned how to stay focused on the present moment. If he felt his anxiety level rising, he could take a moment to focus on his breathing.

Ross tried consciously to focus more on the patient and what he or she was feeling. What must it be like to be sick in the hospital and have this huge group of residents come in and start asking so many questions? He noticed that it seemed like the residents talked about the patients as if they weren't even in the room. They were so busy trying to impress each other they forgot they were dealing with a human being, not a medical diagnosis. Ross found that focusing on the patient helped him worry less about himself and how he was coming across.

Over the next four to six weeks, Ross became proficient at using the cue-controlled relaxation. When he felt himself becoming nervous and worrying about his eyes, he was able to quickly relax his entire body, take a deep breath, and say the word "relax." By doing this, he was even better able to redirect his focus onto the patient, what the other residents were saying, and what he was supposed to be learning from his professors.

You've seen how the techniques in this chapter worked for Ross. Now remember that speech you imagined yourself giving at the beginning of the chapter. Instead of focusing on the beads of sweat on your brow and how the audience is evaluating you, what else could you do?

After reading this chapter, you probably have some pretty good ideas. But in case you need a brief review, here's a chart that summarizes the key points we've made.

INSTEAD OF FOCUSING ON THIS:	FOCUS ON THIS:
Your physical symptoms • Blushing • Sweating • Shaking	**Your presentation** • Your expertise • What you are saying • The point you're trying to make
Your appearance • How you look • Your hair • Your weight • Your clothes	**The other person(s)** • What they're saying • How they're feeling
Your body language • How you're standing • Where your hands/arms are • Eye contact	**Relaxing your body** • Diaphragmatic breathing • Cue-controlled relaxation
The impression you're making • How your "performance" is going • What others are thinking of you	**Relaxing your mind** • Remind yourself you don't have to be perfect • Stay in the present

The skills you've learned in this chapter are skills for living life fully in the present. Whether you're an athlete trying to perform your best or a presenter focusing on giving a speech—to name just a few examples—these skills will help you remain relaxed, focused, and able to put forth your best effort to the task.

Record-setting Olympic athlete Carl Lewis put it this way:

My thoughts before a big race are usually pretty simple.
I tell myself: "Get out of the blocks, run your race, stay relaxed.
If you run your race, you'll win . . . Channel your energy. Focus."

Chapter 8

Face Your Fears

Avoiding danger is no safer in the long run than outright exposure.
Life is either a daring adventure, or nothing.

—Helen Keller

We've all heard the advice: If you fall off a horse, get right back on or fear will set in. In many cases, this makes good sense. For instance, when a friend of mine totaled her car in an accident last year, she didn't want to drive again. She was quite shook up, and she worried that something else bad might happen. Although her hesitancy and anxiety were understandable, I encouraged her to begin driving again as soon as possible. The longer she waited, the more difficult it would be.

Facing your fears can be powerful, especially when you stay in the situation long enough to learn that you *can* cope with it and that a catastrophe isn't likely to occur. This process is called "exposure" or "exposure therapy." Most clinical research studies have shown that to reduce fear and anxiety, the treatment process must include an exposure component. You can't simply sit in a therapist's office exploring how and why you developed your fears; you have to confront them head-on.

Exposure works exceedingly well for simple phobias, such as a fear of snakes or a fear of heights, and it can prove effective for other anxiety disorders. Unfortunately, it's not so clear-cut in the case of social fears. Social situations are different each time, so it can be difficult to build up the repeated exposures necessary to conquer your fears.

Caleb explained it this way: "I force myself into social situations every day, but it doesn't get any easier. One day I may talk to some coworkers in the hallway and it's okay. The next day there may be one extra person in the group, and my heart races, I get short of breath, and I clam up. The next day, I'm too scared to even try."

Miriam, too, had tried exposure therapy with a psychologist and also experienced difficulty. "It was next to impossible to control the situations so my anxiety didn't skyrocket and completely overwhelm me," she said.

In this chapter, we'll first explain in more detail what exposure is and how some experts think it works. Then, we'll show you ways to overcome the special problems in applying exposure methods to social anxiety. Despite the unique challenges socially anxious people face in using exposure, many find it's worth the extra effort. There's often no better way to make significant and lasting changes in your social comfort level.

A Simple Example of Exposure Therapy

When I first explain exposure to my socially anxious clients, I almost always use the treatment of a simple phobia as an example. This makes it easier for them to understand the basic principles involved—to see how exposure works in its ideal form. From there I show them how to adapt these principles to fit their situation. We'll follow the same format in this chapter, first describing the basics of what exposure is and what makes it work. Then we'll offer tips and suggestions for making exposure work for you.

Let me introduce you to Jean, a woman who came to see me

because of a disabling fear of heights. Jean couldn't attend meetings past the fifth floor of an office building. She selected her doctors on the basis of where their offices were situated. She even offended several friends because she wouldn't attend social functions in their high-rise apartments. The impetus for seeking help came when her oldest son was going away to college. He was assigned to the fourteenth floor of a dormitory. She desperately wanted to attend parents' weekend and not have to deal with her height phobia.

I spent the first session with Jean getting a good feel for her situation. I wanted to make sure we were dealing with a simple height phobia and not something more complicated. Her fears, in fact, did seem limited to heights. When she was any higher than the fifth floor of a building she felt dizzy and short of breath. The physical sensations intensified the higher she was, and she had suffered panic attacks on several occasions. When Jean was near a window or an open area her anxiety soared. She kept asking herself, "What if I jump?" or "What if I fall?" I assured Jean these were typical thoughts that go along with a height phobia—she wasn't going crazy.

During the second session I provided Jean with a rationale for exposure therapy and taught her some breathing techniques. She grasped the concepts quickly and was motivated to get to work. By the third session, we were ready to carry out her first exposure. We met at a nearby twenty-one-story hotel—a hotel with a glass elevator in the center of the lobby. Each floor has an interior balcony that overlooks a large atrium.

Jean and I picked the sixth floor to begin the process. This level would arouse her anxiety to a moderate degree without completely overwhelming her. Starting slowly also increases Jean's chances for success, making her feel more confident to move to the next level. We rode the elevator together up to the sixth floor. As we got off, I asked Jean to rate her anxiety on a scale of 0 to 10, with 0 being completely relaxed and 10 being a severe panic attack. She rated her level at an 8. Interestingly, despite her feeling quite anxious on the inside, she appeared calm. I pointed this out to her and she was shocked. "I thought everyone could see what a nervous wreck I am," she said.

As we walked around the hotel, I periodically asked Jean to rate her anxiety level. By the time we had made our way around the walkway one time, her level had dropped to a 6. We continued walking until her level had dropped to a 3. I coached her as we went, reminding her to focus on taking deep breaths. I also encouraged her to walk as "normally" as possible. She tended to clutch the railing as if her life depended on it.

Next, Jean repeated this entire procedure while I waited in the lobby. This was more difficult for her as I represented a safety net of sorts, but she wanted to try. By the time she got back to the lobby, she was beaming, feeling confident she could move on to the seventh floor.

Over the course of about six weeks, Jean and I worked our way up the hotel. She also did exposures on her own between sessions. Later, we moved on to other buildings and added new challenges to the exposure sessions, such as looking out windows or over balconies. In addition, we met in my office periodically to process what she was learning. I wanted to know how her thoughts and beliefs were changing, and how her body was reacting physically to the exposure challenges.

Below is a list of the things Jean reported gaining from her exposure therapy:

- "I learned I can function when I'm feeling anxious. I used to think I wouldn't be able to walk if I felt so dizzy and shaky."

- "I can walk without holding tight to a balcony or railing."

- "I learned I won't pass out from anxiety."

- "Anxiety goes away with time. It doesn't last forever."

- "I don't like feeling anxious, but I can tolerate it now. I think my body got used to those weird sensations."

- "I know it's highly unlikely that I would fall or jump. That's just my anxious mind playing tricks on me."

- "Having this phobia doesn't mean I'm weak or crazy. Most people have something they have to cope with."

Jean had worked hard for several months, and her work paid off. She was able to visit her son at college on parents' weekend. She teased later that maybe she would've been better off not seeing his dorm room, given how messy it was!

So why did walking in circles in a hotel atrium relieve Jean from her fear of heights? You've seen with her case *how* exposure works—what Jean had to do to reduce her fear. Now let's look at *why* it works.

Why Exposure Works

No one knows for sure why exposure works, but there are two main theories. Some researchers believe in a theory called habituation, while others think exposure works primarily through cognitive processes. We'll say at the outset: From our clinical experience, we believe a combination of factors is involved.

The theory of habituation

One theory asserts that exposure works through habituation. This means that the more you become accustomed to doing or seeing something, such as a situation or a behavior, the more you can tolerate it. It becomes such a part of your life—a habit—that it no longer seems like a big deal. In the case of social fears, the occasions or other stimuli that once provoked anxiety now cease to do so. Let's look at an example.

When I was in graduate school, I moved to an apartment complex that was very close to the campus. Unfortunately, it was also right by the airport. The airplanes were so loud when they flew overhead that I couldn't concentrate on anything. Sometimes they startled me, and I practically jumped from my chair. They even woke me up at night. I had no idea how I was going to stand it.

About a week after I'd moved, I was talking to someone on the phone long-distance and they commented on the noise in the background. By that time, I hadn't even noticed. The noise of the airplanes had stopped provoking any kind of reaction from me.

This is how habituation works. By repeated exposure to something, you stop reacting to it. In laboratory studies, habituation is usually de-termined using physiological measures such as pulse rate or blood pres-sure. When I work with clients, we use instead the same 0 to 10 ratings we've mentioned throughout the book. Using the scale—in which 10 is a near panic attack—clients rate their anxiety levels at frequent intervals. In each case I can tell if we need to adjust the exposure.

Cognitive explanations

Another theory is that exposure works by helping you change your expectations about what will happen in particular social situations. If all goes well with your exposures, you learn that the chances of something awful happening are pretty slim, and if something awful did happen, you could cope.

Of course, anyone can tell you, or you can tell yourself, "There's nothing to be afraid of." But the words certainly are not enough. Anyone who's ever tried to tell a frightened three-year-old that there are no monsters in the closet knows the futility of mere words. You have to *show* the child it's safe by shining a flashlight in the closet, poking all around, encouraging the child to look in, and so on. For beliefs to truly change, they must be disproved on a very basic, "gut" level.

Look back at the list of what Jean learned from her exposures. Many of her statements reflect a change in her thoughts and beliefs. For example, she no longer believed that experiencing any anxiety meant she was weak. She also realized that anxiety was uncomfortable, but it wasn't something dangerous to be avoided. In addition, she proved to herself that the chances of her jumping or falling from a high place were about as good as her chances of winning the lottery.

Proponents of the cognitive interpretation of how exposure works believe that being in the fearful situation "activates" one's beliefs, thus making them more amenable to change.

The Keys to Effective Exposure:
Make It Graduated, Repeated, and Prolonged

As you can see from Jean's experience, exposure therapy is not complicated, at least in the case of simple phobias. You really need to follow only three principles to maximize its effectiveness.

Take the gradual approach: Don't do too much too soon.

A key to successful exposure treatment is to go slowly and don't take on more than you can handle. Obviously, exposures are going to create some anxiety. That's necessary for habituation to take place. But there's no reason to overwhelm yourself. This will only make you more fearful and discouraged.

The trick is to break your fears into a series of steps, with the first few steps being only mildly challenging, with later steps increasing in difficulty. To do this, you create what's called a "hierarchy"—a list of the situations that elicit anxiety, rank ordered by the amount of distress each would lead to if you entered the situation.

For Jean, constructing a hierarchy was relatively easy and looked like this:

Jean's Hierarchy

1. Go to the sixth floor and walk around the balcony overlooking the atrium. Do with therapist first. Continue with this step until anxiety level decreases by at least 50 percent.

2. Do step one without therapist.

3. Look over the edge of the balcony on the sixth floor for at least ten seconds. Gradually increase time. Therapist assists.

4. Do step 3 without therapist.

5. Complete 1–4 on the seventh floor.

6. Complete 1–4 on the eighth floor, and so on.

7. Do the above in various other buildings. Add looking out the windows.

We made some adjustments to Jean's hierarchy as we went along, but this one gave us a good initial game plan to follow. Again, by starting with small steps we maximized the chances of her meeting with success early. This helped motivate her to continue, even when the exposures got a little tougher for her.

Make it a habit: Carry out your exposures repeatedly.

For exposure therapy to be successful, you also need to practice consistently and frequently. If you expose yourself to a fearful situation and then wait three months before you do it again, you'll likely not benefit much from either the first or the second experience. Jean and I met once a week to start with, and as I mentioned, she also practiced exposures on her own between sessions. I usually ask people to try to practice their exposures at least three times a week. Obviously, the more you can practice, the more rapidly you'll overcome your fears.

Exposures should be prolonged: Remain in the situation until your anxiety level drops.

How long should exposure sessions last? The usual guideline is to remain in the situation until your anxiety level begins to decline, preferably to a mild level. The theory is that if you leave the situation while your anxiety level is still high it reinforces your fear and can do more harm than good. Because of this guideline, the process of completing an entire exposure session can be quite time-consuming. Many of the treatment manuals used in research studies specify ninety-minute exposure sessions.

Actually, the issue isn't the length of time per se; it's remaining in the situation long enough to realize that fear doesn't persist indefinitely, that catastrophes aren't likely to occur, and that you can handle the situation. Once you get going with the items on your hierarchy, you may find it takes progressively less time to complete an exposure session. This is because you take with you what you've learned from one session to another. For example, after Jean had made it up several floors, she had become familiar with the process. She was already experiencing changes in her thoughts and beliefs. Plus, her body wasn't reacting with quite the same intensity.

Special Challenges in the Case of Social Anxiety

By now you have a good understanding of how exposure works in its ideal form. But as we said at the beginning of the chapter, there are special challenges to using exposure therapy for social anxiety. We'll describe these challenges below, and then we'll show you how to effectively work around them.

It's not always easy to develop a hierarchy.

Social situations tend to be complex and unpredictable and involve many skills, all of which make it difficult to develop a hierarchy of gradual steps.

For example, think of all the aspects involved in dating: You must read nonverbal cues, make pleasant conversation, listen and show interest to your dating partner, and perhaps eat in restaurants or go to other social places. Simultaneously, you must manage any of your physical symptoms of anxiety such as trembling, sweating, or blushing. Also, you must cope with negative thoughts ("He hates me" or "I'm being too quiet") and try not to let them affect your social skills. That's a lot to do at once. Add to the scenario that you have little control over the other person and how he or she will act. With so many unknown variables, no wonder dating is often dreaded by people with social anxiety.

Of course, there are ways to break the fear of dating into small steps. But even what might seem to be an easy step, such as talking to someone of the opposite sex for one minute, might still be too challenging and involve practicing too many skills at once for some people. In reality, creating a gradual hierarchy is not very neat and tidy in the case of many social situations.

Even if you come up with a workable hierarchy, you're likely to encounter other problems. First of all, situations may arise that you're not ready for—they're too high up on your hierarchy—but you have no choice in the matter. For example, imagine your boss surprises you by inviting you to lunch with an important distributor from out of town. The thought of having to go on the spur of the moment, without having time to prepare, is terrifying. This lunch would be especially difficult for you because you feel uncomfortable with authority figures, such as your boss. You know your hands will shake, your stomach will churn, and you'll have trouble eating and sounding intelligent at the same time. But what can you do? You certainly can't say, "Sorry. That's too high up on my hierarchy."

In another case, an opportunity might come along that you don't want to pass up. Maybe someone you've been wanting to get to know better calls and asks you to a movie. You don't feel ready for such a social outing, but you also don't want to risk his not asking a second time. Or, perhaps you're invited to join a professional organization and you know this will give your career a real boost. You're not sure if you could handle the social obligations that would go along with membership. But again, you don't want to pass up the opportunity.

With Jean's height phobia, it was easy to follow a linear, gradual format. But as you can see from these examples, trying to follow the principle of making exposure gradual can be much more difficult when it comes to social situations.

Repeated exposure isn't always feasible.

Another difficulty is that repeatedly exposing yourself to the same situation isn't always possible. Some things like dating, socializing with friends, and going to parties are just a few examples of social situations that don't follow a particular schedule. You don't always have control over whether or not you can practice your exposures three times a week.

Opportunities for things like interviewing for a job, taking an oral exam, or public speaking are even less likely to occur on a regular basis. When I was promoting *Dying of Embarrassment*, I did frequent radio interviews, and my anxiety significantly decreased over time. I got to the point where I could do an interview, feel few if any physical symptoms, and not obsess for days about how I sounded. I grew confident in my ability to get my ideas across, and I also didn't worry as much when I wasn't perfectly polished. It was truly a case of exposure at work; the sheer quantity and frequency of the interviews made me relax, physically and mentally.

However, now that I've been in more of a writing phase and

haven't done any media appearances lately, I know I will be anxious again when the time comes to do more interviews and public speaking. Hopefully, I'll be able to call upon my previous positive experiences and realize that I'm up to the task so that the anxiety won't overwhelm me.

There are ways to simulate situations when the actually opportunity isn't available. But in terms of the traditional guideline of repeating your exposures frequently, it's not always practical.

Social situations are often brief, making prolonged exposure difficult.

Remember that to habituate to something, you have to remain in the situation long enough for your anxiety level to diminish—to become more comfortable. Again, this principle can be difficult to follow. Think of all the social situations that are brief by nature: a handshake, answering the phone, smiling at someone on the street, introducing yourself at a meeting . . .

There's no way to prolong these situations so that your anxiety level can come down naturally. In seconds or minutes, the event is over, but you're left with your racing heart and trembling hands. By virtue of the brief nature of the experience, you don't have the opportunity to learn that your anxiety will dissipate.

You're also left with the doubts in your mind about how the situation went. It happened so fast and while you were so acutely anxious, it's easy to misinterpret things. In other words, you don't get the positive shifts in your thoughts and beliefs that come with prolonged exposure.

What does this all mean?

If you've tried exposure before and it wasn't helpful, don't think that it's your fault or that you've failed. As you can see from the above discussion, there are many reasons why this may have happened. You may experience more success by following some of our suggestions below. Or, it may be that at a different time and in different circumstances you'll see more positive results. Also, you could be someone who would benefit from some medication, a topic we'll cover in the next chapter. In any case, read on and don't give up. If one thing doesn't help, something else will.

Making Exposure Work for You

To deal with the special challenges we've just described, the main things to remember are remain flexible and be creative. Below we'll describe a number of different options we've successfully used with clients. Read through them and see which of these ideas might be helpful in your situation.

Use imaginal exposure.

The type of exposure Jean used to overcome her height phobia is called *in vivo* exposure. This simply means the exposure takes place in the actual situation. There's also another type of exposure, *imaginal* exposure, which can be very useful in reducing social fears. The procedures and principles are essentially the same; the only difference is that the exposure is carried out in your mind.

Imaginal exposure can sidestep many of the problems we discussed in the previous section. With imaginal exposure, you can control more of the variables that can be unpredictable in actual social situations. You can also carry out exposures that might not otherwise be available to you. In addition, imaginal exposure can help you prepare to complete exposures in real life.

How can you implement imaginal exposure? Just as with exposures, you carry out in the actual situation, the first step is to develop your hierarchy. Then, for each step on the hierarchy, you create the scene. Most people find they need to actually write a "script," although a few people may be able to skip this step. In the script, include as many details as possible about the situation, especially details about the things you fear will happen. You'll need to include any troubling physical sensations, thoughts you may experience, other people's reactions, and so on.

Let's look at how Donald, a thirty-five-year-old engineer, used imaginal exposure to help overcome his fear of speaking and reading in public. Donald needed to take several continuing education courses related to his job, but he was terrified that class participation would be required. Whenever he'd spoken in front of a group before, his heart raced, he became short of breath, and he had trouble getting the words to come out of his mouth. He felt so embarrassed. He was sure everyone could tell how nervous he was and think he was incompetent.

Donald also had some other, more general social fears. He never dated and had just a few, casual friends. He lived by himself in an apartment; his roommate had recently moved out to live with his fiancée. Donald wanted to work on his fear of public speaking first, though, because he felt like it was an immediate problem. He didn't know how much longer he could put off taking these classes.

Donald and I created several scenes to use for his imaginal exposures. In the first scene, Donald is in class, and he asks the teacher a simple question. This is a relatively low-risk situation—an easy exposure. Of course, in real life Donald would be anxious about having to say anything in front of the class, but in this scene everything goes smoothly. Donald asks the question and the teacher even comments that he raised an excellent point.

In the next scene, we introduce a little more risk to the situation. Donald makes a comment or two in the class, asserting his opinion about something. Someone in the class disagrees with him. Donald is a bit shaken up, but he maintains his composure.

In each case, Donald imagines the scene, allowing himself to become fully immersed in it, experiencing the accompanying anxiety. His anxiety rises to a moderate level during the exposure. He's uncomfortable, but he stays with the scene for however long it takes for his anxiety to subside. After Donald was able to imagine one scene with little or no anxiety, we created another one that was slightly harder.

Let's jump ahead to the very top of Donald's hierarchy. This scene will target his core fear—the ultimate catastrophe he believes will occur. And remember, you wouldn't use this kind of scene right away. This would come only after all the easier items on the hierarchy had successfully been completed and could be imagined with little anxiety.

Below is the script Donald used. He tape-recorded it onto a looped tape that repeats itself, like those used in answering machines. Then he listened to the tape over and over again until his anxiety level subsided. This process took him about eighty minutes the first time. As he continued these imaginal exposure sessions over the next few weeks, it took less and less time for his anxiety to decrease because he was habituating to the fearful images.

Donald's Catastrophic Imaginal Exposure Script

You are in a required continuing education class related to your job. You have to take it; otherwise, you'll lose your job. The first day of the class, you recognize some of the other people. You know a couple of them are really sharp. You're already wondering if you'll have to introduce yourself or read aloud.

You can feel your heart racing and your mouth feels dry. You wish you could run out of the room!

You notice someone is looking at you. You wonder what he's thinking. "He can probably tell I'm nervous and will probably be laughing at me behind my back on the break."

The teacher begins the class and asks everyone to say their name and what they hope to learn. You can hardly stand it. What if you stammer? What if you can't even get out your own name? What if you lose control? Somehow, you muddle through that part. But then, he asks everyone to go around the room, reading and answering questions from the book. When it's your turn, you pause a long time. You stumble over the words in the question, but you can't think of the answer. You finally mumble, "I don't know."

All eyes are on you. You feel like you're about to have a panic attack and you leave the room. You're mortified, and deeply ashamed.

The next day one of your supervisors comes and talks to you. He says, "I heard you had some problems in the class last night. It sounds like you really lost control of yourself. We can't have any of that around here. You're fired."

Devastated, you clean out your desk and go home, feeling totally defeated. Over the next few months, you go through all your savings, and have to move back home with your parents. You feel worthless—like a total loser who has no purpose in life.

Does this script sound extreme to you? Are you asking yourself why anyone would purposefully imagine such a horrible scenario? How can that possibly be therapeutic?

These are natural questions to ask. The scenario is extreme, but that is the nature of fears. Also, we are not making up this scenario; this is what's played out in Donald's mind all the time. It's just not usually on a conscious level. By bringing his core fears out into the open, he has the opportunity to habituate to the scene so that it no longer can evoke such as strong emotional response. In addition, completing this type of exposure gives him the chance to examine his deeper beliefs and hopefully move them in a more realistic direction.

Granted, completing such an exposure takes tremendous courage and discipline. You certainly don't need to do this right away, and it's just one option to try.

And remember, while doing imaginal or any other type exposure, use the diaphragmatic breathing you learned in Chapter 5. This can make the process more manageable. You can also use a simple coping statement such as, "The chances of this scenerio actually happening are slim; if something like this did happen, I would find a way to cope." Just make sure you're not distracting yourself from imagining the scene—if you don't pay attention to the exposure, it won't have a chance to work.

Another question you may have is, "How do I know what my core fear is?" As we've said, it's not always apparent. The easiest way to find out is to keep asking yourself: If (what you fear) actually occurs, what comes next? What are the consequences? And then what happens? And then what happens? What next? This is the questioning process I used to help Donald discover his core fear. Looking back over Donald's script, you can track the progression of his fears. If diagrammed, it would look something like this:

**Showing any sign of anxiety → Loss of control → Loss of job →
Loss of independence → Loss of worth as a human being**

Can you can see how his fears move from surface concerns—things he's more aware of and has access to—to deeper, more all-encompassing fears? Ultimately, the more you're able to address your core fears, the more complete and lasting a recovery you'll have.

Of course, you don't have to confront your core fears all at once. And we don't want to leave you with the impression that you'll necessarily eliminate your fears altogether. For many of us, we'll struggle with certain fears and insecurities to some degree for the rest of our life. That's simply part of living and how we grow as human beings. But for those who make the effort to bring their core fears into awareness and to face them directly, the payoffs can be dramatic.

Watch Out for "Safety Behaviors"

At the end of Chapter 1 you completed a survey to assess all the aspects of your social anxiety. Recall that there was a section that asked you about things you may do to limit or control your experience of social situations. We called these things "partial avoidance behavior," and they're also referred to as "safety behaviors." For example, these people don't completely avoid social situations, but they rely on safety behaviors to control their anxiety:

- Vanessa always tries to sit in the back of the classroom, where she won't be noticed or called on.

- Kyle can only go to a party if he has two drinks ahead of time.

- Amanda never arrives early for staff meetings because she dreads having to make small talk. She tries to arrive exactly on time. She also doesn't want to be late, for fear of people watching her walk in the room.

- Mark has to grip his glass very tightly when he is at a restaurant. He feels this will make it less likely that his hand will shake.

- Emily takes her children to a "drop-in-and-play" center, but she avoids eye contact with the other mothers. She doesn't want to have to talk to anyone.

- George can give presentations only if he has every word memorized and has slides so that people won't look at him. He also tries to avoid taking questions from the audience. He wants to maintain as much control as possible.

So what's wrong with using these little tricks? After all, isn't it better that the person at least gets through the situation rather than avoiding it altogether?

The problem with safety behaviors is that the person attributes the absence of a catastrophe to the safety behavior. Looking at Vanessa and Kyle, let's see what this means:

- Vanessa thinks to herself, "Am I ever glad there was a seat in the back of the class. I would've had a panic attack if I had to sit in the front row." She prevented herself from learning that either she might not have a panic attack in the front row, or that if she did, it wouldn't be the end of the world.

- Kyle assumes that the only reason he could talk to people at the party was because he already had drunk two beers by the time he arrived. He never learns whether or not he would've been able to talk to people without the alcohol already in his system.

The use of subtle avoidance strategies like these is one reason it seems exposure "doesn't work" in the case of social anxiety. You could do every exposure on your hierarchy, but if you're still using safety behaviors, you're probably not learning what you need to be learning.

But our usual caveat applies: You don't have to get rid of your safety behaviors all at one time. For example, once George became aware of his attempts to exert too much control over his presentations, he could gradually try new things, such as allowing for one or two questions at the end of his talk. Mark could loosen his grip on a glass for just a few seconds at a time to see what happens. Who knows, he might learn that his hand actually shakes less if he's not squeezing so tight.

A good question to ask yourself when you're carrying out your exposures is: What could I do that would make this experience more challenging? Answering this can often lead you to noticing the safety behaviors you're using.

Turn exposures into experiments.

Try to remember back to the science classes you took in school. Remember the steps for conducting experiments? First, you state your hypothesis—in other words, what do you think will happen? Then, you design some type of procedure to test the hypothesis. Next, you record and examine the results to see if your hypothesis is supported, or if alternative explanations need to be considered. You can approach your exposures in the same way, making them miniexperiments to test your beliefs.

I had been working with Gail for several months on overcoming her social anxiety. She had made some progress in feeling more comfortable with the social demands at her job. But she still didn't have many friends to do things with on the weekends. She did a lot of her errands on Saturdays, but on Sundays she often found herself bored and depressed.

During one session Gail talked about a movie she really wanted to see, but she said there was no way she'd have the nerve to go alone. When I asked her why she said, "No one goes to the movies alone. It's all couples or groups of friends. People would think I'm a loser if I was there by myself."

I didn't think Gail would listen if I simply told her I thought at least some people went to the movies alone. Instead, I asked her when was the last time she had seen a movie. She couldn't even remember the last movie she'd seen in a theater. Because of her fears, she'd always waited until they came out on video.

This was the perfect opportunity to conduct a miniexperiment. I wanted Gail to test for herself her "hypothesis" that no one goes to the movies alone. We devised a plan whereby she arrived at the theater several minutes late for a movie she wanted to see. She didn't think she could tolerate standing in line or waiting in the lobby by herself. By going a little late, she could miss some of the crowds. After she had her ticket and was inside, she was to sit in the back row on an end, and she would be free to leave after she collected her "data."

Gail's job was to count the number of people sitting by themselves. If the light was such that she could notice anything about these people, she was also to jot down her observations. Did they look like losers? Were they acting like losers? Were they doing anything that called attention to themselves? Or, were they just sitting there watching the movie? She was also to observe whether anyone appeared to be staring at these lone movie watchers.

When I saw Gail for her next session, I crossed my fingers that there were in fact a few people there by themselves. Sure enough, Gail had counted twelve people who were watching the movie alone. She laughed when I asked if any of them looked like losers, and said, "I don't know. I got so into the movie I stopped paying attention to them." Gail anticipated my next thought when she added, "I guess since I wasn't paying attention to them, no one would really be paying attention to me."

You can develop miniexperiments to test all sorts of beliefs you may hold. Here's another example to help get your creative juices flowing.

Situation:
Lacey claimed that everyone in the grocery store engages in friendly conversation with the checkout person. She hated the task of buying groceries specifically because she felt stupid checking out. She could never think of anything "appropriate" to say.

What she thinks other people are thinking:
The checkout person must think I'm rude because I don't say anything. The people behind me must think I'm strange because I don't talk.

Miniexperiment to test this:
Go to the grocery store and stand in a place where she can see the checkout lanes. She could pretend she's waiting for someone. If this is too difficult, she could go through the line, but make sure she doesn't

look down like she usually does. She should consciously notice how many people are smiling and talking to the checkers. How many are staring off into space? Looking at their watches? Trying to keep their kids from tearing apart the candy display?

New ways she could view the situation.

People might not think I'm rude. They might think I have other things on my mind. Or they might not be thinking anything.

▼▼▼

By viewing exposures as miniexperiments, it no longer matters if you follow the usual principle of making exposures prolonged. The time factor isn't the issue as much as is collecting the data you need to test your beliefs.

Try a paradoxical approach.

Sometimes the best suggestions go against common sense. For example, have you ever heard the advice given to insomniacs that they should try to stay awake for as long as possible? Paradoxically, this approach leads them to fall asleep more quickly.

The same can be true in the case of social anxiety. Sometimes the best thing you can do is to stop fighting. We don't mean give up, but stop working so hard to prevent your anxious reactions.

Norman, a sixty-five-year-old recently retired business executive, came to see me because of a problem with blushing. He reported that he had a few instances of this earlier in his life, but he had forgotten about it until recently when the problem returned with a vengeance. He described an incident that took place about a month ago when he'd gone to the dry cleaners to pick up some clothes. He couldn't remember what had triggered it, but he felt himself getting hot in the neck and face. "I was burning up. I know I must have been bright red," he said. Norman was accustomed to being calm and in control. This experience unnerved him.

Other blushing episodes occurred when he was at the bank, buying clothes at a department store, or even when some of his wife's friends came over to play bridge. He began to anticipate when he might blush, and to avoid any situations in which he thought it might happen. Despite his avoidance, the blushing continued in an unpredictable manner.

I knew from experience with some of my other clients that blushing problems aren't easy to overcome. Sometimes relaxation techniques helped diminish the excessive physiological arousal, but I'd often found that such straightforward techniques weren't enough.

Norman's therapy involved many of the methods we've already described in the book, but I won't go into all of those details. What I will tell you is this: What seemed to help Norman the most was when he "invited the symptom." Let me describe what we did.

Norman probably thought I was crazy at first because I gave him the assignment of purposefully trying to blush for five-minute periods, three times a day. He was to keep a log of these sessions and note how successful he was at producing the blushing. He could do this at home to begin with. Later, I wanted him to try to blush on command while out in public. I also asked Norman to keep a tally count of the number of times he blushed when he wasn't purposefully trying.

What do you think happened?

Norman's blushing episodes decreased dramatically. When he first came to see me he had reported he was blushing almost daily. After a few months of "inviting the symptom," Norman was blushing about once every two weeks. When he did feel himself blushing on those occasions, he wasn't devastated by it. Of course, our sessions involved helping him to examine his beliefs about the blushing—what it meant about him that he sometimes blushed and what the consequences of blushing might be.

Ultimately, Norman learned two important things. One, he had more control than he thought he did. And two, he could tolerate the uncertainty of not having total control.

Make mistakes on purpose.

Related to the paradoxical approach, you can also practice intentionally making mistakes. In so doing, you not only expose yourself to your fear of disapproval, you also test your hypotheses about what you expect will happen. So often, socially anxious people tend to be perfectionistic. We don't want to make mistakes. In fact, we often wear ourselves out trying to avoid making mistakes. Although it might not be at the surface of our awareness, we're likely to believe making mistakes is somehow catastrophic. This exercise was designed to combat such thinking.

In *Dying of Embarrassment*, my coauthors and I listed twenty-nine examples of intentional mistakes, which are shown below. Some of these mistakes might not apply to you; you'll need to think of mistakes that will target your particular fears. For someone with a fear of trembling in public, purposefully making one's hand shake while signing a check would be a useful exposure. If this isn't a problem for you, it wouldn't make any sense to do. Read through the list and make note of any items that apply to you and your fears.

Intentional Mistake Practice List

1. Trip in front of someone.

2. Pay for something with the incorrect amount of money.

3. Drop something (for example, a fork, a coin, your glasses) in front of others.

4. Order something that isn't on the menu.

5. Greet someone by the wrong name.

6. Ask for directions to a store, department, etc., in which you are located or which is very close by.

7. Have your hand tremble when paying for something.

8. Take more than the number of items allowed to try on in a clothing store.

9. Underestimate the size of your feet to a shoe salesperson.

10. Have some aspect of your clothing appear inappropriate such as a label showing, shirttail out, mismatched socks, uncoordinated clothes, fly open (if you're really brave!).

11. Ask for an item that is obviously not carried by the store you are in.

12. Ask an obvious customer for information as if he or she worked at the store.

13. Ask for information or directions and then request that the answer be repeated.

14. Ask a question of someone and either stutter or speak with an unusual accent or tone.

15. Ask someone not to smoke, even though you are in a smoking section.

16. Arrive late on purpose for an appointment.

17. Attempt to purchase something without having enough money along, or without having your checkbook or credit card on hand.

18. Purchase something in a department store and present the wrong charge card.

19. Approach and almost enter the door of a rest room for the opposite sex.

20. Hum or sing so loudly that others can hear you.

21. Order some item and change your mind at least twice.

22. Greet or say something to someone across the room at a volume that is noticed by the other people there.

23. Enter a door inappropriately (push when you are supposed to pull or vice versa), push on a door that is locked, try to open the hinged side of the door, etc.

24. Buy something that you would normally be embarrassed to purchase.

25. Walk against the flow of traffic, stop suddenly, or in some other way bring attention to yourself by how you are walking through the mall.

26. Have yourself paged on a public address system.

27. Bump into something.

28. Tell a store clerk that you've lost something, and ask if it's been found.

29. Incorrectly identify the sex of a baby or child to its parents.

If making these mistakes in real life seems too threatening at first, remember you can use imaginal exposure first. Also remember to try easier mistakes first, working up to ones that seem more difficult.

One of the nice things about mistake-practice is that it doesn't take a lot of time. These are things that you can easily incorporate into your everyday life. In fact, many people find that after they've basically overcome their social anxiety, they maintain their gains by doing mistake-practice on a routine basis. This keeps them from drifting back into their old perfectionistic ways and believing that making mistakes will automatically lead to some kind of disapproval.

Give yourself credit.

Remember how we said that some people can carry out an exposure and still not benefit—not experience a reduction in their fear—because of the way they interpret the exposure? We'll return to Donald's example to illustrate.

As you know, one of Donald's big fears was speaking in public. We worked on this first because he felt his job depended on it. In addition to the imaginal exposures described previously, we created a number of other, real-life exposures. For example, he practiced reading in front of me and later to some of my staff. He also practiced giving brief, impromptu talks on a variety of topics.

One of these "minispeeches" he gave was on sports. I learned he was quite a sports fan, and very well informed. He caught my attention when he mentioned listening to a sports-talk radio show almost every night. He said that he often thought of calling in, but he'd never had the nerve.

I asked Donald if he would like to incorporate calling the show as a part of his exposure assignments. He definitely seemed interested, although understandably apprehensive.

The trick was breaking this task into small steps, ones that he would feel comfortable enough to try. I suggested that he dial the number of the radio station with the intention of hanging up. After hanging up, he was to carry through with imagining the scene. This added a realistic element to the process and also gave him the experience of dealing with his physical symptoms of anxiety which were provoked by placing the call.

After working through a number of steps we'd designed to give him practice, Donald was ready to try his exposure "for real." He couldn't plan what he was going to say because the topics and the guests varied. But we had agreed he was to ask a basic question or make a short comment. He wasn't to go out on a limb and say anything that might be controversial. Of course, we also had to prepare for the real possibility that he wouldn't get on the air. We had no idea what the volume of calls would be like.

The next time I saw Donald he told me what happened. The first night he tried, he got through after only a few attempts. Once on the line, someone asked him what he was going to say and then put him on hold. He waited while he tried to manage his anxiety. After ten minutes he hung up. The next night he only got busy signals. The night after he again got through and was put on hold. He was a little bit more prepared for the process, realizing they must screen the calls first. This time he was on hold for twenty minutes. He managed to deal with his anxiety and although it seemed like an eternity to him, he finally got on the air. He asked a question, but he felt he did poorly. He told me he paused several times and cleared his throat a lot.

I gave Donald a lot of credit for persisting. Wow! Not everyone would have done that. I wondered if he would want to continue, or if the whole thing was too time-consuming and stressful for him. "I always listen to the show, so I may as well keep trying," he said.

Donald became a regular caller on the show. He had amazing luck getting on the air. I thought he was doing incredibly well, but he kept denigrating himself and diminishing his progress. I had tried to hear him on the radio, but had never tuned in at the right time. I asked if he would tape himself the next time he was on the air. I wanted to hear for myself whether he really sounded as bad as he said he did.

At the very next session, Donald had a tape in his hand. I wanted to know what he thought of it before I listened to it. He said he couldn't force himself to listen to it until the next day. When he was calm and relaxed, he put the tape in the tape player and turned it on. He said he surprised himself because he actually didn't think he sounded that bad. "Yeah, I cleared my throat once, but I even heard the guest do that once or twice. It's winter and cold season. No one would know if I was nervous or just plain sick," he said.

By taping himself, Donald was able to listen to his performance when he wasn't caught up in the anxiety of the moment. That allowed him to more realistically evaluate how he sounded. So often when people are anxious, they're looking inward, tuning in to their own experience—and because they feel so awful, they think they are performing poorly. Because of this inward focus, they're not able to notice cues around them that would help them appropriately judge how they're really doing. Notice how this relates back to the previous chapter, "Focus on the Task at Hand."

But what if when Donald listened to himself on tape, he still thought he sounded horrible? What then?

One idea would be for Donald to listen to the tape repeatedly, making this an exposure in and of itself. By doing this he could habituate to the way he sounded, and perhaps he would be able to reexamine some of his beliefs. He could ask himself questions such as: "Of all the other callers I've heard on the show, how many times have I heard others stumble over their words, clear their throat, or pause excessively? Was I worse than 95 percent of them? Was I about average? Do I judge myself against more rigid standards than I judge others?"

What about the possibility that Donald truly didn't sound "good" on the radio (I thought he sounded fine)? Even if that were true, what would it mean? Is he a terrible person because of a flawed performance? Does it mean he doesn't have a right to express his opinions? Of course not.

Donald's case illustrates the importance of evaluating your exposures constructively. There's no benefit in completing an exposure and then haranguing yourself about how you think you did. Give yourself credit for taking a risk. After all, not everyone has the courage to face their fears the way Donald did.

It's Your Turn

In this chapter, you've seen how Donald, Gail, and others used exposure therapy to face their fears. Donald, who once avoided taking classes required for his job, was eventually promoted. Gail, who had greatly restricted her social life, was able to do the things she enjoyed without feeling overly self-conscious.

Indeed, exposure can be a powerful way to fight fear. Although it's a simple procedure in its ideal form, we described some common problems in applying exposure to social situations, and we also showed some ways to effectively sidestep them. Let's review the steps for carrying out exposures.

1. Create an exposure hierarchy. It should include some mildly challenging experiences, some moderately challenging ones, and some very difficult ones. By the time you are at the top of the hierarchy, you should be addressing your core fear(s). If you are doing imaginal exposure, write the script for the scene.

2. Start with the easiest exposure. When you enter the situation your anxiety should raise to a moderate level. Feel free to use your breathing techniques or coping statements, but try to avoid the use of "safety behaviors."

3. Try to remain in the situation until your anxiety level lowers to a mild level.

4. Keep repeating the same exposure (not necessarily on the same day) until it evokes little anxiety.

5. Do the same procedure with the next item on your hierarchy. Continue working your way up the hierarchy.

Now it's your turn. Select something to work on using exposure techniques. Start small; there's no need to change your life overnight. The important thing is to begin.

Chapter 9

Use Medication Wisely

The Lord hath created medicines out of the earth;

and he who is wise will not abhor them.

—Apocrypha: Ecclesiasticus, 38:4

The cultural notion that experiencing an emotional disorder—and

taking medication to recover—is a sign of personal weakness is em-

bedded in our pull-yourself-up-by-your-bootstraps culture.

—Valerie Davis Raskin, M.D.

The approaches for alleviating social anxiety we've described in
Painfully Shy are powerful ones. As therapists, every day we're
privileged to witness people make profound changes in their lives. A
man once unable to participate in Boy Scouts with his son for fear of
having to interact with others can now do so. A woman who previously
turned down a job promotion for fear of having to speak in meetings is
now advancing in her career. And in this book we've watched Christy,
Kim, Ross, and others learn to manage their anxiety and become less
disabled by their unrealistic worry and excessive preoccupation with others' opinions of them.

For some people, however, even the best cognitive-behavioral therapy isn't enough. Remember Garrett from Chapter 2? He had worked
his hardest in therapy, yet he still suffered from severe social anxiety.
Now what? Was this all his fault?

Certainly not. But if you're in a situation similar to Garrett's, it may be difficult to remember you're not a failure. Although considerable scientific evidence shows a strong biological component in anxiety disorders, your family and friends may not know this. They're likely to tell you to "just relax," or in some way imply that you should simply "snap out of it." Unfortunately, even some uninformed doctors may tell you these things.

In Susan Sontag's book, *Illness as Metaphor*, she notes the history of tuberculosis. Until scientists isolated the tuberculum bacteria and found a specific antibiotic to treat it, TB was understood as a "failure of will." In addition, it wasn't too long ago that schizophrenia was believed to be caused by ineffectual mothering. These maligned mothers were called "schizophrenigenic mothers." We now know that schizophrenia is, without a doubt, a brain disorder; if parenting problems coexist, they're certainly not the cause.

Fortunately, as we've said before, social anxiety disorder is gaining recognition. Research studies show certain medications are effective in treating its symptoms, and efforts are being made to educate physicians about these developments.

The decision of whether to take medication to alleviate social anxiety is a personal one, one that ultimately must be made in the context of a trusting relationship with your health care provider. Those able to prescribe medications include psychiatrists, other physicians, and sometimes nurse practitioners under the supervision of a doctor. Although psychologists take courses in psychopharmacology, our primary training involves learning to provide counseling and therapy. Although we can't tell you what to do, we can provide you with information so that you're able to make an informed decision—one that you'll feel comfortable with and, hopefully, one that will ease your pain and suffering.

The Serotonin Revolution

One of the most exciting developments in the past decade has been the release of a newer class of medications called the selective serotonin reuptake inhibitors, commonly referred to as the SSRIs. These new drugs, such as Prozac, Zoloft, Luvox, and Paxil, offer numerous advantages over the previous medications available to treat anxiety and depression. Not only do they target serotonin, a chemical in the brain closely linked to depression and anxiety, they also have fewer side effects than the older medications.

In part, what has made the SSRIs revolutionary is the fact that many medical professionals—not only psychiatrists—are comfortable prescribing them because of their improved safety and side-effect profiles. Doctors can assure their patients that side effects will be minimal and tolerable, and that the medication has a good chance of working. Many people who might not consider seeing a psychiatrist, but who do talk openly with their family physician, can now get the help they need.

Another positive outcome of the release of the SSRIs has been increased public awareness of the disorders they're designed to treat. With Prozac, we learned about depression. With Luvox, we learned about obsessive-compulsive disorder. And now with Paxil, we are hearing about social anxiety disorder, often for the first time. Although some critics lament the fact that the pharmaceutical companies are the power behind the publicity, it seems to us that the result has been positive. Increased recognition leads to increased numbers of people seeking—and receiving—the treatment they deserve.

Making the Medication Decision: Should I or Shouldn't I?

Should I or shouldn't I take medication?" Although we're not medical doctors and therefore can't write prescriptions, we hear this question frequently. Oftentimes, it's a psychologist who forms an initial relationship with a patient and is in the position of helping the person consider the pros and cons of various treatment options. Many issues surface in the context of such conversations, and they often fall under these three areas of concern:

1. Is this problem "real"—one that warrants medication?

2. Is my problem "serious enough" to justify medication?

3. Will the benefits of taking medication outweigh the possible risks?

4. What about the stigma attached to taking these medications?

We'll discuss each of these below.

Is this problem real?

Marie and I had met for about six weeks when the medication issue arose. She was making some progress with the cognitive-behavioral methods, but she was obviously still suffering a lot. She'd begun to push herself to do things she'd been avoiding, but the anxiety often overwhelmed her.

For example, her husband had been taking their daughter to and from preschool each day, which meant he had to leave work at noon to pick her up. Marie didn't feel good about the fact that he sometimes missed meetings because she was too afraid to deal with the car-pool line at the school. You see, the preschool director came out to cars, helping each child get buckled up safely. Although it was only a brief encounter, Marie hated trying to think of what to say to the director.

But as I said, Marie had begun to challenge herself to do more, and one of these things was to pick up her daughter from school. Despite her valiant efforts in using diaphragmatic breathing and other coping skills, she regularly experienced panic attacks while waiting in the car-pool line. Although she felt some pride for facing her fear, these attacks left her drained for the rest of the day.

When I suggested she might consider talking with a psychiatrist in our office to discuss medication options, Marie was besieged with doubts. "Are you sure social anxiety is really a disorder?" she asked. "Maybe I'm just shy and if I try harder, I'll be okay. Anyway, I've never heard of a medication for this sort of thing," she added.

I'd heard Marie's concerns many times. Sadly, it seems so natural to blame ourselves and think if we only tried harder, things would be different.

I asked Marie to tell me about the last time she had taken her daughter to the doctor. "It was just last month. She had bronchitis and a sinus infection. The doctor put her on an antibiotic," she told me.

Of course, no one would dispute taking an antibiotic for a bacterial infection, but somehow it doesn't seem the same in the case of say, anxiety or depression. Marie argued with me a bit.

"I know what you're getting at, but I bring this on myself. I literally think myself into a panic attack," she said. To some extent, Marie was right. Her thoughts did play a role in her condition. But as we've seen in our previous discussions of the mind-body connection, the same could be said for many "medical" illnesses.

I offered Marie the following example to consider. Every year I can count on my husband to become sick, usually with a sinus infection or some other upper-respiratory problem. The timing is predictable. It always happens when he's overextended himself at work. He starts to think he has to solve all the problems at work himself, meeting everyone's needs but his own.

Yes, he's around people all day who are sneezing and coughing, exposing him to all sort of things. But he's also stressed-out and tired, and his immune system isn't able to fend off the germs. I believe getting sick is his body's way of giving him a message: Slow down.

Although psychological factors are involved, does this mean he shouldn't see his doctor and take the medication he's prescribed? Of course not. Should he also review his workload and look at his unrealistic expectations for himself? You bet.

Yes, it is easier to see that a sinus infection or bronchitis is "real." But social anxiety is every bit as real. Our goal is for you to consider all of your treatment options, based on the facts involved in your particular situation.

Is it serious enough?

Marie had other issues with taking medicine. She questioned whether her condition was severe enough to warrant considering this route. Like many of us, she tended to minimize what she was going through. Sometimes it's frightening to let yourself acknowledge how bad it really is. But again, we needed to look at the facts.

Marie had suffered with social anxiety since her teenage years, and her symptoms had worsened with time. For example, she hadn't experienced full-blown panic attacks in social situations until the past few years. In addition to the anxiety, she'd also suffered with several bouts of depression. A few times she had felt so low she considered suicide. These thoughts scared her, and rightly so. She knew her family needed her, but she felt so horrible she just wished the pain would end.

If you're deciding whether to take medication, look at the following issues:

- How long have you been struggling with social anxiety? The longer it's been a problem, the more you might want to consider medication.

- How much does your social anxiety affect your day-to-day functioning? Does it affect your job performance, your relationships, your ability to care for your children? The more it affects your everyday life, the more you'll want to consider medication.

- Do you also experience periods of depression? If so, you may especially benefit from medication.

In general, the more long-standing and severe your problem has been, the more you may benefit from taking some type of medication. But remember, taking medication will likely be in addition to following some of the other approaches we've discussed.

After going through these questions, it became clearer to Marie that yes, her social anxiety was serious enough to warrant considering taking medication.

Will the benefits outweigh the possible risk?

Marie had overcome a number of hurdles in her thinking, yet she still had questions about the specifics of taking medicine for social anxiety. Would there be side effects? Are the medications addictive? Are they safe? Do they work?

These are valid questions. In the next section, we'll go through the various classes of medication frequently prescribed for social anxiety, as well as depression. As we discuss each of the drugs, we'll answer questions about their effectiveness and potential side effects. We've also included a chart at the end of the chapter that summarizes the advantages and disadvantages of various medications. But before we move on, let's address the last of Marie's concerns—the possible stigma attached to taking these types of medications.

What about the stigma?

Marie worried a lot about what it would mean to take a medication for her anxiety. Her thoughts ran along the lines of:

- "Does this mean I'm completely crazy?"

- "What will my husband think? Maybe he'll think I shouldn't need to take medication."

- "Will this affect my ability to get a job in the future? Or get things like life insurance?"

Underneath Marie's worries lay embarrassment—and deep shame. She believed she was somehow defective as a wife, a mother, a person. How could her body betray her like this? How could she be afflicted with such intense anxiety over seemingly mundane events, such as picking up her daughter from preschool?

I understood where Marie was coming from. Not only had I heard many patients describe similar thoughts and feelings, I'd been through it myself.

There was a time in my life—our son Jesse was about three—when I came to the conclusion that I needed to consider medication. It wasn't an easy decision; I fought it kicking and screaming.

You know from Chapter 3 when we talked about acceptance helping to ease suffering that Jesse had numerous health problems the first few years of his life. It was a struggle to keep up with all of his medical appointments while trying to work at the same time. In addition to my usual social anxieties, I worried all the time about Jesse's health, and over time I fell into a deep depression.

I thought to myself, maybe I'm just overly stressed. Maybe some time off would help. It wasn't enough. I worked at acceptance, trying to "flow with the depression"—in effect, giving myself permission to feel lousy. Sometimes this helped for a little while, but it didn't seem to be the total answer. I thought about going to a counselor, but I'd "been there, done that." Perhaps it was my pessimism at the time, but I didn't see the point in talking.

Although it was an intimidating step to take for a number of reasons, I knew I needed to see a psychiatrist. I'd had problems with depression and anxiety before. I was also experiencing many of the physical symptoms of depression, which is often a sign medication is needed. Sure, I'd been under a lot of stress, and it may have triggered this episode. But I also believed I probably had a biological vulnerability toward depression and anxiety.

It wasn't an easy task finding someone to see. I didn't feel comfortable going to a doctor I knew socially or professionally. I also worried about whether I'd run into my own patients in the waiting rooms of doctors to whom I frequently referred. Then, when I gathered my courage to make a few phone calls, I learned most psychiatrists had over a month-long waiting list. Finally, Greg thought of someone he'd worked with in the past who might fit me in sooner if he asked, and sure enough, I got an appointment in two days. To make a long story short, I was prescribed one of the SSRIs, and it's made a remarkable difference in my life.

Certainly, the decision about whether to take medication for depression or anxiety has to be made on a case-by-case basis with your physician. As I said, at first I had many qualms about taking medication. I thought maybe it indicated some sort of psychological or spiritual failure on my part. I sometimes thought I was a "fake"—if only I practiced what I preached I wouldn't have to take medication. But none of that was true. I've finally accepted that my temperament and physiology have interacted with my life experiences in such a way that my brain truly needs the neurochemical help the SSRIs provide.

Although at that time I was embarrassed and ashamed about taking medication, I don't feel that way now, and I hope you won't either. Although there's still some stigma attached to experiencing depression or anxiety, this will change as more people speak out about their experiences. Some studies show that 10 percent of the U.S. population is taking an SSRI, so we're certainly not alone. Look around at the people in your office, your church, or your aerobics class. It's likely that someone you see is taking medication for depression or anxiety.

I don't want to leave you with the impression that medication is a "cure-all." It's not. Most people I know, myself included, find that medication can make a huge difference, but you have to help it along. You can't sit back passively and think the medicine will do everything. And there are side effects to deal with. Sometimes they're only mildly annoying, and sometimes they drive you crazy.

I believe that the most important question to ask yourself after you've looked at all the pros and cons is this: What is the most loving, caring, reverent thing I can do for myself in this situation? Sometimes the answer will be to take medication, and sometimes the answer will be something else.

Navigating the Medication Maze: What Should I Take?

Now that we've addressed some of the more philosophical issues, let's get down to the nuts and bolts. The information below is meant to guide you through the medication maze and help you become an informed consumer. We'll focus mostly on the practical matters, giving you a general description of medicines commonly prescribed for social anxiety, their benefits, and their common side effects. We'll leave you to peruse the "Resources" section if you're interested in more technical pharmacology matters.

Selective serotonin reuptake inhibitors (SSRIs)

As we wrote earlier, the SSRIs are some of the newer medications used to treat anxiety disorders. They include Prozac (fluoxetine), Luvox (fluvoxamine), Zoloft (sertraline), and Paxil (paroxetine). In the early 1990s, the U.S. Food & Drug Administration (FDA) approved the first of the SSRIs, but the drugs have been used in Europe even longer. It's important to note that these medicines often go by different names in different countries.

A medication must undergo extensive testing in large, controlled studies before the FDA officially indicates it is safe and effective in treating a particular disorder. In reality, though, physicians use their clinical judgment to determine what medicine is appropriate for a particular patient. All of the SSRIs have been used to treat social anxiety; however, as we are writing this, Paxil is the only one to have FDA approval to treat it.

The most often cited Paxil study appeared in the August 26, 1998, issue of the *Journal of the American Medical Association*. In that study, 55 percent of the people taking Paxil were "much improved" or "very improved" compared to 23.9 percent of the group taking a placebo. While Paxil is the most studied drug for social anxiety disorder, other SSRIs will likely receive FDA approval to treat it in the next few years.

The SSRIs have become some of the most prescribed medications in the world due to their effectiveness in treating both depression and anxiety, as well as their general tolerability. You may wonder, how do they work?

Although scientists are not 100 percent certain, the general consensus is that the SSRIs work by increasing the available amount of the neurotransmitter serotonin to the brain. The process through which this takes place is a neurochemical chain reaction called "down regulation." Because this process occurs over a period of several weeks or more, you can't expect immediate results from the SSRIs. Most people notice some improvement in their symptoms after taking an SSRI for approximately two weeks but a complete recovery usually takes much longer. Some people do experience side effects from the SSRIs, including jitteriness or agitation, dizziness, drowsiness or insomnia, headaches, nausea, sweating, and sexual dysfunction. Oftentimes, these side effects diminish over the first few weeks of treatment as the body becomes accustomed to the medication. Side effects which persist can be handled in a number of ways, such as adjusting the dose or adding another medication.

Despite the fact that the SSRIs work in similar ways, individual responses to them vary tremendously. You'll need to be prepared for a possible "trial and error" period of finding the right medication and obtaining the optimal dosage.

Monoamine oxidase inhibitors (MAOIs)

Similar to the SSRIs, the MAOIs work by setting into motion a complex neurochemical process that takes place over many weeks. Unlike the SSRIs which affect primarily serotonin, the MAOIs affect three of the brain's neurotransmitters known as the monoamines—serotonin, norepinephrine, and dopamine. After the neurotransmitters do their job of sending messages between brain cells, they get metabolized by an enzyme called monoamine oxidase. The MAOIs work by blocking the action of this enzyme, leaving more of the neurotransmitter substances available to the brain. Numerous research studies have found the MAOIs, including Nardil (phenelzine) and Parnate (tranylcypromine), to be effective in reducing symptoms of social anxiety. Most studies show that about 70 percent of people improve significantly within four to six weeks of beginning treatment. Although these medicines are quite potent, they are frequently not prescribed as a first step because they can cause serious, even fatal rises in blood pressure when combined with certain foods and other medications. They're also likely to cause significant weight gain.

Foods containing the amino acid tyramine must be completely avoided. Although this list is not complete, some of the offending foods include: red wine, beer, aged cheese, soy sauce, foods prepared with meat tenderizers, excessive amounts of coffee or chocolate, smoked or pickled foods, yogurt, and sour cream. In addition, some over-the-counter analgesics and cold remedies must not be taken. People must be willing to strictly follow the dietary and medication guidelines provided by their doctor.

It's a reasonable strategy to consider an MAOI if you've already tried several SSRIs or other medications without benefit. In these cases, most people find the dietary restrictions are well worth the boost in mood and the relief from anxiety they experience.

Benzodiazepines

The high-potency benzodiazepines such as Xanax (alprazolam), Ativan (lorazepam), and Klonopin (clonazepam) are another type of medication used to treat anxiety. The benzodiazepines enhance the function of GABA, another of the neurotransmitters thought to be especially important in regulating anxiety. Whereas the SSRIs and the MAOIs take several weeks or more to begin to work, these medicines act quickly to reduce anxiety, usually within fifteen to twenty minutes. In higher doses the benzodiazepines can be used to promote sleep; in lower doses one hopes to see the reduction in anxiety without the sedation.

While the quick onset of action is a major advantage to the benzodiazepines, they can become addictive over time. This means that your body needs more and more of the medication to experience the same effect, and you're likely to experience physical withdrawal symptoms when you stop taking the medication. Because of this, the benzodiazepines are often used for only a relatively short period of time. Here are some situations in which they're typically prescribed:

- A physician may prescribe a benzodiazepine for someone who experiences jitteriness and agitation when starting an SSRI. Once the SSRI begins to have a therapeutic effect, the benzodiazepine can slowly be withdrawn.

- A benzodiazepine may be prescribed during a period of acute stress and tapered once the crisis is over.

- Another strategy is to prescribe a benzodiazepine to take on an "as-needed" basis, either alone or in addition to an SSRI.

- Some people cannot tolerate any other medication and need long-term treatment with benzodiazepines in order to function. In such cases, the physician and the patient work closely together to monitor issues related to dependence.

It's important to note the issues related to physical dependence; people with known histories of substance abuse may want to steer clear of these medicines entirely. However, in many other cases, individuals with anxiety disorders have such a fear of "losing control" that they typically undermedicate themselves. We've known many patients who have been prescribed Xanax to take when they need it, but they rarely do so. They'd rather "tough it out" than take a pill.

Beta-blockers

Beta-blockers, including Inderal (propanolol) and Tenormin (atenolol), are used to target the peripheral physical symptoms of anxiety, such as rapid heart rate, blushing, trembling, and sweating. As the name implies, these medications work by blocking certain nerve cell receptors—the beta receptors—located within the autonomic nervous system. Their pharmacological action is swift, and people usually notice a reduction in their physical, anxiety-related symptoms within forty-five to sixty minutes of taking the medication.

Beta-blockers are often prescribed on an as-needed basis for performance anxiety, sometimes known as "stage fright." For example, many orchestra musicians take a beta-blocker prior to a concert to keep their hands from shaking. Taking a beta-blocker before giving a speech is also quite common. Some people may even take a beta-blocker to control their anxiety during a job interview. While beta-blockers can be useful for very specific performance situations, they're not thought to be helpful in treating generalized social anxiety.

Other medications that may help

Several other types of medication are being used to treat social anxiety, and by the time *Painfully Shy* reaches the bookshelves, there will likely be more. We'll review some of the drugs we think show promise for relieving social anxiety.

One medication, Neurontin (gabapentin), is primarily an antiepileptic medication used to treat partial seizures. Recently, however, it has been used to treat social anxiety. Initial reports indicate it's effective and has few side effects. No doubt, more studies will be conducted with Neurontin in the future.

Two other antidepressants sometimes used for social anxiety disorder are Effexor (venlafaxine) and Remeron (mirtazapine). These medications are called "combination SSRIs" because they affect the neurotransmitter serotonin, as well as some other neurotransmitters, such as norepinephrine. Because more neurotransmitters are involved, people may experience more side effects with these drugs. Effexor or Remeron are typically tried when someone either does not respond to the other SSRIs or receives only partial symptom relief.

The last drug we'll mention is Serzone (nefazadone). It's often referred to as an SSRI, but it actually displays some unique chemical actions. In an open-trial study of twenty-three patients with social anxiety disorder, 70 percent showed improvement. Although the study included only a small number of people and there was no control group, Serzone holds potential to be an effective medication for social anxiety.

How Long Will I Need to Take Medicine?

Many people believe once they feel better, they can stop taking the medication. This makes intuitive sense. After all, you don't keep taking aspirin once your headache goes away. Although there are no clear-cut guidelines, most psychiatrists believe you must keep taking an SSRI for a year or perhaps two *after* your symptoms improve. Only then is the medication gradually withdrawn over a period of several months.

Why is this? While the medications alleviate the symptoms, they do not necessarily "cure" the underlying "disease." The hope is that after a year or two of taking medication your body's chemistry will have "reset" itself, but for some people this doesn't happen. Indeed, a high percentage of people relapse after medication is discontinued. Admittedly, determining how long someone should take medication is sometimes more art than science. But if you've had several episodes of depression and/or anxiety, don't be surprised if your doctor recommends a maintenance dose of medication for an indefinite period of time.

In addition to following your doctor's advice about how long to take medication, it's also important to learn some of the other approaches we've presented. Having other coping strategies to rely on is your best bet against relapse.

Special Issues for Women and Children

Women's unique health care needs have historically received scant attention in medical research. In the past, studies were carried out exclusively with men; it was assumed the results would hold true for women. Fortunately, the tide has been shifting as we're learning that gender does indeed make a difference.

Valerie Raskin, a physician and specialist in the area of women's psychopharmacology and author of *When Words Are Not Enough: The Women's Prescription for Depression and Anxiety,* writes: "To ignore gender is about as ridiculous as not noticing that one or one's patient is a person of color, a person of another faith or ethnicity, that the life experiences that any two people bring to a healing encounter don't deeply affect the transaction." Her book is an invaluable resource that thoroughly covers unique issues for women such as hormonal fluctuations, pregnancy, breast-feeding, and postpartum adjustment. We highly recommend it.

At this time, there is limited data on the use of medications in socially anxious children and adolescents. Given the early onset of social anxiety, this is an area that demands attention. Luvox and Zoloft are officially approved by the FDA for use in treating obsessive-compulsive disorder in children as young as twelve. In addition, in clinical practice psychiatrists use all of the SSRIs to treat even younger children for a range of anxiety problems and depression. Prozac comes in a liquid form, making it easier for some children to take, which also helps in administering a very low dose.

In general, the SSRIs have been found safe and effective in treating children and are often considered the first-line drugs of choice. In severe cases, benzodiazepines may be used temporarily. Children also benefit from cognitive-behavioral therapy, which we'll cover in Chapter 11.

The Role of Herbal Treatments

In the past few years there has been a surge of interest in herbal remedies for all sorts of problems. Although there have been no studies on the use of herbs to treat social anxiety, there is some related research worth mentioning.

The herbal supplement St. John's wort has been shown effective in treating mild to moderate depression with few side effects. How this works is not well understood. While some studies suggest that St. John's wort works as a mild MAO inhibitor, others point toward its effect on serotonin.

Kava kava and valerian root also have been studied for their anxiety-reducing effects. Again, it's not known how they work, but they seem to be effective for some people. Valerian, in particular, appears to help with sleep difficulties.

Please keep in mind that herbal supplements are actually powerful drugs. Just because a substance is "natural" doesn't mean it's necessarily safe. There are many situations in which taking an herbal product can be dangerous. Herbs may interact with other medications you may be taking, and they may make certain health conditions worse. Before taking any herbal supplement it's vital that you talk with your health care provider.

Andrew Weil, a well-known physician and author, has extensively studied herbs and alternative medicine. If you're interested in this subject, refer to the "Resources" section for a listing of his books.

Getting Good Care

At this point, you've gained an understanding of the potential benefits and drawbacks of taking medication for social anxiety. If you'd like to pursue this option, the next step is finding an appropriate medical professional. A number of options exist.

A good place to begin is with your primary care or family physician. It's important to get a complete physical to make sure there are no underlying medical conditions contributing to the problem. Some women use their ob/gyn as their primary physician, and that's okay. Just start with someone who knows your medical background and with whom you feel comfortable talking.

In many cases, a family physician will be quite capable of assessing your situation and prescribing an appropriate medication. However, if you don't respond to the medication or your situation is complicated in some way, you may want to consider consulting with a psychiatrist. Psychiatrists are adept at knowing what strategies to try for problems which seem resistant to treatment. He or she may:

- Increase the dose of the medication and suggest staying with it for a longer period of time.

- Augment the medication with another drug in order to boost the effects of the first drug.

- Switch to an entirely different medication type.

- Recommend some type of psychotherapy in addition to the medication.

Psychiatrists are also well prepared to deal with side effects. This is an important consideration given the sometimes lengthy duration of treatment with medication. Too often, however, people don't relay their side effects to their doctors—and the doctors are remiss in inquiring— and they stop taking the medication prematurely. No one wants to take a medication that causes them new problems on top of the old ones. But there's usually a way to deal with it if the lines of communication stay open.

We do realize, however, there are times when the doctor-patient match isn't quite right. Some doctors work better than others with certain types of people and certain types of problems. While we're not advocating "doctor-hopping"—switching from one doctor to another because you don't like what you hear—you should be comfortable with

Comparisons of Medications Commonly Used to Treat Social Anxiety

Category of Drug and Some Brand Names	How It Works	Advantages	Disadvantages
SSRIs • Paxil • Prozac • Zoloft	Affects the concentration of serotonin in the brain	• Helpful for many people • Easy dosing, often one dose per day • Side effects generally mild • Safe, nonaddictive • Good antidepressant effect, important given high co-occurrence of social anxiety with depression	• Takes at least two weeks for improvement, often months for full therapeutic effect • May need to take for a year or more • Expense can be prohibitive unless insurance covers it • Sexual dysfunction including low desire and anorgasmia commonly reported • Abrupt discontinuation can cause flulike symptoms
MAOIs • Nardil • Parnate	Inhibits the action of the enzyme monoamine oxidase	• Effectiveness in the 65 percent range • May be a good option for people who haven't responded to an SSRI	• Must follow dietary restrictions • Side effects can include weight gain • Primary care physicians can be reluctant to prescribe

Medication	Mechanism	Benefits	Drawbacks
High-Potency Benzodiazepines • Xanax • Klonopin • Ativan	Enhances the function of GABA	• Fast-acting relief from anxiety in twenty minutes or so. May feel significantly better in one week. • Few side effects, drowsiness being the most common • Helpful for as-needed dosing	• Potential for abuse • Physical tolerance likely with long-term use • Abrupt withdrawal after long-term use is dangerous; medication must be tapered slowly • Can experience "rebound anxiety" when one dose is beginning to wear off and it's about time for the next one • Little antidepressant effect • Generally not a long-term solution
Beta-blockers • Inderal • Tenormin	Reduces ability to produce adrenaline	• Fast-acting • Nonaddictive • Useful for performance anxiety • Reduces tremors, rapid heart rate, sweating, blushing	• Can produce lowering of blood pressure • Can cause depression in some people • Not helpful in cases of generalized social anxiety

your physician. If you don't feel respected and free to ask questions, you may need to think about looking somewhere else for help.

The bottom line to getting good care: Be informed, and trust your instincts. Believe that you deserve to feel better, no matter what it takes to get there.

Chapter 10

Nurture Your Spiritual Self

Spirituality is, above all, a way of life. We don't just
think about it or sense it around us—we live it.

—Ernest Kurtz

We began Part Two of this book with Christy's story—a story
about the power of acceptance, patience, and ultimately, faith.
Christy relied on her faith to provide her with strength and courage:
courage to accept the fact that she had lost her voice and couldn't control
if or when it would return; courage to find meaning in her suffering;
and courage to live life fully in spite of her difficulties. Of course, Christy
wasn't happy about her situation. I imagine she sometimes felt angry at
God and cried out, "Why me?" I know she felt weary and hopeless at
times. But her doubts never deterred her for long, and eventually, even
her voice would not be denied.

In this chapter, we'll first define what we mean by spirituality. Then
we'll show you how nurturing your spiritual self can help you in your
efforts to alleviate social anxiety. Next, we'll take you through four "existential concerns"—some of life's big questions—and describe how re-

flecting on these issues can go a long way toward making life more meaningful and less filled with needless worry.

What Is Spirituality?

Defining spirituality is a slippery task. The concept in many ways defies definition, confronting us with our own limits to describe things in words. In addition, many people have emotional reactions to the word, perhaps because they project their own idiosyncratic meanings onto it. For example, one friend of ours balked at the mere mention of spirituality because she associated spirituality with religion, and religion with guilt.

The definition we like the most comes from a book on parenting called, *Something More: Nurturing Your Child's Spiritual Growth*, by Jean Grasso Fitzpatrick. In the book she writes, ". . . the word spiritual is used to refer to an awareness of our sacred connection with all of life. Our spirituality is our opening to one another as whole human beings, each different and precious, and our exploring how we can truly learn to love." Her point that spirituality is related to love prompted us several years ago to write a book called, *Illuminating the Heart: Steps Toward a More Spiritual Marriage*.

So what is spirituality all about? Below we list a few of our ideas. Of course, your thoughts may be different, and that's fine. Hopefully, our ideas will merely serve as a starting point to get you thinking. Indeed, we invite you to ponder, to wonder, even to doubt. As you'll read below, we believe that questioning is an important part of the journey.

- **Spirituality may or may not involve formal religion.** Traditionally, religion has concerned itself with organized systems of beliefs and has involved, to varying degrees, doctrines, creeds, and adherence to rules. Spirituality is less concerned with these matters, and instead deals with a "way of being" in the world. In effect, spirituality cuts across different religions, uniting all people in the search for meaning and truth in their lives.

- **Spirituality is a process.** Our view of spirituality is one that values process—opportunities for growth along the path, rather than on any particular destination.

- **Spirituality invites questioning.** Spirituality is a quest for meaning and purpose, a daring look at ourselves and our lives with an unflinching but forgiving eye.

- **Spirituality involves everyday experiences.** We believe it's possible to find the sacred in everyday experiences. It's the ordinary moments that yield the raw and rich material for exploring what is meaningful.

- **Spirituality involves not only awareness, but action.** In our view, spirituality is incomplete unless it transforms awareness into action. We must find ways to apply our spiritual insights to our daily lives.

We'll illustrate these ideas more fully as we progress through the chapter, while offering you stories about ourselves and others to make the concepts come alive.

Before we move on, take a few minutes to read through some questions that can help you get in touch with your spiritual self. Think about the questions over the next several days. Jot down any ideas that come to mind. Remember that there are no right or wrong answers. If nothing comes to mind when you read through a particular question, skip it and come back to it at another time.

Getting to Know Your Spiritual Self

1. Do you remember a time when you felt safe and secure, somehow at peace with the world? What were the circumstances? _____
   _____
   _____

2. Was there ever a time when religion/spirituality was important to you? What factors were involved in any changes that have occurred since that time? _____

_____

_____

3. What are your earliest memories of religion/spirituality? What images come to mind when you now think about religion? Spirituality? God? _____

_____

_____

4. Do you (did you) have a spiritual/religious role model? _____

_____

_____

5. What are the miracles in your life? What are you thankful for? _____

_____

_____

6. How do you make sense of the suffering in the world? _____

_____

_____

How Spirituality Can Help with Social Anxiety

Therapist Edmund Bourne, author of *The Anxiety and Phobia Workbook* and his more recent book, *Healing Fear*, is the first anxiety disorder specialist to discuss the role spirituality can play in the recovery from an anxiety disorder. Given our Western culture's emphasis on science as the source of all truth, his move might be seen as a bold one. Let us explain.

Most of the scientific literature about anxiety disorders is rooted in either a cognitive-behavioral perspective or a pharmacological one, and indeed, many advances have occurred thanks to this research. Despite the powerful methods we now have to treat social anxiety, many of which we've described in this book, they're sometimes not enough. A certain percentage of men and women will not benefit from cognitive-behavioral treatment, medication, or even a combination of the two. Even those who do make progress with one of the standard treatments still stand a good chance of relapse.

We don't say these things to discourage you. We only want to point out that our knowledge is incomplete. We must expand our notions of what can be potentially therapeutic.

Although the topic of spirituality and anxiety disorders has not been a subject of scientific inquiry, this doesn't mean the connection doesn't exist. Survey research given to socially anxious people concerning their perceptions and experiences related to spirituality and healing would be a good starting point.

Also, it's not likely that everything of value can necessarily be learned via the scientific method. As physician and author Larry Dossey writes, "Everything that counts cannot be counted."

We believe Bourne's move to add a spiritual perspective as a complement to traditional treatments for anxiety disorders is a move in the right direction. Of course, we will continue to apply the proven techniques at our disposal—namely, cognitive-behavioral therapy and medication. However, we will not close our eyes to other dimensions of healing, and we will look for appropriate ways to study such areas.

In *Healing Fear*, Bourne proposes four specific ways spirituality can help in the recovery process:

1. You feel more hopeful—hope that help is available and that change is possible.

Some type of spiritual framework, a belief in some order or power greater than ourselves, can help us maintain hope even when the road is long. Through faith in something—it doesn't really matter what— we're able to hold strong to the belief that positive change can occur; it's not just wishful thinking.

Psychiatrist Thomas Oxman and his colleagues at Dartmouth Medical School studied 232 patients over age fifty-five who were undergoing cardiac surgery. They found that patients who gained strength and comfort from their religion—who, in essence, had hope—survived longer after the surgery than those without such hope.

One of the most important things I try to do in my first session with new clients is to offer hope. People need the expectation that their lives can be better. Otherwise, what incentive is there to follow through with the necessary and often difficult work ahead? In addition, I routinely tell new patients that different things work for different people, and that I'm committed to doing what works for them. If one approach doesn't work, we'll find another one.

William Shakespeare wrote, "The miserable have no other medicine, but only hope." Fortunately, in our day and age we do have medicines, as well as psychological treatments for social anxiety. But hope will always be our necessary partner.

2. You're open to new ways for handling severe and chronic social anxiety.

As you've seen from the different case examples we've presented throughout this book, the severity of social anxiety can vary tremendously. One person may basically function well except for a fear of public speaking. In contrast, another person may be almost completely disabled by anxiety, unable to work or enjoy personal relationships. And of course, there are situations that fall somewhere in the middle of these two extremes.

Individuals also differ in terms of how long they've struggled with social anxiety. Someone may have been profoundly affected by anxiety his or her entire life. Or, social anxiety may be a more recent problem, perhaps brought on by a change in life circumstances or undue stress.

Sadly, sometimes people who need help the most—those with severe and chronic social anxiety—are the ones for whom treatment fails, or is only partially effective. Then what? What if you've already put forth your best effort with cognitive-behavioral therapy and tried several different medications with little success? Is there any chance left for improvement?

Of course, there is. Please don't ever give up. You should do everything in your power to seek a life free from crippling fear. But sometimes you also have to practice acceptance and realize you can't win the fight alone. Using the language of the 12-step programs, you may need to "turn over" your problems to your "Higher Power."

For many people this translates into some type of prayer. In Larry Dossey's book, *Prayer Is Good Medicine*, he reports the following: "More than 130 controlled laboratory studies show, in general, that prayer or a prayerlike state of compassion, empathy, and love can bring healthful changes in many types of living things, from humans to bacteria. This does not mean prayer *always* works, any more than drugs or surgery always work but that, statistically speaking, prayer is effective."

Keep in mind, prayer can take many forms. Prayer or prayerlike, spiritual moments may involve:

- sitting silently

- gazing at a beautiful sunset

- lying on a blanket while looking up at the stars

- saying, "May the best thing happen" or "Thy will be done"

- offering thanks for life's blessings

- nursing a baby

- meditating

- caring for a pet

- listening to lovely music

- painting a picture or molding clay

- hiking through the woods

- asking for guidance

- reading inspirational books

- writing in a journal

The list is endless, and there are no right or wrong ways to pray. In essence, anything that allows us to pause and reflect on what's central in our lives is a form of prayer.

You may be still be wondering, how can prayer—or taking time to appreciate the spiritual moments of life—help lessen our struggles with social anxiety? The answers are as many and varied as the form of prayer itself.

For me, having a spiritual framework from which to view my life helps me put things into perspective. I realize that my struggles, although not necessarily ones I would've chosen, have helped me to grow and develop into a sensitive, caring person who can understand and help others through their pain. In addition, when I pay attention to the humble, yet awe-inspiring spiritual moments in my life, such as when my son reaches up to hold my hand, I glimpse the futility of my anxiety and can set it aside, even if only for a brief while. And because I believe there is meaning and a purpose to my life, I'm motivated to keep moving forward, to never give up, despite the setbacks that naturally occur.

Bourne describes two scenarios he's seen occur when adopting a prayerful approach to social anxiety. In the first scenario, a person's problem with social anxiety that was once quite serious—not responding well to psychotherapy, medication, or other treatments—goes away on its own. In effect, he says, a miracle occurs. Does this sound impossible, or too good to be true?

Remember how Christy worked diligently for years in therapy to deal with the loss of her voice, among other things. Although her self-esteem increased and she learned to better manage her anxiety, her voice never returned during the time she was in counseling. It was years later that she regained the ability to speak, and it literally happened overnight. Christy believes it was a miracle, and I have no reason to doubt her.

Similar to Christy's situation, we've known other people who improved dramatically in a short period of time, and we can't adequately explain why or how it happened.

If a miracle hasn't taken place in your life, though, don't despair. Equally important, don't think it's because you haven't prayed enough or aren't "spiritually advanced" enough. It may simply be for reasons you don't understand; the timing isn't right—at least not yet.

Probably more common is this scenario. A miracle does not occur, but through your spiritual practices and beliefs, you are better able to cope with your anxiety. You don't view your anxiety in the same way and, as such, it doesn't have the same negative hold on you. The situation hasn't changed, but the way you view it has. In addition, because your relationship with your anxiety has changed, you may not experience your symptoms with the same intensity as before. This, in itself, can be a miracle.

The upshot is, you have to do the work just like Christy did. You can't skip it, waiting for a miracle. Help yourself as much as you can, make use of the resources and conventional treatments available to you, and reach out to others for support. At the same time, pray—in whatever way feels right to you—for guidance, wisdom, and strength for the journey ahead.

You may want to check out the "Resources" section for some inspired, yet practical books on prayer. One we like in particular is, *Prayer Is Good Medicine,* by Larry Dossey.

3. Your attitudes and behaviors naturally evolve in a positive direction.

Bourne also notes that by engaging in spiritual practices—whether it's praying, meditating, attending a church service, or simply spending time in nature—you may experience positive changes in your attitudes and behaviors that will help you in your fight against fear.

For example, learning to trust a power greater than yourself, even learning to trust in another person's ability to lend a hand, may make it easier for you to let go of an excessive need for control. You realize you don't have to go it alone. Sure, as we've said before, you need to take the steps to help yourself. But you can share the load.

Having a spiritual framework on which to base your life also lends a certain sense of security and peace of mind. This serenity can sweep the clutter from your mind, allowing you to focus on what's important, what's real.

In addition, spiritual practices such as prayer and meditation can help you to more easily recognize and separate from the knee-jerk, emotional reactions we all experience. You learn to tune in to the quiet part of yourself that knows the best thing to do at any given moment. You understand that sometimes the best thing to do is accept where you are and simply do nothing for a while. And ironically, this acceptance of what is, this doing nothing, is actually something of great value.

Other changes may also occur. In the context of your faith, you may realize you don't have to be perfect to be loved. You may remember an old saying, "God doesn't make junk." You are unique, special, and worthwhile just as you are. In reality, you don't need to change so much as you need to clear away the anxiety so your true self can shine through.

Keep in mind, we're not advocating any particular religion or spiritual approach. Whatever works for you is fine. In *The Quotable Soul*, edited by Claudia Setzer, there's an apt image of religion offered by Mohammed Naquib, a twentieth-century Egyptian politician and author. He says: "Religion is a candle inside a multi-colored lantern. Everyone looks through a particular color, but the candle is always there."

4. The way you see "the problem" changes.

Finally, by incorporating spirituality into your life and into your recovery, your view of the "problem" of social anxiety is transformed. This relates to what we said earlier about spirituality being a process, not a destination. If your only goal is to reach a destination, then difficult times are seen as unwelcome obstacles. If you view your life as a spiritual process, however, then problems are not obstacles but opportunities for growth and learning. Thus, a spiritual framework that values process allows you to believe that you are right where you need to be at any given moment.

We don't expect you to jump up and down for joy when you experience setbacks with your social anxiety recovery or encounter other difficulties. But after your initial gut reaction of getting angry about the problem or feeling disappointed, you can step back and ask yourself, "What can I learn here? What opportunities are hidden behind this obstacle?"

Now that we've looked at how spirituality can help you with your social anxiety, let's move on to look at what have been called our "existential" or "ultimate concerns."

Our Four "Existential Concerns"

Most religious and spiritual traditions worldwide address the topic of life's basic questions, questions such as "Who am I?" and "What am I here for?" Irvin Yalom, a noted psychologist interested in the interplay between spirituality and psychology and author of *Existential Psychotherapy*, calls such questions the four "ultimate concerns." These concerns include death, freedom, isolation, and meaning. By grappling with these complex issues, you won't necessarily find all the answers, and it's certainly not our goal to tell you what you should believe. However, the questioning process in and of itself will help you, perhaps in some small but significant way, transcend your struggles and pain to find increased fulfillment and joy in your life.

Face the fragility of life.

The first ultimate concern you must face in transforming the nature of your life is the fact of your own finiteness. You might question the therapeutic value of dwelling on something so unpleasant, but considerable clinical and scientific evidence speaks to the benefits of thoughtfully considering the inevitability of death.

In his extensive work with cancer patients and their families, Yalom has found that the monumental shock of such a diagnosis results in far-reaching changes in the patient's life. He summarizes these changes as follows:

- A rearrangement of life's priorities: What is trivial emerges as such, and can be ignored.

- A sense of liberation: being able to choose not to do those things you do not wish to do.

- An enhanced sense of living in the immediate present, rather than postponing life until some point in the future.

- A vivid appreciation of the elemental facts of life: the changing seasons, the wind, falling leaves, the last Christmas, and so forth.

- Deeper communication with loved ones than before the crisis.

- Fewer interpersonal fears, less concern about rejection, greater willingness to take risks than before the crisis.

This last statement, especially, relates directly to social anxiety. When one is fully cognizant of the finiteness of life, others' opinions don't matter so much.

Confronting the idea of death makes us live more fully in the present. We don't know what tomorrow will bring; all we have is today, this moment. Being aware of this can be helpful for anxiety sufferers as worry breeds in future-oriented thinking. When we are fully present in the moment, not thinking about the future, we're less likely to plague ourselves with the "what ifs" of life.

Although I wasn't facing a life-or-death situation, I did receive a "wake-up call" last year when I needed back surgery. It was the type of existential turning point that makes you consider what is truly important in life.

Before the surgery, I had become fairly immobilized with pain. I wasn't able to see many clients (it hurt just to sit), and I couldn't do much around the house. In addition, I had been doing some volunteer work, and now I was forced to say "no" to any such requests. After the surgery, my recovery period was longer than I'd planned. I was limited in what I could do.

Because I'd always tended to judge myself by external standards, particularly by how much I'd achieved or accomplished, I had a lot of "adjusting" to do. I questioned whether or not I had any value as a person since I wasn't able to do anything "productive." What good was I to anyone?

Somehow, slowly, I began to realize that I could still do (or perhaps be) the things that truly mattered: I made Greg smile, I read Jesse a book, I listened to a friend's problems. I came to view myself differently. Before my back surgery, I sometimes made diminishing remarks about myself such as, "I'm too nice" or "I'm boring." Now I thought to myself, "Nice is good. Nice is something of value."

I also lost some of my vanity regarding how I looked. I moved slowly and awkwardly after the surgery, but I didn't care—at least I was moving. I carried a pillow so I could attend church more comfortably; that's an idea I would've shunned before. I wore flat, sensible shoes, and I still do. It may sound trite, but I've found it's true: Good things can come from life's challenges.

Luckily, you don't have to be diagnosed with cancer, have back surgery, or go through anything else catastrophic to live more fully in the present. All it takes is an awareness of the time-limited nature of existence and a willingness and openness to let this awareness inspire your everyday life.

Try this. The next time you find yourself dwelling on what someone else thinks of you, ask yourself, "If I knew this was my last day on earth, would I choose to spend it worrying about this?" Likely you wouldn't want to leave this world worrying about your public speaking skills. So, if you wouldn't be concerned about it then, why worry about it now?

Unfortunately, not all of us are wired that way. You can't simply turn off your anxieties like a light switch. In fact, if I were reading this advice, I'd probably feel guilty for wasting my time worrying. Now don't feel guilty; none of us can live life to the fullest all the time. But asking yourself this question can help put things in perspective. Facing the fragility of life can help us shift gears and focus not on a future we cannot control but on the present, in all of its rich textures.

Accept responsibility.

The second existential concern everyone must face is that of his or her own freedom. You wouldn't think this would be difficult—don't we all relish freedom and independence? Here's the rub: In freedom lies responsibility, and to be responsible is to be, as philosopher Jean-Paul Sartre said, "the uncontested author of an event or a thing." In truth, you are the author of your own fate. You write not only the good story lines, but also the bad ones.

We don't mean this to sound as extreme as it might. You don't necessarily bring on each detail of what happens to you in your life. Certainly environmental and other outside factors exert their influence. We do mean, however, that you *are* responsible for the attitude or stance you take toward what happens in your life. Like the conscious awareness of death, this notion of freedom is frightening, and people seek relief from the fear in a number of ways. A common way people deal inappropriately with the fear of freedom is by displacing responsibility. I'll share a personal example to explain.

Soon after we were married, Greg helped me confront this issue of responsibility; the experience, though difficult, changed my life. I was in therapy at the time, dealing with a number of issues. After seeing this particular therapist for some time, I felt as if we weren't getting anywhere. I developed insight after insight, but all this marvelous understanding didn't change a thing. I kept looking to her for direction, structure, and guidance, but she offered seemingly little. I became even more frustrated when she forgot to show up for several of our sessions and didn't even offer good explanations for her absences.

In sharing my feelings about the entire situation with Greg, he gently confronted me about who bore the responsibility, and indeed the power, to make change occur. He wasn't excusing the counselor for missing our sessions, but he asked me to look at what I might learn from this experience.

After unsuccessfully attempting to work things out with the therapist, I decided to make a go of it on my own. I believe it remains one of the best decisions I've ever made. I comprehended much more fully that I was the one who had to provide the direction, the structure, the guidance for my life—it was *my* responsibility. That summer, after I'd stopped going to counseling, I made more significant and what have proved to be lasting changes in my life than I'd ever done previously. In essence, the one insight that did lead to change was this: If no one else is going to take care of me, not even this person whom I'm paying to do it, then I'd better do a better job of taking care of myself.

We often see people who think we, as psychologists, can somehow magically heal them. And I, myself, fell prey to this unrealistic wish. We're certainly not saying don't seek help. But you do need to keep in mind you're the one who is ultimately responsible. You have to do the work. You're the one who can make change happen.

Connect with community.

The third existential concern we must confront is that of our fundamental isolation. Despite our relationships with others, we die alone. There are limits to relationship: No one can save you from pain; no one can supply you with an identity; no one can provide you with ultimate protection. Yet, once again, it's paradox in action.

Despite the limitations of relationships, the strength we draw from others can help us face adversity. The fact that we're loving, caring individuals can be a large part of our identity. And the acceptance of our own mortality helps us to more fully appreciate the time we have with others.

By recognizing the limits of relationship we're better able to authentically connect with others. As Yalom writes, ". . . aloneness can be shared in such a way that love compensates for the pain of isolation."

Thus, the task of dealing with this existential concern is twofold. First, we must face the fact of our fundamental aloneness and the responsibility that this implies. Then, we must connect with others, not out of dread before the pit of loneliness, but out of a sincere desire to walk the path of life together.

The benefits of community. Connecting with community has been shown to have healing effects on a variety of medical and psychological conditions. About ten years ago, David Spiegel, a professor of psychiatry at Stanford University, conducted what has since become a landmark study demonstrating the power of social support.

His experiment looked at two groups of women with end-stage metastatic breast cancer. Both groups received the same medical interventions; however, one group met regularly with each other to share their thoughts and feelings—to commiserate.

You can probably guess the results. At the time, though, the fact that the group who met regularly for support lived twice as long as the other group was surprising to people. Since then, however, many other studies have replicated these results. We can say without a doubt, enjoying a sense of connectedness is good for your health.

Opportunities for experiencing community. It was within your first family, your "family-of-origin," that you initially experienced the joys and challenges of community life. You developed methods for solving problems; you learned how to express, or not express, your feelings; you celebrated together; you grieved together; and most importantly, you developed your understanding of what it means to belong.

Unfortunately, some of you didn't feel that you belonged. Because of your anxiety, your way of interpreting situations, and the way others reacted to you and your anxiety, you may have felt like a misfit in your own family. Or, perhaps you felt loved and accepted within your family but experienced the pain of not belonging when venturing out into the wider world.

This notion of connecting with community can be daunting for people with social anxiety. Hopefully, by following the methods in this book, you're well on your way to breaking down the barriers that prevent you from enjoying relationships with others and from feeling that you belong.

When we discuss the value of community, many clients wonder whether or not they should tell others about their social anxiety. To tell, or not to tell? It's a question many worry about.

As with any decision, there are pros and cons, and these will vary with the individuals and the situations involved. In general, though, here are some guidelines.

First of all, consider your relationship with the person you might want to confide in. Do you have a close relationship? Is it generally supportive? How has this person reacted when you've shared other things about yourself? Has this person shared personal things about him- or herself? Do you think sharing this information will have a positive effect on your relationship? Of course, you don't know the answers to all of these questions ahead of time. If you did, the decision would be a whole lot easier. But do your best to think through what you hope will happen as a result of telling someone about your struggles with social anxiety.

Next, consider the context of the relationship. Is this person a family member or a colleague at work? That can make a big difference in knowing whether or not to share personal information, and if so, how much detail to disclose.

From the experiences we've heard, telling someone with whom you are close, such as a spouse, a parent, or a trusted friend, can take a huge load off your shoulders. You may feel less shame, and you may also be able to get the support you need in your recovery efforts. After all, people can't help if they don't know about the problem. Also, people may understand you better, and they may make fewer assumptions about your behavior. For example, many people who are shy are sometimes viewed as being aloof or unfriendly. This is hardly the case, but without the knowledge of what you're going through, you can see why others might think this. When you say "no" to every lunch invitation offered, people are going to wonder what's going on.

Depending on whom you're telling, you'll want to vary your approach. If you're telling your spouse or a close family member, you can probably go into more detail than if you're telling a friend at work. If you want to confide in someone at work, you might simply say, "I'm not very good at meeting new people" or, "Sometimes I'm a little shy." Even if the person doesn't understand the full extent of what you're saying, that's okay. You're simply testing the waters, gauging the other person's receptivity and response.

It's always an option to join an anxiety support group or an Internet e-mail list for persons with social anxiety. This will give you an opportunity to practice sharing information about yourself in a minimally threatening arena. Also, although going to church might seem like an impossible task for someone with social anxiety, it can be a wonderful way to experience the benefits of a warm and supportive community.

Keep in mind, even people who look completely confident and self-assured on the outside still have their struggles—it's part of being human. But because of the isolation and avoidance associated with social anxiety, too often we don't realize this. When we take the risk to reach out to others, to share our vulnerabilities, we learn that we're not alone. We also learn that we love and are loved not in spite of our imperfections, but because of them.

Find meaning and purpose.

The final existential concern is to discern a sense of meaning and purpose in our lives. For some people, this comes easily. They've always had a sense of direction—they knew what they wanted to do, and they did it. However, it's not just a matter of deciding "what we want to be when we grow up," or in accomplishing some goal.

In essence, enjoying a sense of meaning and purpose in your life is accomplished by courageously wrestling with the existential concerns of death, freedom, and isolation—and engaging in life, fully aware of these concerns. In other words, the meaning of life isn't so much an answer to be found, but rather a question to be lived. You must find out what matters to you, what captivates you, what enthralls you, and then do it.

Recall how Christy realized she couldn't put her life on hold while waiting for her voice to come back. She had to keep going—keep doing the things that mattered to her. She knew life is too short and too precious to wallow in self-pity.

What would Christy have said about her purpose in life? Although I shouldn't speak for her, I think I know her well enough to come close to what she'd say:

- To be a faithful servant to God.

- To continually build a loving, supportive marriage.

- To help animals in need through my work at the Humane Society.

- To grow closer each day to loving myself unconditionally.

If you don't have your life's purpose clearly articulated, you're not alone. Many of us don't slow down long enough to think about whether what we're doing is what we truly want to be doing. It can help, though, simply to consider a few possibilities:

- The meaning, or mission, of my life is to leave the world a better place to live in.

- My life is dedicated to a group of political/social/spiritual causes that hold special importance to me.

- The purpose of my life is to create a sense of home—a safe haven—for myself, my spouse, and our children.

- My life is about reaching my full creative potential.

- My life is an opportunity to give and receive love, and to know myself and those close to me as fully as I can.

Keep in mind that Christy didn't find meaning in her life by sitting down, trying to figure out her life's purpose on demand. It wouldn't work that way even if she tried. Instead, she had to exercise patience, tolerate uncertainty, and be willing to listen to what life was telling her.

Living the Questions

It seems that we often have more questions than answers in our lives. How did I wind up with social anxiety? What caused it? Why won't it just go away? How can I live like this? What treatment approach should I try? What if I don't get better? What if I do? And the list goes on.

As we've said, it's okay to question, and it's okay not to have all the answers. None of us does. But by giving ourselves permission to ponder the questions, we begin to appreciate our connections to the larger world around us, and we learn we're not alone. In turn, this realization goes a long way toward helping us cope with our fears and lessen our anxiety.

In concluding this chapter, we'll share with you one of our favorite quotes by Rainer Maria Rilke in *Letters to a Young Poet*:

Be patient toward all that is unsolved in your heart
and try to love the questions themselves like locked
rooms and like books that are written in a foreign tongue.
Do not seek the answers . . . Live the questions now.

Chapter 11

Help Your Child
Overcome Social Anxiety

Often, by making relatively minor adjustments in their child-rearing style, parents can promote the development of self-esteem and the skills kids will need to survive in a relentlessly social world.
—Franklin Schneier

Many of my clients have told me that the only thing more difficult than struggling with social anxiety is watching their children struggle with it. Rachel certainly felt this way. Her daughter, in the first grade, was quiet and cautious. She had a difficult time joining in with other children on the playground and sometimes came home saying, "No one likes me." Similarly, Rachel's eighteen-month-old son hid behind her when they were around new people, and he cried each time she left him with a baby-sitter, even a familiar one.

"I am terrified of history repeating itself," Rachel said. "I die inside every day thinking that my children will someday be as miserable as I am."

I understood Rachel's concerns. Her social anxiety had contributed to much loneliness and despair in her life, and she naturally didn't want her children to endure the same pain.

Fortunately, the methods we've presented in this book can also help children cope with shyness and overcome social anxiety. The techniques must sometimes be adapted to fit the age of the child, but the basic principles of reducing fear are the same.

In this chapter, you'll learn to recognize when social anxiety becomes a problem for your child and what you can do to help. The first half of the chapter focuses on the shy and cautious child, while the second half looks at children with more severe social anxiety. Whatever the case may be, you'll gain tips on encouraging your child without pushing too hard, and you'll see how your own experiences, when properly directed, can increase your child's chances for social success.

How Shy Is Too Shy?

How do you know if your child has a problem with social anxiety that needs attention, or if he or she is going through a normal developmental stage? The answer to this question can be tricky, especially if the person asking the question is someone like Rachel, who has herself suffered with social anxiety for much of her life.

Rachel focused on every aspect of her children's lives that could signal a possible problem. While many young children experience stranger anxiety and distress at separating from their mothers, Rachel was convinced this meant her toddler, Sam, was destined to a life crippled by social fears. She was also obsessed with her daughter, Dana, and whether she had played with other children at recess. Every day after school she questioned Dana about how recess had gone, whether she had spoken in class, and so on.

Rachel's concerns, although well-meaning, were misguided. She needed to know when it was appropriate to worry and what constructive steps she could take if her worry was justified.

You can determine whether your child is "too shy" by looking at the following issues:

- Are your child's fears common for his or her age? In other words, are the fears appropriate to the stage of development?

- Is shyness interfering with your child's functioning at day care or school?

- Is shyness preventing your child from enjoying friendships with other children?

- How long has the fearful, anxious behavior been going on? The longer the pattern, the more likely it's not simply a phase the child will grow out of.

There are many ways you can learn about developmental milestones and age-appropriate behaviors. We're fortunate in Missouri to have a wonderful program called *Parents as Teachers*. It pairs parents with a parent educator who visits with you in your home, interacts with your child, conducts developmental screenings, and offers practical parenting advice. Other states offer programs that go by different names; your school district will know what is available. It's important to know that these programs are for all families, not just those with identified problems.

To help her better understand Sam's behavior, I directed Rachel to *Parents as Teachers*. There she learned that Sam's fear of separation and strangers are common for children his age. In this case, his fears are nothing to worry about; he's simply going through a stage. Still, Rachel can use the parenting skills presented later in this chapter to help Sam have positive social experiences.

Rachel had more cause for concern with her first-grade daughter, Dana. Dana had suffered from separation anxiety for as long as Rachel could remember, and she rarely spoke aloud in class. She had a few friends with whom she could play with one-on-one, but when it came to group activities, she stayed on the periphery. Dana also had many strengths. She was doing well academically, and she enjoyed a warm relationship with her teacher. She had a delightful personality when she was relaxed and with people she knew.

Rachel had come to see me because of her own anxiety, but she also wanted information on how to help Dana. This was no problem. As we've said, methods for relieving anxiety are similar, regardless of age. The suggestions I gave Rachel are ones you'll read in this chapter, and ones you can use to help your own child overcome social anxiety. But before we move on, we need to examine the labels we use when talking about our children.

A Look at Labels

Although "shy" is not a negative term in our minds, we realize it's sometimes not considered a desirable trait. Bernardo Carducci, a nationally published researcher on shyness, frequently comments on our society's prejudice against shyness. He says, "The problem is a society that approves being bold and outgoing more than being reserved and quiet." Think about it. When was the last time you had someone tell you, "Wow! It's great that you're shy."

Because of our culture's view of shyness, it's a good idea to give your children other terms in which to think about themselves. For example:

INSTEAD OF SAYING THIS:	TRY THIS:
"You're shy."	"You're talkative with people you know well."
"Don't be afraid."	"It takes a little while for you to feel comfortable with new people."
"You're anxious."	"You're cautious. You like to know what something is all about before you try it."

You might be thinking, "That's all well and good, but what about other people calling my child shy in front of them? I can't do anything about that."

Shari and Dave ran into this situation frequently with their daughter, Emily, who was three years old and naturally cautious around unfamiliar people. But they developed a method for dealing with others' comments. Whenever they were at church, someone would invariably ask Emily a question, and she wouldn't answer. If the person then asked, "Oh, she's shy, isn't she?" Dave and Shari made sure to say something like, "Wait until you get to know Emily. She'll talk to you about anything."

In *The Art of Sensitive Parenting*, Katherine Kersey writes, "Children come into the world not knowing who they are. They learn who they are from those around them." In the next section we'll show you how to encourage your child in a way that avoids labeling and judging and instead focuses on giving your child the words and tools he or she needs to succeed in social situations.

Six Steps to Encouraging Your Child

True, you can't change your child's temperament. If your child is naturally cautious and quiet, you're not going to transform him or her into a gregarious extrovert, and that's okay. Parents can, however, exert a positive influence on their children in terms of how they feel about themselves. You can encourage your child in a way that says, "You're wonderful," *and*, "It's okay to take some risks." Here are six steps to guide you.

Step 1: Start from a position of acceptance.

In Chapter 3 we encouraged you to practice acceptance—to find the good in yourself and your situation—and not berate yourself for your perceived flaws. Now you must do the same with your child. You must appreciate the unique strengths of your child and not try to change him or her into someone else.

Recall the research we presented in Chapter 3 about the shy, sensitive children in China being the most popular. It's good to keep in mind that shyness and sensitivity are not necessarily "good" or "bad" traits, but ones that are valued differently depending upon where you live. There is nothing inherently wrong with you or your child. Of course, you'll want to help your child learn skills to succeed in our Western culture, but that doesn't mean you have to stamp out shyness.

Assure children that you love them just as they are. At the same time, let them know you're available to help them master their social anxiety so they can feel more confident and at ease—and do the things they want to do.

Step 2: Support your child by listening and identifying feelings.

An important part of encouraging children is to listen to them and help them identify what they are feeling. This holds true for any feelings, not just those that involve feeling shy or anxious. Although this sounds easy enough in theory, it can be a tough task sometimes.

For Rachel, the hardest part of listening to her daughter talk about problems at school was keeping her own emotional reactions in check. She told me about the first time Dana came home complaining about recess. "It was my worst nightmare hearing her say that no one played with her—that she went to the other side of the playground and played by herself. I thought I was going to break down and cry on the spot," Rachel explained.

Rachel did indeed have a difficult task. In order to support her daughter, she needed to put her own issues on hold. If she was truly to listen to Dana, she couldn't become consumed with her own thoughts, such as "Oh my God, I've cursed my child with this."

What can Rachel do in such situations? First, she needs to encourage Dana to talk more about it. She can say, "I'm glad you're talking to me about this. I want to hear more." Then Rachel can calmly listen, without offering advice or judgment at this point.

Depending on what Dana says, she can check out possible things she might be feeling. She can say, "It sounds like you felt lonely and sad playing by yourself." Or, "I wonder if you weren't sure how to join in with the other kids."

By listening and helping your child talk about feelings, you're taking away some of the sting and setting the stage for future problem solving.

Step 3: Give your child permission
to go at his or her own pace.

Peggy, a mother of a four-year-old boy, seemed instinctively to know not to push her son too quickly in new situations. Her son, Tyler, had wanted to take gymnastics lessons for as long as she could remember. The first night of class, however, he changed his mind. It was a struggle just to get him to the YMCA for the lessons, and then, he didn't want to participate. He cried when the instructor tried to coax him into joining the other children; instead, he jumped into his mom's lap and grasped her neck so tightly she thought she might choke.

How did Peggy handle the situation? What did she do? Probably just as important as what she did, is what she didn't do. Peggy *didn't:*

- Tell her son not to cry.

- Tell him, "There's nothing to be scared about."

- Tell him, "Don't be so shy."

- Act angry and say, "You were the one who wanted to do this."

While all of these responses are understandable from a parent who is frustrated and embarrassed, they will do nothing to help the situation and, in the long run, will hurt the child's self-esteem.

Instead, here are some of the helpful things Peggy told her son:

- "It's okay to watch first."

- "You like to check things out before you jump right in."

- "New things are hard."

- "I used to feel scared when I tried new things."

By making these types of statements, she validated his concerns. In effect, she let him know his feelings were normal and nothing to be ashamed of.

Other ideas that might help in a similar situation are to talk with your child at home about what to expect. If you've been to the YMCA before, talk about what the building looks like, where the gymnastics room is located, and if neighborhood children you know are also registered for the class. Plan to arrive a little early so your child can become more comfortable before the class begins—perhaps meet the teacher and see where you will be sitting.

Tyler needed to watch for most of the entire first class. Because his mom had told him this was okay and nothing to feel bad about, he loosened up and seemed to enjoy himself, even if he was mostly observing. Toward the end of the class, Peggy walked with him to where the group was, and they sat together on the floor while the teacher demonstrated how to do something. By allowing Tyler to go at his own pace, Peggy turned what could have been an unpleasant experience into a successful one—and one that he would feel comfortable trying again.

Step 4: Break the event into small, manageable pieces.

Sometimes new social situations can be daunting for children because the whole thing seems huge and overwhelming. If possible, break the event into smaller pieces that your child can relate to. For example, Eric's son was nervous about his first den meeting for Cub Scouts. His son had no idea what to expect, and the images he formed in his mind were frightening, not to mention way off base. Eric was able to reassure his son, Collin, with the following pieces of information—information that broke the meeting up into smaller, more familiar pieces:

- "Remember the time you played at Derick's house? The meeting will be at his house, and you'll probably have a little time to play before the meeting, just like you did the other time you were there. I bet he had some neat stuff."

- "You've met Derick's parents before. They seemed pretty nice, didn't they? His dad is the den leader. He'll be there to tell both of us what we're going to do."

- "We'll probably sing some songs, play a game, and eat a snack."

Collin had no idea what a "den meeting" was like, but he could relate to playing at Derick's house, singing songs, and eating a snack. These things were familiar to him and helped him feel less anxious about attending the meeting.

Step 5: Remind your child about past successes.

It's also important to help children remember their previous successes and to build on those. For example, Peggy reminded Tyler that he hadn't wanted to go to Sunday school at first, but he now enjoyed it and looked forward to it. They talked about how it had been scary for him because he didn't know the teacher or the other children. For the first few Sundays, his stomach hurt in the morning and he couldn't eat any breakfast. Peggy told him that what he was experiencing starting gymnastics class was just like what he had gone through in the beginning of Sunday school. He might be nervous for a few weeks, but then he'd get used to it and it would be fun.

Step 6: Give it time.

Encouraging a cautious child takes a lot of time and patience. For example, Peggy didn't expect that by saying a few supportive comments her son would leap off her lap, ready to turn cartwheels without ever looking back. As we mentioned, he sat on her lap during most of the first gymnastics lesson. The second lesson he joined the group only with her staying out on the gym floor with him. The third week she was able to step back a few feet. By the end of the eight-week session, she was sitting with the other parents while watching Tyler enjoy himself. Her gentle encouragement, support, and accepting attitude allowed Tyler to overcome his anxiety and feel successful in the process. They both had reason to be proud.

Some Other Helpful Hints for Parents

In addition to following the above six steps for encouraging your child, there are some other things you can do to help your child become more at ease socially. As you read through these suggestions, see which ones might apply to you and your child's situation.

Give your child plenty of practice socializing.

When shy children frequently avoid or withdraw from social situations, they may not develop the social skills they need. You can help by making sure your child has plenty of opportunities to practice socializing.

Invite another child to play at your house. Children often feel more comfortable on their own "turf." Sometimes shy children are more relaxed playing with slightly younger children, so this is an option to try initially. Have the time period be fairly brief at first, and try to have something planned you know your child will enjoy.

Take your child to places where they can be around other children, even if they choose not to talk to anyone. Call your local library to see if they have a children's story hour, or go to the park when the weather allows. Again, don't force your child to interact, but arrange for outings that make socializing possible.

Depending on the age of your child, you can practice social skills using puppets. There are also some good books for young children on coping with shyness and other fears. They're listed in the "Resources" section.

Perhaps the biggest problem comes when one or both parents are painfully shy. If this is the case for you, many of the suggestions we've made may seem completely out of the question. This was the case for Abby, but she found a way around her problem by enlisting the help of relatives. Let's look at her story.

Abby found it difficult to provide her ten-year-old son, Jacob, with the amount of socializing he needed. Jacob wasn't having problems socially. In fact, he thrived on being around other people. But Abby was quiet, had few friends, and found it extremely difficult to initiate things with other people. She was working in therapy to become more out-going—for Jacob's sake as well as her own—but she still had a long way to go.

"It was so easy when he was little and all he needed was to be fed, held, changed, and kissed. I was good at that," she explained. "But now Jacob's at the age where he wants to be around other people. Just being with me isn't very exciting."

Fortunately, Abby's sister-in-law, Rhonda, was quite outgoing and had a busy household with four children. There were always neighborhood kids coming and going, and she told Abby she wouldn't mind one more child being around. They worked out an arrangement where Jacob went to their house a few times a week after school. This worked out great. Abby spent the time going to therapy and doing her exposures, and Jacob was content to play with his cousins more often.

This type of arrangement can also work with neighbors. Look around to see where several children are playing out in the yard. We know it would be a challenge, but if you were able to become acquainted with an outgoing mom in the neighborhood, it might be a wonderful opportunity for your child to socialize with different people and become exposed to different personality styles.

Talk about the benefits of overcoming social anxiety.

Oftentimes children become anxious, and they aren't exactly sure of the reasons. What they are certain of, however, is wanting to avoid—at all costs—whatever situation is triggering their anxiety. They never realize what they are missing or giving up in the process. It's your job to help your child understand the benefits of mastering his or her anxiety.

This encouragement can be low-key. For example, eight-year-old Danielle was bored at home after school every day. Although her mom offered to play games with her and suggested things to do, none of it interested Danielle. She began whining and pouting on a regular basis, which just about drove her mother, Stephanie, crazy.

Stephanie began casually talking to Danielle about the possibility of inviting another girl from her class home after school. She'd mentioned it before, but Danielle had seemed reluctant and said, "I don't know if anyone would want to come over to my house. And anyway, what would we do?" But Stephanie continued making occasional comments about the fun things she and another girl could do together.

Finally, Danielle agreed to invite someone over for the next afternoon, and the friend agreed. The experience went so well Danielle later told her mom, "That was lots of fun—I should've done that a long time ago!"

Focus on positive reinforcement—not criticism.

The best way to encourage your child to try out new behaviors is to use positive comments and sometimes even small rewards, but avoid criticism and nagging. Again, this is easier said than done.

Stephanie admitted that at times Danielle annoyed her so much with her glum face and whining about being bored that she lapsed into nagging. She'd say things such as, "Just go outside and play" or, "You need to get out of the house. You're driving me crazy." When that didn't work, Stephanie did what we, as parents, all have done—more of the same. We somehow think that if nagging didn't work once, we'll make our point if we say it louder and more often.

Sometimes parents can become even more frustrated and make shameful comments about the child: "Why can't you be more outgoing like your brother," or "You'll never have any friends if you sit around and play Nintendo all day." Shame will never work to make your child less shy, and in fact, will have the opposite effect.

Instead of using negative comments, the best way to shape new behavior is to notice and reward desired behavior consistently and frequently. And remember to start small in what you expect. Don't wait until your child is selected for the school talent show before you show your pride. For a child who rarely speaks to adults, making eye contact with the mail carrier may be quite an accomplishment.

What type of reinforcement works best? Oftentimes verbal praise works well. Just be sure you don't go overboard and make too big a deal out of something as this might make your child more self-conscious. In addition, young children often respond to sticker charts, and this is a fine way to establish a new behavior. For example, your child might receive a sticker every day if they say "hello" to two people. Once the behavior has become a habit, you can phase out the stickers. The "Resources" section lists several good parenting books that can help you design an appropriate behavioral plan.

Separate your issues from your child's.

Another difficult, but important task, is to separate your own issues from those of your child. Because of your experiences, you may project your feelings onto your child, and these may or may not be correct. Let's look at an example.

Jeremy once observed his child on the playground and noticed that his son was shooting basketballs by himself. He felt his heart sink to his stomach. "Poor guy. I know just how he feels. It's miserable to be ostracized from the other kids," he thought to himself.

Later that evening, he asked his son about it. Contrary to what he had imagined, his son was enjoying himself and doing what he had chosen to do. "I played kickball with the other kids for a while, but I felt like practicing my free throws," his son explained. "I was thrilled when no one was playing basketball so I could have the hoop all to myself."

Of course, a parent who knows his child well will often make correct assumptions about how the child is feeling. Just be careful not to go too far and think that you're *always* right. Check things out with your child, and recognize when your reactions may be stemming from your own experiences.

Realize you can't protect your child from all pain.

It's natural that we want to shield our children from adversity in life, but children must also learn—in small, gradual doses—to deal with reality. Swedish writer Ellen Key is cited in *Words of Women—Quotations for Success* as saying, "At every step the child should be allowed to meet the real experience of life; the thorns should never be plucked from his roses."

If you're a sensitive person who has struggled with being painfully shy, this is probably the hardest lesson to take to heart. After all, you remember what it was like to feel sick to your stomach on show-and-tell days. You know how your heart raced when you were called on to answer a question in class. You felt the agony and the unfairness at not being invited to the popular kids' birthday parties. Of course you don't want this for your child. You must realize, though, to some extent there are normal "traumas" that children must go through. If you protect them from everything, they won't grow and mature as they should.

When Social Anxiety Becomes Severe

In this section we'll examine what happens when shyness turns into extreme anxiety—interfering with not only the tasks of daily living, but also with its enjoyment. First, we'll answer commonly asked questions about social anxiety disorder and how it presents itself in children and adolescents. Then we'll look at two closely related conditions—school refusal and selective mutism. We'll suggest things you can do on your own to support your child as well as point you in the direction of appropriate professional help.

Recognizing social anxiety disorder:
When your child is *painfully* shy

You may have recognized your child when reading some of the case examples described above. Perhaps you've already tried some of the suggestions we offered, and they weren't enough to turn things around for your child. Or, maybe your instincts have always told you that your child is more than "just shy." If so, you probably have many questions running through your mind at this point.

Does social anxiety disorder "look" the same in children? Social anxiety disorder in children and adolescents is presented in much the same way as it is in adults. The same types of situations elicit fear and anxiety, such as public speaking or being the center of attention. However, because most children attend school, some of their feared situations may be unique. Some examples include:

- Being called on by the teacher

- Giving a report in class

- Reading aloud

- Eating in the school cafeteria

- Writing on the blackboard

- Using school rest rooms

- Performing in school plays or concerts

Really, any situation which holds the potential for embarrassment, scrutiny, or disapproval can become a source of concern.

When confronted with feared situations, children experience physical symptoms of anxiety, just as adults do. Common complaints include choking sensations, flushes or chills, heart palpitations, shaking, headaches, and abdominal pain. Younger children with social anxiety, in particular, complain of headaches and stomachaches.

The cognitive symptoms of social anxiety disorder are often not as evident in children, especially young children. They may react with intense anxiety, yet not be able to verbalize what is upsetting them. Because of this, trying to address faulty thinking patterns with your child may be difficult.

Parents are likely to witness more behavioral symptoms in these anxious children, such as crying fits and tantrums. Unfortunately, sometimes these kids are wrongly labeled as "oppositional" or "defiant." This is usually not the case. When you consider the fact that children don't enjoy the same freedom as adults to avoid the situations they fear, their behavior makes more sense. When an anxious child perceives he's being backed into a corner and forced into something frightening, "acting out" with tears or tantrums seems like the only option.

Is the prevalence of social anxiety disorder in children the same as in adults? Because the diagnostic categories for children have undergone major revisions, it has been difficult to determine precisely how many children suffer with social anxiety disorder. However, in reviewing all of the research in this area, Deborah Beidel and Sam Turner, psychologists and authors of *Shy Children, Phobic Adults,* conclude that 5 percent of children suffer from social anxiety disorder at some point.

Beidel and Turner also note that the prevalence of problems that coexist in children with a primary diagnosis of social anxiety disorder are similar to those in adults. In their research on a group of children with social anxiety, they found:

- 20 percent had other specific phobias;

- 16 percent had generalized anxiety disorder;

- 8 percent had depression;

- 16 percent had attention deficit hyperactivity disorder; and,

- 16 percent had learning disabilities.

These figures illustrate the fact that children with social anxiety disorder often exhibit numerous problems and complex symptoms. If you recognize your child as having more than one disorder, it's all the more likely you'll need to seek professional help.

My son has always been socially awkward. His language was delayed and he still hasn't caught up to other children his age. Could he have social anxiety disorder? Mostly likely, no. Social anxiety disorder is only an appropriate diagnosis for children who have developed age-appropriate language skills and who demonstrate the ability to interact socially. A child with social anxiety disorder will frequently be outgoing and charming around close family members, for example, yet have difficulty interacting around unfamiliar children and adults. Children with developmental disorders would not be diagnosed with social anxiety disorder.

Won't my child grow out of this? Once your child's difficulties are serious enough to warrant a diagnosis of social anxiety disorder, it's best not to take a "wait and see" approach. Most likely by this point un-healthy patterns of withdrawal and avoidance have become habitual and aren't likely to be changed without some type of concerted effort.

Also, the effects of untreated social anxiety can be detrimental. Beidel and Turner write, "Children suffer both emotionally and devel-opmentally from social phobia. They tend not to play with other chil-dren, do not develop normal friendships, appear unhappy, do not engage in organized activities such as sports teams and birthday parties, and in extreme cases, may refuse to attend school."

Because of these factors, it's best to seek professional help as early as possible. Keep in mind, it may not take long to get on the right track, so don't necessarily think you're looking at years of therapy. We've worked with many children and their parents who've made remarkable improvements in only three to four sessions.

We mentioned earlier that social anxiety becomes more severe when it interferes with the enjoyment of everyday life. So let's turn our attention to two specific examples of social anxiety disorder—school re-fusal and selective mutism—to see what positive steps parents can take to help.

School refusal: When your child won't go to school

Javon and Briana, a couple in their late thirties, came to see me because of problems they were having with their twelve-year-old daugh-ter, Dominique. According to what her parents told me, Dominique had always found transitions difficult. Whereas their other two children would get into the swing of a new school year in a few weeks, it took Dominique many months before she felt even somewhat comfortable.

This year was the first year of middle school, and things had gotten off to a rocky start. Dominique was extremely nervous about going to a new school, one that was much bigger and farther away. She had to take the bus, something she hadn't done before. On top of that, her best friend from grade school moved to another state over the summer. Dominique had seemed "down in the dumps" ever since her friend left.

Briana told me Dominique complained of abdominal pain nearly every day. She had taken her to the doctor, but nothing seemed medically wrong. By the second quarter of school, Dominique had been absent numerous times and her grades were lower than they'd ever been. Several of her teachers commented on her report card that she did not participate in class discussions and did not seem to be working up to her potential.

When Dominique did go to school, she made Briana drive her because she hated taking the bus. She said she was intimidated by the other kids and couldn't find a place to sit. Although this resulted in Briana being late to work, she went along with her daughter's requests because she appeared so visibly distressed. She didn't want to make Dominique feel any worse than she already did.

One day, the school counselor caught Dominique skipping a class. When the counselor asked Dominique what was going on, she burst into tears and explained she was terrified of giving an oral book report due that day. The counselor called and asked the parents to come in for a conference, and the family was subsequently referred to me for help.

While it's beyond the scope of this chapter to detail every aspect of Dominique's treatment, we want to provide you with some general suggestions of what to do if you're in a similar situation.

What you can do:

- If your child is complaining of physical symptoms, have your child checked by a physician to rule out medical problems.

- Set up a conference with the teacher and the school counselor. Both parents should attend if at all possible.

- Approach the conference with an open mind. Don't assume the teacher or the school has done something wrong. Similarly, teachers should not assume the problem lies with the parents.

- Talk with your child about what's bothering him or her, while at the same time making it clear that a plan will be made to return to school.

- Do not make it appealing to stay at home. Let children know that if they're truly ill, they will need to see the doctor, stay in bed and rest, keep the TV off, and so on.

- Look for patterns of when children complain of illness. Do they wake up with a stomachache or headache? Do they complain of these things when they're busy and distracted? Do they feel ill on Saturdays?

- If your child complains of being sick often, make it a policy that unless he has a fever, he will need to go to school. If he continues to feel ill, he can go the school nurse and she can evaluate the situation. This takes the parent out of the power struggle.

- Remember that the longer your child remains home, the harder it will be to return to school. In most cases, consider "home-bound" schooling only as a last resort; at the very least, make sure your child knows from the start that this is a time-limited arrangement.

- Some parents find it helpful to have someone else take their child to school until the situation is resolved.

Although it's unsettling to see your child intensely distressed about attending school, it's imperative that you remain calm and supportive, but ultimately firm. By following the above suggestions and seeking help from an experienced therapist, there's good reason to believe your child will triumph over fear and go on to achieve his or her full potential.

Selective mutism: When your child is "scared speechless"

Children with selective mutism do not speak at school or in other public places where others might hear them, or they speak only in a barely audible whisper. These children speak freely and easily, however, when they're at home with family members. This condition used to be called "elective mutism," reflecting the thinking that these children were deliberately not speaking, perhaps being stubborn or simply trying to get attention. Current theories argue that the problem is *not* elective. Rather, it's as if these children's voice boxes are frozen with fear, preventing them from communicating with words.

Olivia became concerned about her daughter, Jenny, when she was in preschool. She never said a single word to her teachers or the other children. One day she fell on the playground and cut her knee deeply, but she didn't tell the teacher what had happened. When someone noticed and directed her to the nurse's office, she became hysterical.

Later, when Olivia came to pick up her daughter after learning what had happened, Jenny admitted she was afraid to talk to her teacher and she definitely didn't want to talk to the nurse. When Olivia took her daughter to the pediatrician—both to check out her knee and to ask about her not speaking at school—the doctor said, "She's just shy. She'll grow out of it." Olivia wasn't convinced, but she didn't know what else to do.

Jenny did not speak the entire year at her preschool, although she was quite talkative at home. Olivia hoped and prayed her daughter would start to talk at school in kindergarten—even just a few words— but it didn't happen. Fortunately, her kindergarten teacher recognized Jenny as being extremely anxious, and they were referred to me for evaluation and treatment.

My work with Jenny and her family involved many of the methods we've described in this book, especially those in Chapter 8, "Face Your Fears." Although an abbreviated version, I want to share a bit about Jenny's treatment to give you an understanding of what's involved. Then we'll offer some suggestions for what you can do as a parent if your child has selective mutism.

At first, Jenny wasn't comfortable talking with me. But we worked with puppets, and she was able to make them move their heads to indicate "yes" or "no" responses to my questions. I like working with children, in part because their imaginations let me be creative when explaining basic concepts for relieving anxiety and reducing fear. For example, I taught Jenny some basic breathing techniques—children usually learn these quite easily—by having her imagine a balloon expanding and contracting in her belly. I taught her progressive muscle relaxation by having her pretend to squeeze a lemon in her hand and then release it, and so on.

We drew pictures of ladders to show how she could overcome her fear of speaking by climbing the ladder, one rung at a time.

After some preliminary work of educating Jenny and her family about the process, we constructed a hierarchy of situations she was to complete. We also devised a reward system in which she would earn stickers for completing the items on her hierarchy. In addition, Jenny would be able to buy a stuffed bear she had been wanting after a specified amount of progress had been made. The hierarchy we used is below. After Jenny worked her way through it, we developed another one using more challenging tasks, such as asking aloud in class, "May I get a drink of water please?"

Jenny's Hierarchy
1. Whisper aloud to Mom or Dad so that Jill (same-aged neighbor) can hear.

2. Talk aloud to Jill with Mom or Dad present.

3. Talk aloud to Jill without Mom or Dad present.

4. Talk aloud to Mom or Dad in front of Jill's mother.

5. Say one sentence to Jill's mother.

5. Say a few words to an unfamiliar adult, such as a bank teller who gives her a piece of candy (for example, "thank you").

6. Say "hello" to an adult, such as the mail carrier.

7. Say "hello" to teacher at school—no children present.

9. Say "hi" to a classmate.

10. Talk to teacher in presence of one other child.

In addition to working with Jenny behaviorally on her hierarchy, I also met with the family to teach them to stop reinforcing Jenny for not speaking. Jenny's siblings had become quite skilled at knowing what Jenny wanted or needed when they were in pubic and she wouldn't speak. This commonly happens when a child has selective mutism, and unless these dynamics are addressed, little progress can be made.

Fortunately, Jenny's family was cooperative when they realized they weren't doing Jenny a favor by "helping" her in the ways they had been. Meanwhile, Jenny worked diligently to complete the items on the hierarchy. Of course, her parents were there to encourage her and keep her on the right track. Once the pattern was broken, though, it didn't take much time to see progress.

If you suspect your child has selective mutism, here are some general suggestions to follow.

What you can do:

- Selective mutism is best treated early. If your child has not spoken in the classroom by midyear of kindergarten at the very latest, seek an evaluation from a mental health professional who is familiar with selective mutism.

- Don't speak for your child or allow siblings to do so. Once a child learns he or she can communicate without speaking, it is much more difficult to break the cycle. In addition, over time the extra attention the child receives can be reinforcing and keep the problem going.

- At the same time, do not "force" your child to speak or use any type of punishment to correct the problem. Instead, encourage your child to meet small speaking-related goals in a gradual fashion. See the sample hierarchy below. A therapist may be needed to assist with this.

- Not all cases go as smoothly as Jenny's did. Some children may require medication as an adjunct to behavioral treatment. Don't be afraid to try medication if things are not going well using therapy alone.

- Check out the *Selective Mutism Group* on the Internet. There are tips for parents and teachers, support groups, an "Ask the Doctor" program, book listings and reviews, and two forums for those with selective mutism—teens and adults—to share thoughts and concerns. See the "Resources" section for the web address.

Regardless of how your child's anxiety manifests itself—be it social anxiety disorder, school refusal, selective mutism, or some combination—chances are good that you'll need to work with your child's school to maximize progress and ensure success.

Working with the School

Because your child spends so much time at school, it's important to work closely with the teacher and other staff members to ensure that they understand your child and know best how to help him or her feel comfortable. The key to success in working with the school is to maintain a positive attitude about your child and the teacher. Begin with the assumption that the teacher has your child's best interests at heart.

Talk with your child's teacher before the school year begins. Tell the teacher your child takes a while to warm up to new people. Explain that your child can become very uncomfortable if put on the spot. In short, share whatever information you think will be helpful. You certainly don't want the teacher to mistake lack of verbal participation as a lack of interest or intelligence. We list numerous other tips for teachers in an appendix of this book—feel free to share ideas that seem appropriate with the school.

If you believe that psychological factors are interfering with your child's learning, you have a right under federal law to request a "behavioral evaluation." A behavioral evaluation is a comprehensive assessment of your child completed by a mental health professional who is not employed by the school district. The point of such an evaluation is to have an independent party determine what problems may be hindering the learning process and to recommend steps the school should take to help your child overcome these problems.

During the course of a typical evaluation, the mental health professional conducts clinical interviews with both parents and the child and performs psychological testing, if needed. Parents and teachers also fill out behavior rating forms, and the mental health professional may observe the child in the classroom setting.

Be sure to submit your request in writing; the school district then has a responsibility to respond in writing, and in all likelihood they'll honor your request. If your child's grades are an issue, you can also request that he or she be evaluated for learning disabilities. Given the high percentage of socially anxious children who have coexisting learning problems, this isn't an unreasonable request.

There are legal protections you will want to learn about if your child is found to have a disability. For example, accommodations should be made for your child which aid the learning process. In the case of test anxiety, which is often a form of social anxiety, the student can be given extra time to complete the test, or take the test in a room away from others. The National Alliance for the Mentally Ill (NAMI) is an excellent resource for this type of information.

Seeking Professional Help

There are many times when parents, through no fault of their own, need the help of a mental health professional. It's important to recognize such times and not wait too long, hoping the problem will go away on its own.

Seek a professional consultation for your child if he or she:

- Seems sad or withdrawn most of the time for more than a few consecutive weeks

- Talks about wanting to die or has made suicidal gestures

- Has not responded to your efforts at following the suggestions in this chapter

- Exhibits significant changes in sleep and eating patterns

- Becomes noticeably more agitated, irritable, and has difficulty concentrating

- Displays intense and severe anxiety and is difficult to calm

A good first step is a visit with your family doctor or pediatrician. Anxiety can mimic several medical problems, and you want to make sure this isn't the case. Once medical problems have been ruled out, ask for a referral to a psychologist who works with children and has experience treating anxiety. If your child needs medication, your family doctor may be able to prescribe it, or you may also need to see a child psychiatrist.

Be sure to prepare your child before an initial visit with a psychologist or psychiatrist. Tell your child you're going to see a doctor who talks to people and helps them with their problems. Make the point that such doctors don't give injections. For adolescents who may be embarrassed, reassure them that even successful athletes and movie stars get help from psychologists, and it doesn't mean they're crazy.

We understand that it can be painful for some parents to admit they need help with their child or that their child has problems. But there's nothing to be ashamed of. Start by taking the blame off yourself and giving up the guilt—you have not failed your child. Instead, if you've made some parenting mistakes—we all have—learn from them and move on. Channel your energy into seeking the help your child needs.

Next, realize that many people must cope with a child with special needs. Seek out a support group of other parents in similar situations. And always remember that social anxiety doesn't make your child any less unique and wonderful.

We also know, however, that this can be an exhausting and draining process. So be sure to take care of yourself, too. That way you'll be able to enjoy the benefits of seeing your child master social anxiety.

Epilogue:
Reclaiming Your Life

And the day came when the risk to remain tight in a bud
was more painful than the risk it took to blossom.

—Anaïs Nin

"Come to the edge," he said.

They said, "We are afraid."

"Come to the edge," he said.

They came. He pushed them . . .

and they flew.

—Guillaume Apollinaire

I've been open with you throughout this book about my own recovery from social anxiety, and I won't lie to you now. It's not easy this business of blooming—sometimes it seems better, certainly easier, to remain in a tight bud.

I had one such experience while writing this book. I was scheduled to do a telephone interview with a radio station in Canada. I hadn't done an interview like this in a long time, and I was apprehensive. My stomach felt queasy and my hands shook a little as I waited for the phone to ring.

But all in all, I managed my anxiety pretty well. I concentrated on breathing deeply. I thought about what I wanted to say. I reminded myself, "I have an important message, and it doesn't matter if I deliver it flawlessly. What matters is I have the opportunity to reach out to others who may not yet know about social anxiety disorder."

Sure, sometimes I think, "It's not worth it. I still feel anxious. Maybe I should just get a job where I never have to speak in public." But something always keeps me from giving up. I think, at least in part, it's because I believe God has plans for me, and it's my job to follow the plan, regardless of whether I feel anxious or not.

As I finish this book, I feel like a mother bird about to nudge her babies out of the nest. I know you're ready to spread your wings and fly, but there's some sadness in letting go. You see, as I've written these pages, I've imagined you—your hopes, your dreams, the challenges you face. I'm not sure whether we've shared any of the same hopes and dreams, but I know we've faced similar challenges. I wish I could follow each one of you on your journey to overcome social anxiety and find peace within yourself. I know you can do it; there's no doubt in my mind. Still, I'd love to catch a glimpse of you blooming, soaring, and all of those good things you so richly deserve.

Appendixes

Recognizing and Coping
with Coexisting Problems

I f, after reading this book, you're thinking to yourself, "I can see I have social anxiety, but I think there's something else going on," the information here will help clarify things for you. You may be absolutely right about another problem complicating your recovery from social anxiety. Coexisting disorders are common. In fact, some studies show that up to 58 percent of individuals with social anxiety disorder have at least one additional disorder, the most common being another anxiety disorder, depression, or substance abuse.

Below are some questions for you to answer. Although this isn't a substitute for talking with your doctor or a mental health professional, you'll get an idea of what other problems may be impeding your progress. These questions are based on *The Diagnostic and Statistical Manual for Mental Disorders—Fourth Edition (DSM-IV)*, which we mentioned in Chapter 1. After you answer the questions, we'll offer some suggestions on how to deal with your situation.

Are You Depressed?

(Consider the previous two weeks when answering these questions.)

1. Have you felt down in the dumps, sad, or empty nearly every day?

2. Have you lost interest or pleasure in almost all of the activities you used to enjoy?

3. Has your appetite changed? Has your weight changed? (increased or decreased)

4. Are you experiencing sleeping difficulties—either sleeping too little or too much?

5. Do you feel uptight, restless, or edgy?

6. Do you feel tired and have low energy nearly every day?

7. Do you feel worthless and/or guilty?

8. Are you having trouble concentrating?

9. Do you have frequent thoughts of death and/or are you considering attempting suicide?

If you answered yes to questions #1 or #2, and you answered yes to four or more additional questions, and these symptoms have been occurring together for two weeks, you may be experiencing a clinical depression.

Do You Have Panic Disorder?

A panic attack is a discrete period of intense fear or discomfort, usually lasting about ten minutes, in which four or more of the following symptoms are present: rapid heart rate, sweating, trembling, shortness of breath, choking sensations, chest pain, dizziness, nausea, numbing or tingling sensations, chills or hot flashes, feelings of unreality, fear of losing control, or fear of dying. If you've experienced a panic attack, please continue.

Do your panic attacks occur in some circumstances other than social situations? If so, answer the questions below to see if you have panic disorder.

1. Do you experience recurrent, unexpected panic attacks? By unexpected, we mean they seem to come from "out of the blue."

2. Has at least one of these attacks been followed by at least a month-long period of concern about having another panic attack?

   and/or

3. Have you worried a great deal about the consequences of a panic attack? ("Am I having a heart attack?" or "Am I going crazy?")

   and/or

4. Has your behavior changed since having the panic attack?

If you answered yes to question #1, and you answered yes to at least one of the questions under #2, you may have panic disorder.

Do You Have Agoraphobia?

(Note: You can have panic disorder with or without agoraphobia.)

1. Do you experience anxiety in places or situations where escape may be difficult or embarrassing should you have a panic attack? Or, do you worry about whether or not help would be readily available if you had a panic attack?

2. Do you avoid these situations or endure them only with great distress?

If you answered yes to questions #1 and #2, you may have panic disorder with agoraphobia.

Do You Have Generalized Anxiety Disorder?

1. Have you worried more days than not for at least six months about a number of events or activities, such as work or school?

2. Do you find it difficult to control the worry?

3. Do you experience any of the following symptoms, with at least some of the symptoms being present on most days?
    • restlessness or feeling keyed up or on edge
    • being easily fatigued, tired
    • difficulty concentrating
    • irritability
    • muscle tension
    • difficulty falling or staying asleep, or restless sleep

4. Do the worry and physical symptoms cause you a great deal of distress? Or, is your functioning affected?

If you answered yes to questions #1 and #2, have at least three of the physical symptoms listed under #3, and answered yes to #4, you may have generalized anxiety disorder.

Do You Have Obsessive-Compulsive Disorder?

1. Do you experience obsessions, as defined below?
    • recurrent and persistent thoughts, impulses, or images that are experienced as intrusive and inappropriate and cause a great deal of distress
    • the thoughts are not simply excessive worries about real-life problems
    • the thoughts are extremely difficult to ignore or suppress

2. Do you experience compulsions, as defined below?
   - repetitive behaviors, such as handwashing or checking, that you feel driven to do in response to the obsession
   - the compulsions are aimed to reduce distress or prevent some dreaded event from happening, and are clearly excessive

3. Do you spend a significant amount of time dealing with your obsessions and compulsions (more than one hour per day)? Or, do your obessions and compulsions interfere with your day-to-day functioning and relationships?

If you answered yes to each of the above questions, you may have obsessive-compulsive disorder.

Do You Have Post-traumatic Stress Disorder?

1. Have you been exposed to a traumatic event in which both of the following statements are true?
   - you experienced or witnessed an event that involved actual or threatened death or serious injury, to yourself or to others
   - your response was one of fear, helplessness, or horror

2. Are you "reexperiencing" the traumatic event in one or more of the following ways?
   - recurrent and intrusive recollections of the event, which may include thoughts or images
   - recurrent and distressing dreams about the event
   - feeling as if the event is recurring—"flashbacks"
   - intense distress when confronted with reminders of the event

3. Are you avoiding things associated with the traumatic event?
   - efforts to avoid thoughts or feelings associated with the trauma

- efforts to avoid people, activities, places associated with the trauma
- inability to remember certain aspects of the trauma

4. Do you feel "jumpy" or irritable? Are you having trouble sleeping? Are you having problems concentrating?

If you answered yes to each of the above questions, and if the symptoms have lasted a month or more following the trauma, and these symptoms are adversely affecting your functioning, you may have post-traumatic stress disorder.

Do You Have Problems with Substance Abuse?

1. Have you developed a tolerance to a substance, such as alcohol? If you answer yes to one or both of the following questions, it's likely that you have.
   - Do you notice less of an effect over time from the same amount of the substance?
   - Do you need increased amounts of the substance to achieve the desired effect?

2. Do you experience withdrawal symptoms when you stop taking the substance?

3. Have you tried to cut down on your use of the substance?

4. Have other people encouraged you to cut down on your use of the substance?

5. Do you use the substance in situations that might cause physical harm, such as driving a car while under the influence of alcohol?

6. Have you experienced legal problems related to your use of the substance?

7. Is your use of the substance leading to failure at work or school?

8. Is your use of the substance affecting your personal relationships?

The more of these questions to which you answered yes, the more likely it is that substance abuse is a critical issue to address.

After answering these questions, take some time to catch your breath and relax. If you feel overwhelmed after learning the extent of your problems, try not to worry. Having more than one disorder to deal with is more the rule than the exception, and this certainly doesn't mean your problems are insurmountable. Also keep in mind you may need to see a mental health professional to help you sort through your responses, more fully evaluate your situation, and devise an appropriate treatment plan. In the meantime, below are some suggestions to point you in the right direction.

Coping with More Than One Anxiety Disorder

Many people with social anxiety disorder also have another anxiety disorder to contend with. In addition, people with a "primary" diagnosis of another anxiety disorder may have social anxiety disorder as a "secondary" diagnosis. For example, studies show that 24 percent of individuals diagnosed with obsessive-compulsive disorder (OCD) receive an additional diagnosis of social anxiety disorder. Let's look at a brief example.

Janine is a thirty-eight-year-old married woman with two young children. She obsesses continually about whether her house is neat and clean enough. She frequently stays up until three in the morning scrubbing and straightening. Janine is also painfully shy and has few friends. She worries about what other people think of her and is terribly afraid of rejection. Some of her neighbors get together with their children to play in a nearby park or each others' homes, but Janine never joins them.

Janine has OCD *and* social anxiety disorder. If her social fears are not recognized up front, it's likely she'll run into roadblocks in her efforts to overcome the OCD.

Several years ago I coauthored, along with psychologist Monica Frank, an article for the OCD Foundation's newsletter. In that article we described key issues people with OCD and social anxiety disorder need to address in order to ensure a full recovery. The following suggestions are adapted from that article and can apply to any situation in which social anxiety coexists with another anxiety disorder.

1. Understand that self-help may not be enough.

If you you're dealing with social anxiety disorder in addition to another anxiety disorder, recognize that self-help approaches may not be enough. Why not go ahead and seek a consultation with a mental health professional now, rather than spinning your wheels trying to go it alone? This doesn't mean that following the suggestions in this book or seeking other support isn't important. But when you're dealing with a combination of anxiety disorders, approaching the situation from more than one angle is likely your best bet for a full recovery.

2. Recognize the importance of the therapeutic relationship.

As you know, people with social anxiety disorder desire relationships with other people but are fearful of possible rejection or disapproval. This is true even in a relationship with a therapist. Before you can make progress in treatment, you need to feel comfortable enough in the therapeutic relationship that you know your therapist will not reject you for making a mistake or for getting angry, for example. The development of this trust can be a slow process for many people but especially for those with intense social fears.

This is a critical point. We've known and heard of therapists who tell clients who are not completing their behavioral assignments that they're not ready for treatment—and abruptly end it. As you can imagine, such a stance can be devastating if you have social anxiety disorder. If you feel rejected by your therapist, you may become even more sensitive to possible disapproval and avoid further treatment opportunities.

Therapists need to recognize that although someone may not be ready for behavioral assignments, such as exposures, he or she may still need therapy to address irrational fears regarding social situations. As these beliefs are effectively challenged, then he or she may be able to engage in the more behavioral aspects of treatment.

3. Determine your core fear.

Recall in Chapter 6 we described how to trace the path of your unrealistic thoughts. This technique can help in determining whether the fear of being evaluated or judged is at the root of your anxiety.

Imagine this dialogue between a therapist and a client. You can also ask yourself these same types of questions.

THERAPIST: Tell me about your fears.

CLIENT: I'm afraid of being contaminated.

THERAPIST: What would happen if you were contaminated?

CLIENT: I'm afraid I'll get sick.

THERAPIST: What would happen then?

CLIENT: I might die.

At this point, the therapist and client have uncovered the innermost fear and the questioning stops. In this case, the client's fears seem consistent with OCD, in which a fear of death is typical.

Now contrast the above dialogue with the following one.

THERAPIST: Tell me about your fears.

CLIENT: I'm afraid of being contaminated.

THERAPIST: What would happen then?

CLIENT: Other people won't approve of me.

THERAPIST: What would happen then?

CLIENT: They would reject me.

THERAPIST: What would happen then?

CLIENT: I'll be alone.

As you can see, the surface fear appears the same, but the underlying fear is very different. In such a case, even the outward behavior may be similar. For example, both individuals may avoid contaminated items and engage in extensive cleaning or washing rituals. As a result, OCD may be easily diagnosed. However, the obsessions and compulsions may hide the social anxiety, and in our experience, if the social anxiety is missed, it may wreak havoc with treatment.

Although we used an example related to OCD and social anxiety, the same principle also holds true in the case of other coexisting anxiety disorders. Whether you go through this questioning process alone or with the help of a therapist, the key is not stopping too soon. Continue asking, "What would happen then?" until you've exhausted all possibilities. When you reach that point, you've determined your core fear. This core fear, then, is what establishes the direction for treatment.

4. Accept that progress may seem slow.

There's no doubt it can be a struggle when you have social anxiety disorder and another anxiety disorder stacked on top. It can sometimes seem like you're not getting anywhere in your recovery.

You may need to examine your beliefs about the process of change. Do you think that therapy must proceed quickly in order to be considered successful? If you do, you're likely setting yourself up to feel frustrated and like a failure.

Although it would be nice if everyone were able to overcome their problems quickly, it often doesn't happen so easily. If it feels like you're taking two steps forward and one back, remember that is normal. Also keep in mind, the goal is progress—even slow progress—not perfection.

Dealing with Depression

If you're struggling with depression in addition to social anxiety, you face some unique challenges. First of all, you may not have the energy needed to participate fully in cognitive-behavioral therapy for your anxiety. As you know from reading this book, many of the steps you must take to overcome fear are very action-oriented—steps that can prove difficult if you're suffering from fatigue as a result of your depression.

In addition, because depression can also leave you feeling hopeless and discouraged, you may ask yourself, "Why even bother?" or "What's the use?"

If any of this rings true, you may need to work with a therapist to alleviate your depressive symptoms—at least somewhat—before you're able to do the work necessary to confront your social fears.

Below are some other suggestions:

- Start an exercise program. Of course, exercising is probably the last thing you're thinking about when you're depressed, but the boost in mood you'll receive will make it worth the effort. See Chapter 5, "Treat Your Body Well," for additional information.

- The methods in Chapter 3, "Practice Acceptance" and those in Chapter 6, "Think It Through," may be particularly useful to you in dealing with depression.

- Be sure to recognize your accomplishments. Every step you take—no matter how small it may seem—takes courage and moves you closer to your goals.

- If depression is moderate to severe, consider medication as an option. Many of the commonly prescribed medications work to relieve depression and anxiety. See Chapter 9 for details.

- If you feel imminently suicidal, seek help immediately. Tell a friend or family member and have them take you to the emergency room of your local hospital.

- Refer to Appendix D for several books on depression and managing your moods.

Quitting Alcohol and Drugs

If you've developed a problem with substance abuse from trying to "self-medicate" your social anxiety, you're not alone. Many people turn to alcohol to calm their nerves, and because it's often readily available in social situations, it's an understandable coping strategy. The good news is that as you overcome your fears, you'll likely not have the same motivation to drink or use drugs. Of course, the substance abuse may have become a habit with a life of its own, and for this reason, you'll need to deal with both problems.

Here are some suggestions and things to think about:

- Be sure to give your doctor an accurate account of how much you drink, or what drugs you use. Although it can be embarrassing to share this information, your health depends on it.

- It can be dangerous to drink while taking many prescription medications for depresssion and anxiety. Know and follow the guidelines for your particular medication.

- Realize that despite the immediate perception that alcohol has a calming effect, it actually increases anxiety over the long term.

- Studies show that people drinking a placebo (something they thought was an alcoholic beverage) did just as well socially as those drinking alcohol. Furthermore, even the placebo served to decrease inhibitions—leaving these people feeling more relaxed and outgoing.

- We know going to Alcoholics Anonymous meetings can be an overwhelming prospect for those with social anxiety. You may need to work individually with a therapist before this option even becomes a possibility. If you do go to an AA meeting, you can be sure there will be others there with social anxiety, just like you.

- The book, *Changing for Good*, listed in Appendix D, may be particularly helpful.

Encouraging Those with Social Anxiety: Tips for Family Members, Teachers, and Others Who Care

Social anxiety disorder impacts not only the sufferer, but also family members, friends, and others who care about the person. Below are some tips on providing support for your loved one, while taking care of yourself in the process.

General Tips for Caregivers

- Realize that if someone has just received a diagnosis of social anxiety disorder, he or she may feel a mixture of emotions. There may be relief at finally having a word for the problem, or there may be anger and frustration over the years of suffering, when no one knew what was wrong or how to help. Remember that all these feelings are okay.

- Remember that it's not possible to reason away social anxiety any more than it is to reason away a broken leg. If people could simply "snap out of it," they would've already done so.

- Maintain a positive mental attitude. Social anxiety disorder is real and serious, but it's not irreversible. Several effective treatment options now exist. There is every reason for hope.

- Encourage your loved one to follow his or her treatment plan. For example, medication should be taken according to a doctor's instructions. It should not be discontinued abruptly.

- Learn as much as you can about social anxiety disorder. Having a good understanding of the disorder will help you feel more in control and better able to help your loved one.

- Provide support, listening, and feedback, but avoid minimizing the problem or offering quick solutions.

- Keep in mind that change is possible, but that it doesn't happen quickly. Try to be patient.

- Praise all efforts—even those that might seem small.

Tips for Spouses/Partners

- Maintain your own friendships and outside social interests. Isolating yourself will only put more stress on your relationship.

- Recognize that you may have a variety of intense feelings about your partner having this disorder. All of these feelings are normal and okay. However, you must express them appropriately and in a way that does not hurt your partner or damage your relationship. (See *Illuminating the Heart* in the "Resources" section for guidelines on communicating effectively.)

- Be open to looking at the well-meaning ways you may have helped your spouse avoid certain social situations. As one example, do you always answer the phone? *Gradually* encourage him or her to assume more responsibility in these areas.

- Remember that you cannot solve your spouse's problems.

- Let your spouse know your needs, too. In other words, you shouldn't always need to be the caretaker.

- Know that many commonly prescribed medications for anxiety and depression can cause sexual dysfunctions. Keep the lines of communication open, and encourage your spouse to talk with his or her doctor if this is an issue.

Tips for Parents *(Read Chapter 11 for our suggestions on helping your child overcome social anxiety. Some general points are below.)*

- Accept your child as being unique and wonderful. Avoid giving your child the impression that you'd prefer him or her to be a different way.

- Focus and build on your child's strengths.

- Don't criticize or punish your child for being shy or quiet.

- Give up any guilt you may feel. If you're reading this book, chances are you're taking constructive action if needed.

- Also remember that good parents make time for their marriage.

Tips for Teachers: Working with Children Who Are Shy

- Figure out what your shy students are interested in. You can ask them, use interest inventories, notice what they wear (sports jerseys? T-shirts with dinosaurs on the front?), have them write a book about themselves, bring in pictures from home, and so on. Use the information you learn as starting points for conversation or educational activities.

- Assign them to work with other children in the class who are more outgoing. This may help promote interaction and new friendships.

- Capitalize on strengths. If a shy student excels in math, have him or her tutor another child who needs help in this area.

- Arrange desks or seats in such a way that shy children are grouped with either some children they know or children who are good at including others.

- Teach children how to join in group activities. For example, on the playground, prompt the child to ask someone, "Can I play, too?"

- Give them a task to do that will encourage moving around the room and interacting with others. Or, give them something to do that will make them feel important, such as erasing the blackboard or hanging up their work on a bulletin board.

- Take time to check in with shy students each day. Engage them in conversation. If they are able to establish a warm relationship with you, they may feel more secure and able to take risks in the classroom.

- Avoid placing shy children in situations that might be embarrassing or overly stressful for them.

- Teach children to deal with teasing. Give them words to use to protect themselves ("Teasing is not nice. I don't like it when you tease. Please stop . . ."). Be prepared to intervene. Although some teasing is inevitable, adopt a no-tolerance policy on bullying.

- Maintain contact with the parents. Ask what the children are saying about school at home. Although a child may be quiet in the classroom, he or she may speak quite positively about school.

- Encourage parents to volunteer in the classroom whenever possible. Having a parent visit the class, at least in the primary grades, can be a source of pride for children.

- Keep in mind, though, that some of your shy children may have shy parents. These parents may fare better in the classroom if you have something structured prepared for them to do. Something simple, such as cutting, would allow a parent to observe without the pressure of talking. Check it out ahead of time with the parent if you can.

- Find out what resources the school counselor has. He or she may have books and games that can help promote self-confidence and social skills.

- Watch for warning signs, such as: The child never speaks or speaks only in a whisper, doesn't use the rest room, doesn't eat lunch, appears sad and withdrawn much of the time, looks visibly anxious if called upon, never or rarely plays with others, looks down at the ground when spoken to, complains of stomachaches or headaches, and so on. If you have concerns, or are not noticing progress, ask the parents to consider seeking a consultation with a mental health professional.

Some of these tips for teachers were adapted from the ERIC Digest (Clearinghouse on Elementary and Early Childhood Education), Working with Shy or Withdrawn Students, by Jere Brophy. ERIC Digest reviews are funded by the Office of Educational Research and Improvement of the U.S. Department of Education and are in the public domain.

Managing Social Anxiety
Related to Medical Conditions

The *Diagnostic and Statistical Manual* of Mental Disorders (DSM-IV) makes note of several medical conditions that may contribute to "secondary" social anxiety—that is, social anxiety that is at least partly a result of a medical condition. The medical conditions *DSM-IV* lists include:

- Benign essential tremor

- Parkinson's disease

- Stuttering

- Obesity

- Disfigurement secondary to burns

Notice these are all conditions in which people may potentially experience embarrassment as a result of their symptoms. For example, people with Parkinson's may worry others will notice their trembling and shaking. While a realistic element exists—some people do stare—the worrying may be problematic and, in fact, make the Parkinson's symptoms worse. Although there has not been much research in this area, some studies show social anxiety is a common problem in those with Parkinson's, affecting up to 40 percent of these patients.

Whether you have Parkinson's disease or one of the other medical conditions listed above, there's every reason to believe the current treatments for social anxiety disorder will prove effective for you, as well. Here are some general guidelines:

- Join a support group. Hearing other people share similar concerns will make you feel less alone. You may also gain some tips on how to handle others' reactions gracefully.

- Realize that some people will stare. This doesn't automatically mean they disapprove of you or are judging you. They may lack information. Children, especially, are just naturally curious.

- Pay particular attention to the suggestions in Chapter 5, "Treat Your Body Well." For example, caffeine will worsen tremors and is best avoided.

- Make sure you get plenty of rest, and manage your stress levels.

- Provide your friends and family with information about your condition. This will help them understand what you're going through and know how best to assist you.

- Don't isolate yourself for fear of what other people might think of you. Most people are well-meaning, and those who aren't don't deserve your concern.

- See the "Resources" section for related books and web sites.

Seeking Additional Help and Information: Resources, Recommended Reading, Web Sites, and More

As we compiled this section, we were amazed at the wealth of information that now exists on social anxiety disorder. Ten years ago, when my colleagues and I wrote *Dying of Embarrassment*, there was virtually nothing else written about this common problem; now that certainly isn't the case. What was once called the "neglected anxiety disorder" is neglected no more.

Below you'll find lists of books, newsletters, organizations, and Web sites that you may find useful in your efforts to understand and overcome social anxiety. Knowledge truly is a source of power—make good use of the resources available to you.

Books

Anxiety Disorders

Bourne, E. 1998. *Healing Fear: New Approaches to Overcoming Anxiety*. Oakland, CA: New Harbinger Publications. Excellent resource on all anxiety disorders. Includes information on cognitive-behavioral techniques as well as spiritual growth. Bourne has fought his own battle with anxiety and writes with understanding and compassion.

Bourne, E. 1995. *The Anxiety & Phobia Workbook, 2nd ed*. Oakland, CA: New Harbinger Publications. Basic, step-by-step instructions for using cognitive-behavioral methods to overcome anxiety and phobias.

Hallowell, E. 1997. *Worry: Controlling It and Using It Wisely*. New York: Pantheon Books. Hallowell's writing style makes this book a good read, while at the same time con important information about the fundamental nature of anxiety. Includes a short chapter on social anxiety.

Ross, J. 1994. *Triumph Over Fear: A Book of Help and Hope for People with Anxiety, Panic Attacks, and Phobias*. New York: Bantam Books. An inspiring and practical book written by the president of the Anxiety Disorders Association of America. Contains chapters on each of the anxiety disorders.

Change

Prochaska, J., J. Norcross, and C. DiClemente. 1994. *Changing for Good*. New York: William Morrow & Company, Inc. Explains the six stages involved in making lifelong changes. Shows readers how to free themselves from bad habits—from smoking to overeating—and includes applications for anxiety and depression.

Children and Parenting

Kurcinka, M. S. 1991. *Raising Your Spirited Child*. New York: HarperCollins Publishers. A lifesaving guide on understanding and working with your child's temperament. Highly recommended.

Turecki, S. 1994. *The Emotional Problems of Normal Children: How Parents Can Understand and Help*. New York: Bantam Books. A reassuring book on how every child can have problems and how parents can help. Good information on the topics of communication and effective discipline. Also offers tips on knowing when to seek professional help.

See also:

The Hidden Face of Shyness, Chapter 17, "Parenting the Shy Child," listed under "Shyness."

Beyond Shyness, Chapter 3, "Good Intentions: The Parents' Role in Social Avoidance," listed under "Shyness."

For children's books on shyness, see www.parentingpress.com and www. polaris.nova.edu/~malouffj/shyness.htm.

Depression

Copeland, M. E. 1992. *The Depression Workbook: A Guide for Living with Depression and Manic Depression.* Oakland, CA: New Harbinger Publications.

Kinder, M. 1994. *Mastering Your Moods: Recognizing Your Emotional Style and Making It Work for You.* New York: Simon & Schuster.

Herbal Supplements

Bloomfield, H., M. Nordfors, and P. McWilliams, 1996. *Hypericum & Depression.* Santa Monica, CA: Prelude Press. A helpful reference guide on St. John's wort.

Bloomfield, H. 1988. *Healing Anxiety with Herbs.* New York: HarperCollins.

Tierra, M. 1990. *The Way of Herbs.* New York: Pocket Books.

Weil, A. 1997. *Eight Weeks to Optimum Health.* New York: Alfred A. Knopf.

See also:

Beyond Prozac, listed under "Medication."

Medication

Gorman, J. 1995. *The Essential Guide to Psychiatric Drugs.* New York: St. Martin's Press. A good reference for commonly prescribed psychiatric drugs. Updated frequently.

Norden, M. 1995. *Beyond Prozac: Brain-Toxic Lifestyles, Natural Antidotes & New Generation Antidepressants.* New York: HarperCollins Publishers. Offers a variety of natural solutions to the problem of serotonin deficiency. Also supplies information on the newer antidepressant medications.

Preston, J., O'Neal, J., and M. Talaga. 1998. *Consumer's Guide to Psychiatric Drugs*. Oakland, CA: New Harbinger Publications.

Raskin, V. 1997. *When Words Are Not Enough: The Women's Prescription for Depression and Anxiety*. New York: Broadway Books. Covers the important, yet often neglected topic of how women can respond differently to medications. Full of useful tables and charts. Must reading for any woman considering taking medication for anxiety or depression.

Meditation and Relaxation

Davis, M., E. Eshelman, and M. McKay, 1988. *The Relaxation and Stress Reduction Workbook, 3rd ed*. Oakland, CA: New Harbinger Publications. Provides full and detailed scripts for every type of relaxation imaginable. A classic.

Kabat-Zinn, J. 1990. *Full Catastrophe Living: Using the Wisdom of Your Body and Mind to Face Stress, Pain and Illness*. New York: Delacorte Press. Presents a new way of thinking about illness that can transform suffering into something more. Offers useful information on breathing, meditation, and awareness. Includes a chapter devoted to working with fear, panic, and anxiety.

Obsessive-Compulsive Disorder

Foa, E., and R. Wilson. 1991. *Stop Obsessing: How to Overcome Your Obsessions and Compulsions*. New York: Bantam Books.

Schwartz, J. 1996. *Brain Lock*. New York: HarperCollins Publishers.

Steketee, G., and K. White. 1990. *When Once Is Not Enough: Help for Obsessive-Compulsives*. Oakland, CA: New Harbinger Publications.

Panic Disorder/Agoraphobia

Wilson, R. 1996. *Don't Panic, 2nd ed*. New York: HarperCollins Publishers.

Zeurcher-White, E. 1998. *An End to Panic, 2nd ed*. Oakland, CA: New Harbinger Publications.

Parkinson's Disease

Duvoisin, R., and J. Sage. 1996. *Parkinson's Disease: A Guide for Patient and Family*. Philadelphia, PA: Lippincott-Raven Publishers.

Post-traumatic Stress Disorder
Matsakis, A. 1996. *I Can't Get Over It: A Handbook for Trauma Survivors, 2nd ed.* Oakland, CA: New Harbinger Publications.

Professional Texts
Beidel, D. C., and S. M. Turner. 1998. *Shy Children, Phobic Adults: Nature and Treatment of Social Phobia.* Washington, DC: American Psychological Association.

Heimberg, R. G., M. R. Liebowitz, D. A. Hope, and F. R. Schneier (Eds.). 1995. *Social Phobia: Diagnosis, Assessment, and Treatment.* New York: The Guilford Press.

Leary, M. R., and R. M. Kowalski. 1995. *Social Anxiety.* New York: The Guilford Press.

Rapee, R. M., and W. C. Sanderson. 1998. *Social Phobia: Clinical Application of Evidence-Based Psychotherapy.* Northvale, NJ: Jason Aronson Inc.

Yalom, I. D. 1980. *Existential Psychotherapy.* New York: Basic Books.

Shyness/Social Anxiety/Social Phobia
Aron, E. 1996. *The Highly Sensitive Person: How to Thrive When the World Overwhelms You.* New York: Birch Lane Press. A perceptive book that will speak to many socially anxious people. Highly recommended.

Berent, J. 1993. *Beyond Shyness: How to Conquer Social Anxieties.* New York: Simon & Schuster. Particularly useful is information for parents seeking help for adolescents and grown children with social anxiety disorder. Guides parents in empowering their children to accept responsibility and shows how to tell the difference between nurturing and rescuing.

Markway, B., C. Carmin, C. A. Pollard, and T. Flynn. 1992. *Dying of Embarrassment: Help for Social Anxiety & Phobia.* Oakland, CA: New Harbinger Publications. A classic resource on the cognitive-behavioral treatment of social anxiety. Guides readers step-by-step in assessing their fears and developing a personalized recovery program.

Schneier, F., and L. Welkwitz. 1996. *The Hidden Face of Shyness: Understanding and Overcoming Social Anxiety.* New York: Avon Books. Effectively combines research findings with case histories to provide an excellent account of the nature and treatment of social anxiety.

Simon, G. (Ed.) 1999. *How I Overcame Shyness: 100 Celebrities Share Their Secrets*. New York: Simon & Schuster. An inspiring collection of short selections by famous people telling how they overcame shyness.

Spirituality

Dossey, L. 1996. *Prayer Is Good Medicine*. San Francisco, CA: HarperSanFrancisco, HarperCollins Publishers.

Fitzpatrick, J. G. 1991. *Something More: Nurturing Your Child's Spiritual Growth*. New York: Penguin Books.

Markway, B., and G. Markway. 1996. *Illuminating the Heart: Steps Toward a More Spiritual Marriage*. Oakland, CA: New Harbinger Publications.

Meberg, M. 1998. *I'd Rather Be Laughing: Finding Cheer in Every Circumstance*. Dallas, TX: Word Books.

Substance Abuse

Birkedahl, N. 1990. *The Habit Control Workbook*. Oakland, CA: New Harbinger Publications.

Fanning, P., and J. O'Neill. 1996. *The Addiction Workbook: A Step-by-Step Guide to Quitting Alcohol and Drugs*. Oakland, CA: New Harbinger Publications.

Newsletters

ASPIRE! Newsletter
Anxiety and Social Phobia Information and Resources
  Rosemary Moore
  83 Fairholme Crescent
  HAYES, Middx, UB4 8QU
  ENGLAND

SP Newsletter: Social Phobia—The Patient's Perspective
  Editor: Eric Joffe
  P.O. Box 58281
  Cincinnati, OH 45258-0281
  www.spnewsleter.com

Organizations

Alliance for People with Social
Phobia
  P.O. Box 58281
  Cincinnati, OH 45258-0281

American Psychiatric Association
  1400 K Street, N.W.
  Washington, DC 20005
  (202) 682-6220

American Psychological Association
  750 First Street, N.E.
  Washington, DC 20002-4242
  (202) 336-5500

Anxiety Disorders Association of
America
  11900 Parklawn Drive, Suite 100
  Rockville, MD 20852-2624
  (301) 231-9350

Anxiety Disorders Network
  1848 Liverpool Rd., Ste. 199
  Pickering, Ontario
  LIV 6M3, Canada
  (905) 831-3877

National Alliance for the
Mentally Ill
  200 N. Glebe Road, Suite 1015
  Arlington, VA 22203-3754
  (800) 950-NAMI

Phobics Anonymous
  P.O. Box 1180
  Palm Springs, CA 92263
  (619) 322-2673

Social Anxiety Disorders Coalition
1-800-934-6276
  You can call for a free brochure
  about social anxiety disorder.

Relaxation Tapes

New Harbinger Publications, Inc.
5674 Shattuck Avenue
Oakland, CA 94609
1-800-748-6273
www.newharbinger.com

Web Sites

The Internet can be a valuable source of information on social anxiety disorder. Keep in mind, though, it is not a substitute for advice from your physician or a mental health professional.

We reviewed these sites and found them to be user-friendly and full of helpful information. However, because of the rapidly changing Internet environment, it's possible that some of these sites will be inactive at the time this book reaches publication.

Also, particularly in chat rooms or on e-mail lists, misinformation abounds. Realize that not everything you read will be factually correct.

American Psychiatric Association
www.apa.org

Anxiety Disorders Association of America
www.adaa.org

Anxiety Network International
www.anxietynetwork.com

Association for the Advancement of Behavior Therapy
www.aabt.org

Behavioral Consultants
www.behavioralconsultants.com

Berent, Jonathon
Center for Shyness and Social Therapy
www.socialanxiety.com

Canadian Psychiatric Association
http://cpa.medical.org

Chat group for people who suffer from social anxiety

www.groups.icq.com/
group.asp?no=1312513

Cognitive Therapy
www.cognitivetherapy.com

Freedom from Fear
www.freedomfromfear.org

Internet Mental Health
www.mentalhealth.com

Markway, Greg and Barb
www.painfullyshy.com

Mayo Clinic
www.mayohealth.org

National Depressive and Manic-Depressive Web Site
http://www.ndmda.org

Open Mind
www.open-mind.org/SP/

Panic/Anxiety Disorders
www.panicdisorder.about.com

Saint Louis Behavioral Medicine Institute
  slbmi.com

Selective Mutism Group
  www.selectivemutism.org

Shawns Mental Health Pages
  www.community-1.webtv.net

Shy and Free
  http://www.shyandfree.com

Social Anxiety Disorders Coalition
  www.allergictopeople.com

Social Anxiety Network
  www.social-anxiety-network.com

Social Anxiety Organization
  www.social-anxiety.org

Soc-Phob Mailing List
  www.colba.net/~audiotex/

Social Phobia Program, Temple University
Philadelphia, PA
  www.temple.edu/phobia

The Anxiety-Panic Internet Resource (tAPir)
  www.algy.com/anxiety/social

The Place
(pen pal and dating web site for Soc-Phob Mailing List members)
  www.fast.to/theplace

Toastmasters Program
  www.toastmasters.org/

Wilson, Reid
  www.anxieties.com

World Wide Web Mental Health Page
  http://www.mentalhealth.com

Index

▼▼▼▼▼▼▼▼▼▼